"Architecture...should not define how people behave, but rather allow them to develop over time their own relationships with the space they inhabit."

————————————————————————————— Sou Fujimoto

Ethereal

Sou Fujimoto Architects
Humans since 1982
Tuomas Markunpoika
Maiko Takeda
Sissel Tolaas

Designers create forms that shape space, time, light, or air, sometimes defying permanence and weight in favor of ephemeral materials or fleeting effects. An object or building might exist in the space between or the space left behind more than in the thing itself.

Sou Fujimoto Architects

— TOKYO, JAPAN, FOUNDED 2000 —

The work of Sou Fujimoto (Japanese, b. 1971) embraces contrast, harmonizing architecture and nature, public and private, transparency and opacity. Moving to Tokyo from rural Hokkaido to study architecture at Tokyo University, Fujimoto found early inspiration in the tension between the built environment and nature. One can see this in his built work. The Serpentine Pavilion (London, 2013) is a temporary structure of interlocking grids upon which glass planes formed multi-purpose surfaces: steps, seats, tables. The pavilion became landscape through density, blurring into the sky and challenging ideas of space and form. Here Fujimoto demonstrates the dexterity of his craft, creating atmospheric, sensual experiences of space from rigid, austere forms (the grid) and materials (steel). Conceptual projects continue this integration of opposites. Souk Mirage (2013) is a master plan for a city in the Middle East. It proposes stacks of structural arches to comprise an undulating topography of public and private spaces, invigorating the inherent beauty in vernacular Islamic architecture. The grid again generates spatial rhythm, an elegance emerging from complexity, ambiguity paired with order. It is perhaps not surprising to learn that Fujimoto initially studied physics, the most elegant of scientific fields. — ANDREA LIPPS

——What were your early inspirations; what led you to architecture?

SOU FUJIMOTO: I was a child who liked to make stuff. I remember flipping through my father's Gaudí book and seeing pictures of his buildings. That was the first time I came across architecture.

In high school, I became interested in physics. Einstein was my role model. It was through reading his theories that I learned the concept of "space." I was fascinated by the fact that natural phenomena are governed by physics and, through theories of which, organized and further integrated into clear principles. This has ever since served as the foundation of my architecture practice.

When I entered college, I decided to pursue architecture as a profession. However, I would say what led to this decision was not determination but rather an incidental attempt. I think I was fortunate.

——Tell me about your current way of working.

When I approach a design problem, I often look at several explorations and develop them in parallel. On a sketchbook, I put my ideas into conceptual forms. I also look to my team members for inspirations that can only be obtained through dialogue. Sometimes these dialogues lead to a design approach that is greater than what I would have conceived by myself. Then I set up a few experiments, each with a hypothesis, and observe their growth as I do different tests to them. Physical study models and computer modeling are also methods I use to explore possibilities, through which I often find new values.

——How do you engage the user with your architecture?

I want people to use and experience my architecture—namely, the building I have designed—in whatever way they want. And because of that, architecture, in my opinion, should not define how people behave, but rather allow them to develop over time their own relationships with the space in which they inhabit. The pavilion I designed for the Serpentine Gallery in 2013 is a space that brings about interactions between architecture and people.

——You have described your aesthetic as "primitive future." Can you elaborate on what this means to you?

When we try to conceive architecture for the future, we should look back more often at the fundamentals of architecture: the relationship between body and space, between internal and external, between nature and architecture, between individual and commons. We may find new inspirations by revisiting these fundamental ideas.

——How does beauty factor into your process? And in the final work?

When new ideas and concepts form relationships with many other things and matters in ways that have never been done before and they become somewhat an integrated whole, that, to me, is beauty. I also find a similar kind of beauty in the clarity of physics and mathematical formulas.

——In what ways do you engage with architecture as manifesto?

In my architecture practice, I always design with the idea in mind that the architecture-to-be would be a new typology of its kind, be it a house, a library, an apartment, or a tower. And besides creating new typologies, I seek to investigate the integration of architecture with nature.

——What comes to mind when you hear the word "beauty"?

Integration, orchestration, mergence, and clearness.

——What is the most beautiful time of day?

A silent evening.

——What is the most beautiful place you've visited?

Marrakesh, Morocco.

— INTERVIEW WITH ANDREA LIPPS

Serpentine Pavilion, London, England, United Kingdom, 2013

Renderings, Souk Mirage / Particles
of Light commercial building complex,
concept master plan, 2013

Humans since 1982

—STOCKHOLM, SWEDEN, FOUNDED 2010—

Humans since 1982 forge graphic and mechanical expression to create conceptual objects that expand traditional function. A specimen study of LEDs serves as a light. Analog clock hands become typography. Their work is unified in its elegance, if not its color palette—black and white—and most often explores the ephemeral qualities of time or light. Their kinetic projects include the clock *A million times* (2013), made in collaboration with electrical engineer David Cox. The hands of 288 analog clocks rotate each minute until they pause to unveil a digital presentation of the time; a moment that is lost as the clock hands rotate again. The piece comments on the ephemerality of time, while also creating a new visual expression in its presentation. Having met during their MA studies at Sweden's HDK School of Design and Crafts, founders Per Emanuelsson (Swedish, b. 1982) and Bastian Bischoff (German, b. 1982) remain deeply curious about the natural and material realms, reflected through the lens of their respective fields. Emanuelsson had previously studied mechanical engineering; Bischoff, graphic design. — ANDREA LIPPS

————Your work exists somewhere between functional design and art object. What is important in your design?

BASTIAN BISCHOFF: We wrote our graduate thesis about function and experience, proposing that the experience, or the fascination of people looking at an object, is also a function. It is the function of fascination.

————We can see from your work that you are creating objects that are collectible design and not mass produced.

BB: Yes, everything we have done so far is only collectible, limited edition. But we're also planning out for the future more serially produced objects.

PER EMANUELSSON: That was mainly because there was no producer that picked up our early pieces.

BB: We started to work with different galleries, and they supported the development of unique work. I'm quite happy that we ended up this way, because for us this field is more interesting than serial furniture production.

————Why is that?

BB: There is more space for conceptual thinking without the restriction of cheap producibility. Often a producer requests a lot of change and compromise in an object so that it is mass producible. Without that, we have more freedom.

————How do you work together? What are your processes and methods?

PE: In the beginning, we didn't have any clients, so it was more open and we would look for a starting point. But now it often happens that the gallery comes to us and asks for a new work, or a client comes to us and asks for an installation in a particular space.

BB: We've tried to follow technology or social phenomena, and then if one of us has an idea about a certain topic, we just tell each other, and it's going back and forth. And if we think it's strong enough, then we go for it. But there are a lot of ideas that have never happened because we don't find the right way to make it really good, or at least not yet. Maybe in the future we'll find a little tweak that might make a particular idea great.

————And do you have certain roles in the process? Your backgrounds are so different: technical engineering [PE] and graphic design [BB].

PE: When it comes to the idea, the core, we are on the same level. But of course, we each have practical skills to solve different problems in the process.

————Can you use A million times as a reference? How did you work with that?

BB: It started as a font. We made this clock showing letters, and then it developed into showing digits with clocks, and then showing the time with clocks. It was all digital in the beginning, and we made a little video and uploaded it to YouTube. It got quite a lot of reactions, just based off this. Some people were wondering if it was a real thing or just animated.

And then we got in contact with Saatchi Gallery, who wanted to have it for an exhibition. We had to kind of make it real within a quite short time—maybe two months or something. David Cox, who is the electrical engineer behind this project, helped us to turn it from a digital version into manual clocks that are interconnected and run by a small computer.

————Are there other people, aside from David, who you work with during your process?

BB: For production, we have to use companies that are specialized in producing pieces of aluminum and other components that we cannot produce by ourselves.

PE: We also cooperate with different galleries, so far in Brussels, New York, and Mumbai. Victor Hunt often manages the production of the housings in Belgium; other times we produce here in Sweden. We always develop the electric technology, so it's partly assembled before we install it into the aluminum. We are a quite small studio, so we need some support to finish up all the projects.

————What comes to mind when you hear the word "beauty"?

PE: People. Beauty is very connected to people and image.

BB: Yes, in the media, beauty is very connected to the image. Two hundred years ago, it was more philosophical or deeper. But I think that in perhaps the last eighty to hundred years, beauty has become more about the surface.

————And how does beauty relate to your work or your aesthetic?

BB: It's more like intuition. For example, our objects are very simple and black-and-white. It's what we like in an aesthetic sense.

PE: It's quite difficult to describe. For us, one part is to create or to push ideas through the work.

BB: [Another part is to c]ommunicate something in the most clear way. So we don't add any extra element and try to not add decorations. The concept is the core of it, and then to communicate that concept. So what we design is relying on intuition as a presentation.

————What is the most beautiful time of day?

PE: The morning. I enjoy the morning light so much that I get almost stressed when the daylight sets in.

BB: For me it is evening, when I can sleep.

————What is the most beautiful place you've visited?

BB: In the Alps between Milan and Zurich. If you take the train there in the spring, it's beautiful to see the contrast between the snowy mountains and the valleys.

PE: The north of Scandinavia, close to Kiruna [Sweden]. It's very beautiful and very calm, no people.

— INTERVIEW WITH SUVI SALONIEMI

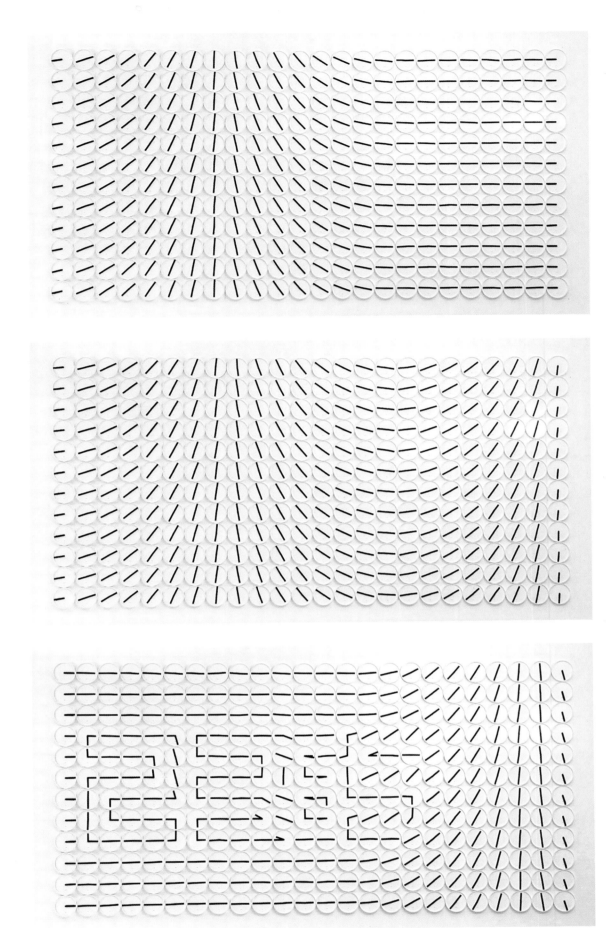

Clock prototype, A million times 288 H, 2013;
Aluminum, electric components, powder-
coated clock hands, screenprinted dials;
180 × 344 × 5 cm (5 ft. 10⅞ in. × 11 ft. 3⅞ in.
× 1¹⁵⁄₁₆ in.); Courtesy of Victor Hunt Gallery

OVERLEAF: Installation view.

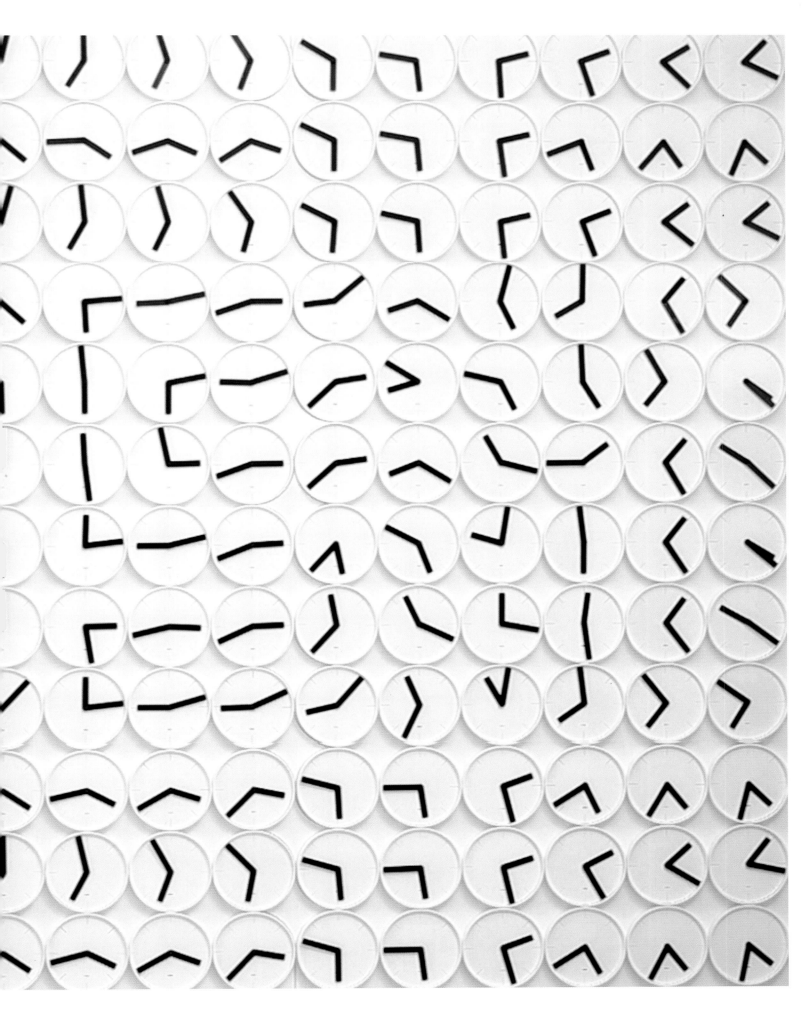

Tuomas Markunpoika

—FINNISH, ACTIVE IN NETHERLANDS, B. 1982—

Tuomas Markunpoika explores metaphysics in the design of objects. Inspired by his grandmother, whose memory was fading in the grip of Alzheimer's, Markunpoika's design for his Engineering Temporality cabinet (2012) evokes two fundamental experiences of being: memory and impermanence. The object is made from hand-cut rings of tubular steel that he welded over a traditional wooden cabinet. The cabinet was burned away, leaving behind the blackened metal rings, a shadow of the original form. Almost ghostly in appearance, the cabinet expresses fragility. Markunpoika, born in the provincial city of Jyväskylä, Finland, was trained as an industrial designer at Finland's Lahti Institute of Design and Fine Arts. After an exchange at the Danish Design School in Copenhagen and an internship with Marcel Wanders's studio in Amsterdam, he pursued a more conceptual path for design. Markunpoika graduated with a master's in contextual design from the Design Academy Eindhoven in Netherlands and set up his practice in Amsterdam, where he currently lives and works. —ANDREA LIPPS

————Describe yourself as a designer.
I was trained as an industrial designer; I studied furniture and products for mass production at Lahti University [Institute] of Design in Finland. After my bachelor's degree, I started looking for something more conceptual and experimental. I found the environment in Finland very suffocating and very small. It was difficult to do anything outside the established framework. Attending the Design Academy Eindhoven for two years was a big shift in my career and perception of design.
————How has your Finnish background affected your design practice? It is a country with a powerful design history.
I feel that the Finnish design heritage is a burden to me. As a younger designer, you have to support this framework that was set by the previous generation of world-class designers. Finland is a small country that has produced a few international designers. You are always working in the shadow of these people. We

need a complete cultural shift. There needs to be something new. This is one of the reasons I left Finland. I don't want to fight against the windmills but rather do my thing somewhere else. I guess it's something you cannot get rid of. You just need to unlearn things.
————Describe your current way of working.
My approach is conceptual. I am not solely concerned about functionality, but more about the metaphysics in design, and how philosophy can resonate through objects. An object doesn't need to solely be functional to be important and valuable. I don't define function as solely practical, but also as psychological and metaphysical—that the object gives something more than it is.
————Tell me about your Engineering Temporality collection?
The topic for the work was my grandmother, who was suffering from Alzheimer's. It was a stressful time for me and my family. We were

seeing a person that we knew start to lose her memories and personality—we were seeing her deteriorate in front of our eyes. Engineering Temporality was about the idea of how and why we make objects that are so different from people. How and why do we make objects that try to achieve some sort of perfection in terms of aesthetics or in terms of durability? For me, it is hard to connect with objects made with a mass-produced perfection. They don't resonate any kind of human nature. The objects in this collection become vessels for memories, almost elevating the tedious functionality of everyday objects.

I chose tubular steel for the material because it is commonly used in the furniture industry. It became a symbol of a perfectly mass-produced, symmetrical material. I wanted to mutilate the material and make it imperfect. So I started cutting pieces manually from a steel pipe and started rendering each one individually. I welded the steel rings onto wooden furniture, which I then burned away to leave an exoskeleton. It became like a naked memory, a physical memory of the furniture—kind of a smoky, shady, semi-transparent memory.
————Many of your works are made through a physical process. Do you need to make things yourself?
It's hard for me to work on a computer. For me, it's much easier to think in three dimensions when I have material in front of me and I can see how it behaves, what I can do with it. You can work in any material and do anything on the computer, but that doesn't necessarily mean it the piece will work in reality.
————What comes to mind when you hear the word "beauty"?
Beauty is nature's way of seduction. Beauty is also highly subjective. Everybody has some sort of general idea of beauty: symmetry or asymmetry, certain colors or shapes. I think beauty can be found in objects that are not necessarily beautiful in a visual way. There can be something in the object that renders it beautiful as soon as you know something about it, like a process or a history that makes you look at it in a very different way. I think beauty mutates and transforms very easily.
————What is the most beautiful time of day?
The moments when the sun sets or rises. There is a lot of energy in the moments when something is changing. You can visually see something is going to happen.
————What is the most beautiful place you've visited?
I don't have any particular place at the moment that I would revere as the most pristine and beautiful.
— INTERVIEW WITH SUVI SALONIEMI

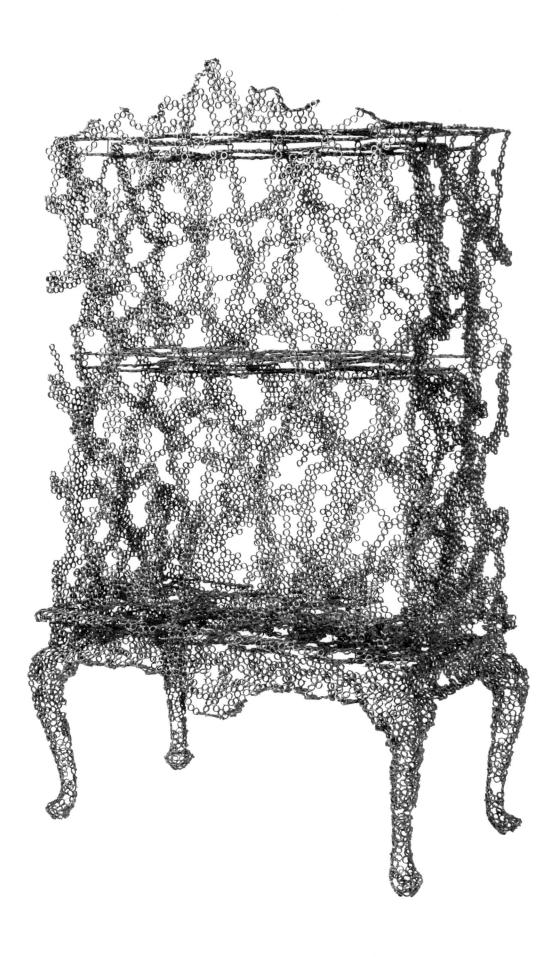

Cabinet, from Engineering Temporality series,
2012; Welded and burned steel rings; 175 ×
95 × 50 cm (5 ft. 8⅞ in. × 37⅜ in. × 19¹¹⁄₁₆ in.)

OPPOSITE: The wood cabinet is burned away.

Maiko Takeda

—JAPANESE, B. 1986—

Maiko Takeda is a milliner and jewelry designer whose work proposes new expressions of body adornment. Having grown up in Tokyo, Takeda moved to London to study at Central Saint Martins College of Art and Design and later the Royal College of Art. The influence of nature is apparent in her work. Inspired by environmental phenomena such as shadow, clouds, and wind, Takeda's work is sensual, exploring ephemeral and immaterial effects. Atmospheric Reentry (2013), for example, is a collection of headpieces with bristles that emanate from a wearer's head to create an aura-like effect. The edges blur into the surrounding environment in softened forms. Made of thinly shredded acetate tinted with color gradients, the pieces have an inviting tactility, evocative of a protective, synthetic fur. — ANDREA LIPPS

———Could you describe your starting point for the Atmospheric Reentry collection?

I had this thought that it would be quite cool for a hat or a piece of accessory not to have a distinct edge to itself, so that when it blurs into its surrounding space you don't know where it starts or where it ends. Like a cloud. You can't really grab it. You can't keep it in a box. I thought it would be nice if someone wore something like that on the body as an

accessory. That was just a simple question I had. So I started experimenting with a lot of materials and techniques to achieve this effect visually. I found that printing colors on acetate sheets—which I then shredded and layered— created an aura, an effect on the surface.

At that time, I happened to go to an opera, *Einstein on the Beach* written by Philip Glass and directed by Robert Wilson. I loved its sounds and colors and movement, the whole spatial experience. That became a main inspiration for this collection, which guided me through the whole process.

———What were the challenges in creating the collection?

The biggest challenge was to discover a way to incorporate sheets of acetate to create a structure that is flexible enough to be worn on the body. At first I was making a lot of sheets of pointy acetate. I was folding the bottom then stitching these sheets onto fabric, but it could only bend in one direction. The head is round and has to be sculpted around freely. Plus, I wanted to make it as transparent as possible, which stitching on the fabric didn't allow.

I ended up using laser-cut acrylic discs. You sandwich the acetate with two discs of acrylic, and each disc has a hole on each corner, so you just close the holes with a metal jump ring. There's no glue or stitching. The acetate stays in place, and when you link those units with other jump rings, it becomes a module that you can build on. By linking these small units, I could build a flexible structure on the body. That enabled me to do many different shapes. These spikes are waving in the wind, and as the body moves, the piece follows as well. It became a lot more sophisticated and natural. That was the biggest breakthrough in my process.

———Your work transcends traditional ideas about personal adornment. Can you speak to this?

Millinery is a profession with such a long and rich tradition. The materials used for hats are often still quite limited, though. So in that sense I wanted to change the conventional idea about headwear.

Experience is very important in my work. With Atmospheric Reentry, it lives its life when it's on the body, when someone's moving in it, when people around it see and experience the whole moment.

———What comes to mind when you hear the word "beauty"?

Poise.

———What is the most beautiful time of the day?

When the sun is setting and the colors of the sky change.

———What is the most beautiful place you've visited?

I don't know exactly where it was, but it was somewhere up in a mountain in Japan. I was very small, and my parents took me and my sister to watch shooting stars.

— INTERVIEW WITH JUSTIN ZHUANG

Atmospheric Reentry series, 2013–14; Acetate films, acrylic discs, rhodium-plated metal jump rings, plastic base, fabric-covered metal wire

OPPOSITE: Atmospheric Reentry series, 2013–14; Acetate films, acrylic discs, rhodium-plated metal jump rings

Sissel Tolaas

—NORWEGIAN, ACTIVE IN GERMANY, B. 1962—

Sissel Tolaas is a smell designer, artist, chemist, researcher, odor theorist—a "professional in-betweener" as she calls it, working amid research, commercial, and creative innovation. Smell is Tolaas's medium, but her interest is not a conventional approach to scent, which is characterized by perfumes that camouflage, deodorize, and sanitize reality. For Tolaas, smell is information. She composes provocative smells to stimulate memory, recreate place, capture seasonality, and arouse emotional and intellectual responses. She simulates complex and often transgressive olfactory experiences to enhance smell sensibilities. She investigates and develops language to communicate smell. She values sensory experience as a way to heighten reality. Tolaas is smell's biggest advocate. Born in Norway but currently based in Berlin, Tolaas studied mathematics, chemical science, languages, and visual art in Norway, Poland, Russia, and the United Kingdom. In 2004, with support from International Flavors & Fragrances Inc. (IFF), Tolaas founded the SMELL RE_searchLab, a workspace to research, develop, and execute smell-related projects for institutional, educational, and individual clients. — ANDREA LIPPS

——How do you describe what you do?
I live life with all of my senses, first and not last starting with the nose. I let my nose do most of the job, in terms of identifying, understanding, and perceiving the world.

——What were the early drivers that led you to working with smell?
Coming from Scandinavia, the large topic of concern in my life was weather. So at a very early stage in life, I started to ask questions about this massive "invisible nothingness" that surrounds us called air. Atmosphere. It seemed to be very important for our well-being and our existence. I made chemical experiments to see if I could discover dimension beyond what I knew about the existing weather that could help me understand it better.

The air that we breathe contains particles: smell molecules, information beyond our conscious understanding. And we have this amazing tool on the body called the nose. But why is it that we are so nose-disabled? What is a smell? Why don't we learn about chemistry of smell and how we can use our noses?

We have a body. I call it the hardware. We also are equipped with software called the senses. We largely navigate and understand our surroundings based on the look of things. But the nose knows long before any of the other senses start processing. In humans, this process happens subconsciously. In animals, it happens consciously. I wanted to check out if I could have a more conscious relationship to smell and could train my nose, like I would train other parts of my body.

From the beginning, questions of concern have been: Would I then be able to smell in a conscious way? What if I could relate to smells in a rational, rather than an emotional, way? What about smell and language? Smell and hedonics? Smell and tolerance?

——How do you train your nose?
I have an archive of 6,730 smells from reality, collected from seven years of fieldwork all over the world. Other people would write a diary; I collected smells for the same purpose. I also have a professional chemistry lab, with 4,000 chemical components. Every morning, I have my smelling session. That's how I start my day. I smell a certain amount of molecules or smell compositions.

——How has your life changed by using your nose to gather information from your surroundings?
Tolerance. I never thought that I would become as tolerant as I am now. I can go into situations where other people just turn around and leave. I can go beyond the borders that I put up for myself before and discover constellations of life and parts of my surroundings that I didn't know existed. It adds a quality to life. I now use all of my senses in a more conscious way! I use more than one sense to understand my life and to understand my surroundings. I confront a situation; I walk into a city; I meet a person; and I decide: how am I going to approach and perceive this situation? Do I use my nose, my ears, my eyes, touch, or all of them, or a combination? Adding the nose to understand and perceive reality, you gain joy, playfulness.

——Dimensionality.
Yes. With my topic of concern, I have to be everywhere and all the time! Everyone has known, still knows what playing incorporates. It's very important not to forget this. I see when I do workshops with different types of professionals or age groups; there is never a situation where people are not leaving the workshop without big smiles on their faces. Smelling and the nose bring back joy!

——Yet we don't have much language to articulate smell. We assign a value to it.
Exactly. There are hardly any terms or words in most languages. Mostly we describe smells as bad and good, and through metaphors. Having said that, language is a very important aspect of my work. I do believe it is possible to speak about smells with very precise terms and words, even if it has to be abstract. Look at for instance naming colors. It is also very abstract!

——What comes to mind when you hear the word "beauty"?
Tolerance. Real smells: pure and honest stuff. For me, that is quality beauty, and I prefer that rather than a perfumed and sanitized reality. By camouflaging, we remove a lot of important information about a situation, a person, a city. . . . This information is there for a purpose. "Tolerance" is the key word for a new approach to our surroundings and us. We have to learn to live together in a different way. To be able to do this, we have to go back to the body and learn the functions of the tools we have. A very important aspect here is that these tools are free! This process can start with the nose! Nothing stinks, but thinking makes it so.

——What is the most beautiful time of day?
The early morning. My nose is smartest in the morning.

——What is the most beautiful place you've visited?
Iceland.

— INTERVIEW WITH ANDREA LIPPS

OPPOSITE: Tolaas doing field research.

SmellScape Tokyo display, Museum of Contemporary Art, Tokyo, 2013

OPPOSITE: *Fear* display, Museum of Contemporary Art, Tokyo, 2013

Intricate

Whether handmade or mass-produced, intricate images and objects revel in richness of detail, complexity of form, or a multiplicity of elements. Performing astonishing feats of craftsmanship and physical construction, designers and artisans create textured or patterned surfaces that engage the eye in a wandering journey.

"When you do everything yourself by hand and you put so many hours into something, it's like it has your hair inside, it has your tears inside, it has your food inside . . . the work is really personal."

———————————————————————————————— Sandra Backlund

Sandra Backlund

—SWEDISH, B. 1975—

Sandra Backlund's knitwear has no comparison. Operating outside the fashion cycle, her voluminous, textural, and layered forms evoke both organic and cyborg origins to exaggerate and distort the body's silhouette. "I mean to shape the idea of the body using clothes," she says. The tessellated form of a dress that she created in Fall 2013, for instance, operates as a type of soft armor. The natural, undyed cotton emphasizes the garment's shape and highlights Backlund's extreme dexterity with the craft of crochet. Her creations flow organically from the techniques and materials of knitting and crochet, much as her sculptural designs borrow from the avant-garde and from conceptual art. Backlund graduated from Beckmans College of Design in Stockholm, Sweden, in 2004, and subsequently established her eponymous company. In 2007, Backlund was the Grand Prix winner of the Festival International de Mode et de Photographie à Hyères. — SARAH SCATURRO + PENNY WOLFSON

———Could you tell me about your way of working?

Knitwear is my specialty, but I also do other traditional handicraft techniques like crochet, usually with yarns. I have also done some projects with paper, like origami. I don't sketch; I just start off from the material. Then I start building a 3D collage on the mannequin. It's almost like sculpture. I don't really plan for an outfit and then execute the silhouette; I just do it while working. What's good with knitting and crochet is that you can create your own fabric while working. You don't have to cut them. You just go ahead and add. I do everything myself by hand. I invent the pieces while doing them.

———It seems like the material is very important to your work. Is that the main source of your ideas?

No. I would say maybe the techniques are most important, and then I try to find a color or special yarn or something that adds to the idea of the technique. Sometimes, also, it's what I can find in the local store when I'm inspired. It depends, it's not so planned, it's very . . .

———Spontaneous?

Artistic, in that sense. Sometimes the materials are really important for the idea, and sometimes it's just a matter of getting to the result.

———How do you do that?

I like working alone. I usually lock myself up and concentrate really hard. I don't listen to music or anything that can possibly distract me. I usually don't get inspired so much by places or objects or situations. When you do everything yourself by hand and you put so many hours into something, it's like it has your hair inside; it has your tears inside; it has your food inside, in a way—in them. The work is really personal.

Often you have to be very patient because sometimes you need to knit for four or five full days just to understand if it was a bad idea or if it gave you something. I guess it's a constant struggle—the combination between the passion of finding a good solution and the frustration when you don't find it.

——— How do the techniques or things that you take away from each project inform the work that you do later on?

It's always like an evolving story. I'm never going to stop working. It's always something I found from the last thing I did or something I couldn't do within that idea I put for myself for that time. I save it and use it again in another situation.

Everything is linked together. I work sometimes with a collection, but it's more like chapters. It's not really separated. It's an ongoing process.

———What comes to mind when you hear the word "beauty"?

For me, it's a matter of execution in the traditional handicrafts, like a pattern-maker point of view when someone is really good at doing nice silhouettes or creating shape for clothes, but it's unique or something extra. I consider [beauty] a big part when I work, but it's not the most important. Sometimes I'll just choose to do something that I know is not conventionally beautiful. I work a lot starting from the human body and thinking about different ways to either show or hide, and also to exaggerate.

I mean to shape the idea of the body using clothes. In fashion it's always been about this. This is why we have all the high heels and corsets and things like that.

I don't work starting from "I want to do a beautiful piece of clothing." Sometimes my clothes end up being very flattering and beautiful, and if the right person wears it, it's really great. Then, sometimes it's something beyond that.

———What is the most beautiful time of day?

The night. It is when I solve a lot of the most difficult problems within my work.

———What is the most beautiful place you've visited?

The ocean.

— INTERVIEW WITH TIFFANY LAMBERT

SECTION OPENER: Dress, from Fall/Winter collection, 2013; Crocheted cotton

Homa Delvaray

—IRANIAN, B. 1980—

Typography provides the building blocks for the imaginative visual constructions of Homa Delvaray. Three-dimensional letterforms interconnect with buildings, interiors, and objects in her remarkable graphic works, which seek to surprise and engage viewers with mysterious, multifaceted depictions of language in space. Whether creating a poster for a recycling project or designing the cover of an architecture book, Delvaray uses the raw materials of Iranian visual culture and Persian traditional arts to build detailed works that confront the polarities between East and West, tradition and modernity, and local and international design vocabularies. Since earning a degree in visual communications from Tehran University in 2006, Delvaray has applied her deeply personal, culturally situated approach to projects for Iranian arts and culture organizations as well as for overseas clients in London, Berlin, Los Angeles, and beyond. Her poster designs have been recognized with numerous awards including the 2009 jury prize at the Trnava Poster Triennial in Slovakia, and exhibited at the 2015 CO2 Global Poster Biennial, Colorado, USA. — JUSTIN ZHUANG

————How would you describe yourself as a designer?
As a graphic designer, I like to create a richly detailed graphic work that functions as a communication medium as well, and I like to combine contemporary formal and conceptual elements with Iran's traditional visual culture. Being in love with unusual, unrelated, mismatched things, I am passionate about creating colorful, detailed images. My works have been called maximalist, orientalist, eclectic, mysterious, and ambiguous, but I don't care about the labels. This is the way I think, work, and live. I would like to enrich or expand the audience's taste and perception. In my opinion, graphic designers can change the collective taste of a society and culture by respecting their viewers' intelligence and educating them through provocative and powerful designs.

————Tell me about your work process.
My work is centered on typographic designs with architectural structures. I look for new, unusual ways to combine traditional and modern elements by creating intricately constructed illustrations. Despite its seemingly formal nature, my style does not defy "concept"; concepts in my work are nudged to deeper layers and placed in between intertwined forms that require decoding, as has always been the case in Eastern art.

Nearly all of my works are digitally finalized versions of hand sketches. Sometimes I look at traditional visual elements as raw materials to work with, and I rejuvenate them by using them in contemporary contexts. I used to scan my drawings, transfer the files to software, and refine the imagery from there. Nowadays, to shorten the process, I prefer to start my work directly in software and render my drawings in vector format. However, I've always begun the ideation/design process by sketching on paper. The resulting work becomes a fusion of past as well as contemporary properties.

My Iranian-Islamic background is an inexhaustible source of inspiration, both visually and conceptually. Sources include architecture, calligraphy, manuscripts, lithography, book decoration, Persian painting, carpet patterns, folkloric symbols, and more. By taking this experimental approach, I have created a visual language that is both progressive and based in tradition. My works are a reflection of where I live—Tehran, a paradoxical city that also reflects my personal life. Novels and art history, literature and movies, music and visual arts—these are inseparable parts of my life. Graphic design, in my opinion, is a multidimensional and interdisciplinary profession. I believe any graphic designer must expose him- or herself to a variety of art forms, ideas, and social contexts.

————What comes to mind when you hear the word "beauty"?
This question is connected to the sources of inspiration that I mentioned earlier. So my answer is Iranian-Islamic arts.

————What is the most beautiful time of day?
Afternoon.

————What is the most beautiful place you've visited?
Istanbul.

— INTERVIEW WITH SUVI SALONIEMI

Poster, Tehran Touch, Iranian Graphic Design
New Scene, 2014; 100 × 70 cm (39⅜ × 27⁹⁄₁₆ in.)

Poster, Silver Cypress, The Third Biennial of the
Iranian Graphic Designers Society, 2013; 100 ×
70 cm (39⅜ × 27⁹⁄₁₆ in.)

Poster, Tehran Monoxide Project, Photos From
Four-to-Eighteen-Year-Olds' Viewpoint, 2014;
100 × 70 cm (39⅜ × 27⁹⁄₁₆ in.)

Hechizoo

—BOGOTÁ, COLOMBIA, FOUNDED 2000—

Founded by Jorge Lizarazo (Colombian, b. 1968), Hechizoo is a weaving atelier based in Bogotá, Colombia, that produces textiles for rugs, upholstery, window treatments, and architectural meshes. Lizarazo is a self-taught weaver, having trained as an architect at University of Los Andes. He practiced in the Paris offices of Massimiliano Fuksas and Santiago Calatrava before returning to Colombia to establish Hechizoo, bringing on artisans with diverse expertise in their country's rich weaving traditions. Hechizoo's textiles revel in detail with a deep tactility—copper wire and nylon thread are hand-wrapped around fique-plant fibers to create a luminous rug (2014). Other textiles evoke landscape—the colors of one large woven rug (2014) mimic the subtle gradations of deepening water. Lizarazo's architectural training certainly plays out in the scale and proportion of many of Hechizoo's pieces, not to mention its focus on material experimentation. The workshop mixes indigenous natural fibers—jute, raw silk, and wool—with unconventional materials—copper, twine, steel wire, and nylon monofilament—resulting in textiles that filter and reflect light to transform space. — ANDREA LIPPS

———What is the meaning of your workshop's name, "Hechizoo"?

JORGE LIZARAZO: I didn't want to name my workshop Jorge Lizarazo. I'm an architect; I'm not a weaver, so if I was by myself I couldn't do that many things. I need a lot of people; I need a lot of knowledge. Our textiles try to translate the knowledge of the people of my country. And we saw the reaction of people when they see our pieces—they are enchanted. They can't describe very well where the textiles are coming from, but they recognize a cultural heritage. So like that, the name became Hechizoo. *Hechizoo*—in Spanish, it means "enchantment."

———How do the notions of cultural heritage and traditional craft play out in your work?

For example, let's talk about a new research for a project that I'm doing. Colombia has a very important river called the Magdalena River, along which there is a heritage of fishermen that have an unbelievable culture of weaving nets for fishing. I've started doing an investigation of the meshes that they weave along the river. And when I was in Peru and in Chile, I realized that this weaving is the same part of the cultural tradition passed for more than two thousand years. They're intact and beautiful. It's a very long tradition.

Looking at the way the fisherman handle their yarns, I say, "Why not show this tradition?" But if I show the same way that they're doing it, of course people will say, "OK, no. This is the same that we have been seeing for a long, long time." That's why metal is very important for all my research, because every time as

we show anything in metal, people realize that we are evaluating the technique.

I always say that metal is a silent witness of tradition. To us, metal is like the DNA that we always want to avoid in our work, but at the end it always comes back to us. I always wanted to change metal for something else. But people are delighted by shiny surfaces. It makes our work so much easier when we have this reaction of the people; it's the best way of introducing the old techniques into our present world.

———A weaving of the industrial and the organic, if you will.

Exactly.

———And it creates the enchantment you spoke of earlier.

Yes! Exactly. There you are.

———You're an architect, not a weaver. What drew you to weaving?

I was working in Europe with Massimiliano Fuksas. I was the person in charge of the Materiotech, the materials library. Massimiliano said to me, "Jorge, remember that a material always has more than one use. It's in your guts to experiment with them." I think that was the beginning of Hechizoo.

We love to experiment with yarns. We started with three yarns, and in my workshop today there are more than two thousand different yarns. We just kind of mix one with the other.

I always say to the people that to me the beauty of the culture are *mestizos*. It's the mélange, it's the mix of different bloods. In our textiles, we want to do that. We want to mix the blood of mineral yarns with the "blood,"

we might say, of vegetable yarns, or animal yarns, or industrial yarns, and that creates the product that to us has become unique.

———Your work is incredibly materials based, and it also references nature. Is that a large inspiration for you?

Very much. The color in nature, the texture. I am very lucky that I was born in this country that has such a complicated nature and such an untouched nature, which makes it beautiful. That's what's beautiful about the Amazonas, which inspires the project that we're doing for the Triennial. The Amazonas is amazing, because you realize how beautiful the world was at the beginning, and how beautiful it is now. In the night, you start hearing a whole world, a world for the insects, a world for the birds, a world for the mammals. It's a world for everyone that is there, and they just communicate well together. The project will be an homage to the Amazonas and in a way an SOS to keep the Amazonas safe from all of us, for all of us.

———What comes to mind when you hear the word "beauty"?

Love. Love is like beauty because it is overwhelming. When you see beauty, you have this moment of silence, of stillness. In this world that's so noisy, and that you don't have time for anything, to keep those two constants of stillness and silence together, just for a moment, that's beauty. That's love. That's happiness.

———What is the most beautiful time of day?

Between five and five thirty in the evening, when the sun is coming down in Bogotá, is one of the most beautiful, purple lights.

———What is the most beautiful place you've visited?

The Chicamocha Canyon in Colombia. There is this little river between these two giant, gray-pink mountains, stripped naked and with no other distraction. It is powerful only because of its presence. I've found beauty coming from the landscape.

— INTERVIEW WITH ANDREA LIPPS

Wire and thread are hand-wrapped around fique-plant fibers to create an iridescent rug, 2014.

Leandra rug, 2013; Silver-plated wire, colored wire, nylon; 4.5 × 6 m (14 ft. 9 ³⁄₁₆ in. × 19 ft. 8 ¼ in.)

OPPOSITE: Detail of Caribbean Rain rug, 2013; Embroidered tin wire and colored copper wire

Detail of Pangea dress

OVERLEAF, LEFT: Pangea dress, from Spring/ Summer 2015 ready-to-wear collection, 2014; Main body: nylon tulle; Contrast 1: 38% polyethylene, 32% polyurethane, 15% cotton, 15% polyester; Contrast 2: 50% cotton, 50% PVC; Lining: silk

OVERLEAF, RIGHT: Dam C coat, from Fall/Winter 2015 ready-to-wear collection, 2015; Collar, placket: wool; Main bodice: polyester; Skirt overlayer: polyester; Skirt underlayer: wool; Embroidery: PVC; Lining: silk

Mary Katrantzou

—GREEK, ACTIVE IN UNITED KINGDOM, B. 1983—

Trompe l'oeil prints featuring huger-than-life renderings of geometric jewelry elements propelled Mary Katrantzou onto the world stage straight out of her graduation show at London's Central Saint Martins fashion textiles course in 2008. She sold prints to Bill Blass while she was still a student, and she won support from the British Fashion Council's NewGen program, enabling her to develop six seasons of graphically complex ready-to-wear collections. Moving beyond her initial focus of mapping captivating surfaces onto strong silhouettes, Katrantzou is now exploring a heady, almost Victorian mix of pleats, folds, embossing, and embroidery. Her modernist attention to shape and structure is colliding in new ways with her ongoing fascination with intricate pattern and optical opulence. — ELLEN LUPTON

————**You studied architecture at the Rhode Island School of Design. What influence does architecture have on your approach to fashion?**
Architecture is still something I'm interested in, and I think form and structure play a significant role in my collections. For my Fashion Week 15 collection, we worked with automotive technology to mold and sculpt entirely seamless bustiers and tops. Structurally they were a real challenge to create, from their initial foundations to the dimensions. Everything was very technical!

————**What ultimately led you to fashion?**
I transferred from Rhode Island School of Design to Central Saint Martins to study textile design. Most people there were applying their textile and fabrication developments to clothing, and it looked interesting and ultimately inspired me to sign up for the MA fashion course. If you'd told me ten years ago that I'd be a fashion designer, I'd have laughed!

————**You've pioneered the use of digital prints in fashion, engineered in perfect proportion to the body. Where does your interest for such bold, colorful prints come from?**
My work has always been about perception and creating an identifiable visual language. Print is an excellent way of demonstrating this, and color is very communicative. However in recent collections, we've shifted the creative direction to demonstrate it through lace, embroidery, the craftsmanship, and a feminine silhouette. As a designer it's important to evolve and allow yourself to explore the depths of your identity.

————**Your most recent collections are inspired by evolution and modernism/Victorianism. Tell me about your process. What is the starting point for a new collection? Where do you find inspiration?**
At the beginning of the design process, my initial ideas tend to stem from a visual image, which I then expand upon in terms of researching materials and silhouettes. I try not to niche myself too much in terms of an identifiable theme at the beginning; the theme often evolves to encompass more than one idea as we develop the collection. I travel a lot, which certainly helps the get the creative juices flowing! I carry a scrapbook with me when I travel, collecting anything from stamps and menus to scraps of fabric, and I'm forever with my iPhone in hand, snapping pictures. My iPhone holds my archive!

————**Your recent collections have shifted away from a focus on prints to the use of embroidery, embossing, texture, and unexpected materials. What do these new materials, textures, and techniques bring to your practice?**
It's exciting to work with new fabrications and textures, as they really add another dimension to the collection. We work with embroidery factories in India and have a fantastic in-house embroidery team who hand-embroider super-intricate garments and really allow us to innovate in new areas of luxury design.

————**What draws you to the rich detail and patterned surfaces seen throughout your work?**
Surface innovation is something that will always resonate strongly with me. I've always had an eye for detail, and print, textiles, and embroidery allow us to explore that. Many of the details in the pieces are missed on the catwalk, so when people have the chance to see them up close, they can see each tiny glitter flock, each embroidered panel and seam detail.

————**What comes to mind when you hear the word "beauty"?**
The focus of the brand has always been about turning filtered beauty into applied design and design into function. Beauty is entirely subjective; it's more about individual interpretation, which is something I've tried to capture and translate through the collections. From footwear, to interiors, to stark Kenophobia, to priceless Chinese objets d'art and verbose Victoriana—it's about finding functionality and beauty in design, and demonstrating it through innovation.

————**What is the most beautiful time of day?**
Dusk. There's something so peaceful about a sunset!

————**What is the most beautiful place you've visited?**
Croatia and Montenegro are both beautiful, so unspoilt with the bluest sea I've ever seen!
— INTERVIEW WITH ANDREA LIPPS

Richard Niessen
—DUTCH, B. 1972—

Graphic elements collide, converge, and overlap—more by chance than by design—in the work of Richard Niessen. Faceted spaces emerge from saturated colors and gilded planes. Working in Amsterdam as an independent designer, Niessen studied design at the Gerrit Rietveld Academy, graduating in 1996. Alongside professional clients that include museums and foundations, Niessen pursues collaborations, publications, and self-authored projects in the cultural realm. *Palace of Typographic Masonry* (2015) is a series of screenprinted posters that distill the elements of Niessen's distinctive design vocabulary into a "memory palace." The three main wings of this gamelike space are Sign, Symbol, and Ornament, categories of expression that animate Niessen's rich body of work. — ELLEN LUPTON

————Tell me about your practice.

I've always worked by myself, but I share the studio with my wife, Esther de Vries, and besides helping each other out, we do a magazine together called *1:1:1*. Esther's work is more about book design and image editing—she's maybe more for the pixels, and I am more for the vectors. My work is very graphical and based on signs, ornaments, and typographic systems. I forge these elements into amalgams, which are used in mostly nonlinear structures. I call this method "Typographic Masonry."

I like to work on identities. When an identity continues for a while, I can develop a layered language or sign system over time. It feels like I'm talking in a new language. I also like to work densely with artists. I have worked a lot with Dutch artist Jennifer Tee. It started when I designed a book about her work and made several typefaces that played a role in this book. Then she took some of these typefaces back into her work. And then I made a publication about that work again. We were developing a language together.

————You have personal projects and then more commercial client-driven tasks. Tell me about this range of work.

I like to collaborate closely with the client to develop something new. It's quite difficult for a commercial client to accept this method. This is happening in the cultural field as well; there is always a communication manager or someone who comes between me and the one who is really in charge. If there are more people in between, then collaboration gets quite difficult.

I've worked on a broad range of high-end limited editions with different materials. I have made works in wood, a coin, my own fabrics, and ceramic tiles, but also a lot of print work in silkscreen. It's the translation into all types of materials and all kinds of forms that interests me.

————Where do your ideas come from?

Often it's quite chaotic. Sometimes I keep sketches, and I place them in order so I can look back on the process. I have a few of these process books now. When I show them to students or to whoever's interested, I find out that after one hour, I already have the idea, and then I just start.

But then it takes a long time until I'm satisfied about the concept. I just start collecting images, and it's like one big labyrinth that I'm

Preparatory photograph for Palace of Typographic Masonry.

going through. When I look back on the end results, I see that everything I've touched along this journey through the labyrinth is somehow reflected in the final product.

What comes out is never one clear image. For me, it's a bit like poetry. If you make a poem, you have to look at the rhythm, and you want to put in some content; you want to talk about something. But slowly, the poem takes over. And when it's finished, you can't really tell what it's exactly about—it refers to all kinds of things. My work is good when it points in different directions.

Again, it really does feel like a labyrinth. I always tell my clients that it's going to be like that. I notice that they can't really follow the path that I'm taking because I'm changing ideas all the time. I just take them along on the journey. Afterward, they realize what happened.

———Tell me about the Palace of Typographic Masonry.

A "memory palace" is a traditional method of ordering and retrieving information through symbolic spaces. The Palace of Typographic Masonry is an imagined architecture in which I can place my sources and structure my input. I am "building" the "palace" through a series of workshops with students around the world (who, by following the workshop, become initiated, passed, and raised into the first degree of the craft of Typographic Masonry). As of now I have made the Pavilions of Honor (ECV Aquitaine in Bordeaux), The Rhythm Section (COMA workshop with Boston University students), and the Gate of Ciphers and Codes (Lebanese American University in Byblos, Lebanon). The "building bricks" are literally the building bricks: I construct the parts of the palace by playing with the bricks, and I will add more bricks in each episode, thus creating a growing "language" (inspired by, for instance, the symbolic language of freemasonry). Then there are the Seven Rulers, seven values translated from *The Seven Lamps of Architecture* by John Ruskin (1849). These rulers are moral tools to help to build the palace; they sometimes appear on the posters as well.

———Do you consider yourself a graphic designer or illustrator or both?

I'm a graphic designer, not an illustrator. I'm not looking for the image; I'm looking for the system. There's always some sort of toolkit that I'm making. In the posters, I'm trying to apply this toolkit in a way that is almost animated. There's some sort of randomness to it. So I'm thinking in a systematic way rather than in an illustrative way.

———Your work often takes some time to understand. Tell me about how you communicate.

I don't try to directly bring out the message. I am aware you could work in a clearer and more communicative manner. But I try to make a poster or book more layered and more beautiful, so it also functions in another way.

What is designed now is forced to be more and more efficient. What you see on the street is pure commercial seduction in a way. The Netherlands were seen as some sort of design paradise in the eighties and nineties. We had beautiful stamps and beautiful money and a very rich poster culture. Right now, there's not so much of that still visible in public space, because posters and graphic design have to deal with all the demands of the clients, these communication managers. They forget that graphic design can add to society in another way. When you're surrounded by beautiful communication in the city, instead of posters that only shout or seduce, they show that another language, another rhetoric, is possible.

It's just like when you hear people talk in a lovely way, you might also want to talk that way. When you focus only on how words can send a basic message, then the language becomes flat, because you don't need that many words to make yourself clear. The language dries out. This is where beauty plays a role. It's a human activity that you should not deny.

———What comes to mind when you hear the word "beauty"?

You can't measure beauty with an economical system. It's something in a work that is not directly functional. It's something extra. Beauty is somewhere in this area of the non-necessity of design. For a long time, you could not talk about beauty. When I was teaching, it was all about the concept. Last year I was studying a text by John Ruskin to find some values to talk about graphic design, and one of these values was beauty. He proclaimed that beauty always has to do with natural forms. Well, nowadays, you can't really say that. When I was thinking about this and arguing about it with my students, we decided that beauty can be found in very well-worked-out concepts. Design becomes convincing,

and beautiful, when it's worked out in a very consequential way, and then it can be guided by some sort of a natural law. And in this way, I could reuse this value by John Ruskin in this age, as one of my Seven Rulers.

———What is the most beautiful time of day, and what is the most beautiful place you've visited?

I think while we were still living in Bijlmermeer area [in Amsterdam], I had to bring the children to school. We would bike through a small piece of land where there were birds and some horses and a cow. I was doing that in the morning, around eight or half past nine, and the sun was rising. This is really like the most beautiful time and the most beautiful place. The land is what we call a *polder*. It used to be a lake, but they pumped out all the water, and then it was farming land for a long time. They didn't build anything on it, so it was sort of a leftover space that reminded you of the farmland that it used to be. It felt special because all the land around it was used so densely. It wasn't a park, but also not really farmland. Because we had to go there every day, we noticed the small differences each day. So you could focus on the light or on the kind of weather or when a bird had made a nest.

— INTERVIEW WITH SUVI SALONIEMI

CLOCKWISE FROM TOP LEFT: Poster, The Plan, Palace of Typographic Masonry, 2015; 118 × 84 cm (46⅞₁₆ × 33¹⁄₁₆ in.)

Poster, The Gallery of Modernity & Nostalgia, Palace of Typographic Masonry, 2015; 118 × 84 cm (46⅞₁₆ × 33¹⁄₁₆ in.)

Poster, The Conversation Room: "De Nieuwe Cultuur," Palace of Typographic Masonry, 2015; 118 × 84 cm (46⅞₁₆ × 33¹⁄₁₆ in.)

Poster, The Gate of Ciphers and Codes, Palace of Typographic Masonry, 2015; 118 × 84 cm (46⅞₁₆ × 33¹⁄₁₆ in.)

OPPOSITE: Poster, Building Bricks, Palace of Typographic Masonry, 2014; 118 × 84 cm (46⅞₁₆ × 33¹⁄₁₆ in.)

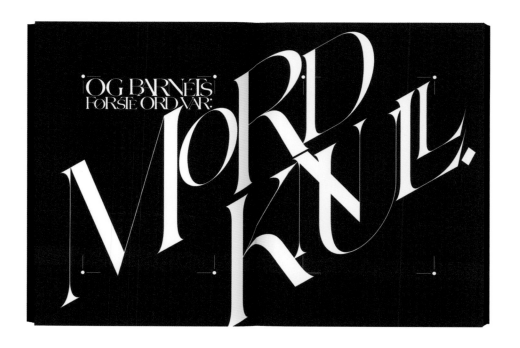

Non-Format

—OSLO, NORWAY, AND MINNEAPOLIS, MINNESOTA, USA, FOUNDED 2000—

Kjell Ekhorn (Norwegian, b. 1965) and Jon Forss (British, b. 1966) founded the contemporary graphic design practice Non-Format in 2000 while they were both living in London. Since 2007, when Jon moved to Minneapolis and Kjell returned to Oslo, Non-Format has been working as a two-man practice divided by four thousand miles of land and sea and a seven-hour time difference. From early clients like the music magazine *The Wire* to new clients like fashion designer Rick Owens or software giant Adobe, Non-Format keeps on refining their unique combination of custom typefaces and extraordinary images. Non-Format's typographic approach is hyperelegant and lushly abstract, as seen in posters for the Tokyo Type Directors Club and the book design for Norwegian writer, actor, and comedian Odd-Magnus Williamson's darkly humorous love story *Ord For Dagen Mordknull*, which are among their recent accomplishments. — SUVI SALONIEMI

————Tell me how you work together.

JON FORSS: We both police each other, in terms of figuring out whether something is working, whether it's really answering the brief, and whether it's doing anything new. We keep a check on each other, and we trust each other's judgment.

————Have you had any challenges in this method of working?

JF: We have fairly normal working hours, but we're located seven hours apart from each other. If we're lucky, there's a four-hour overlap between when I start work and when

Kjell finishes work. From a client's perspective, this can work quite well, inasmuch as our combined working day covers about three-quarters of a twenty-four-hour day. So a client can give us a correction in London, for example, and I can work on it and have it done so that they can receive it first thing the next morning. That can be a positive thing from a client's point of view, but it can also be something of a burden if it creates an expectation that any progress will be delivered first thing in the morning. We just have to be careful not to overpromise.

————Do you make your own artistic projects?

JF: Most of our work is commercial. We don't tend to self-initiate projects just for the sake of producing something. But there is a certain amount of experimental work that we create that we know will channel into our commercial work. We're not creating art for the sake of art. We experiment in the hope that it will lead to something that we can use on a future commission.

————How do you get your clients, or how do they find you?

JF: Mostly by word of mouth or by reputation. There are quite a few advertising agencies from all over the world that will have seen something that we've done and will contact us directly. There are publishers that want us for specific projects. There are fashion designers—for example, Rick Owens, who saw our work and asked us to design look-books for several of his collections.

KJELL EKHORN: There is one record label in London that we have worked with since we started. We have a couple of regular clients in Oslo as well, but our work is worldwide.

————How do you describe yourselves as designers?

JF: We like to think of ourselves as being quite contemporary. We're trying to push things along in terms of form, but there's a rigorous backbone to everything we create. Anything that looks like surface style is usually the result of intensive investigation. How would you describe it, Kjell?

KE: We trust our own guts in the way we approach stuff. If we do something and we think it looks good or looks interesting and feels interesting, then we trust that there will be other people who also will find it interesting. It's seldom that we have a brief and we find that the best way to serve this brief would be to do a pastiche of, for example, a seventies poster. We try to draw from ourselves rather than be too influenced by something we've seen.

JF: There's no agenda. We're not aiming for a particular kind of expression. If we create something that appeals to us—if we feel an emotional connection to something, then we trust that it's also going to resonate with the public.

————How about your concrete methods of working?

JF: Sometimes the quickest way is just to sketch it out, but neither of us is really

Non-Format for Cappelen Damm; Creative direction by Anti; Illustration by David Bray; Book, *Ord For Dagen Mordknull* by Odd-Magnus Williamson, 2014; Edges in black foil, blind-debossed cover; Closed: 26 × 19 cm (10¼ × 7½ in.)

hands-on. We're not getting out the paint-brushes or other tools of the craft trades. Once we have an idea, we generally pursue it on the computer. The invention of the Mac made it possible for me to be a graphic designer. Without that technology, I'm sure I would have ended up in a different kind of job. The computer allows us to create something and then say, "There you go. This is what it's going be."

KE: We try to be playful with the software we use. We like to sketch and play with things so that we don't really know how it's going to come out or what's going to happen. We use software as a playground for exploration.

————Tell me about your work with custom typefaces and typography.

KE: It started with customizing existing typefaces and developed from there. Creating our own typefaces has been a way of creating something unique for a project.

JF: Yes, you could argue that there are plenty of typefaces in the world, and there isn't that much need for many more of them, but we get such pleasure from creating a typeface—not necessarily the full alphabet, but enough characters for what needs to be written. It's a way of expressing something that's intrinsic to the project, but in our own voice. Generally we try to create our own typography rather than just choose a font.

KE: This also creates a sense of ownership. If you create your own typefaces, then that much more of the design feels unique to you. Custom typography creates unique value for clients. They get something that nobody else has, and that's part of what you get when you come to Non-Format. It isn't an add-on; it's the way we work. It's the way we look at design.

————Tell me about the Type Directors Club [2014] posters and Elsewhere [2014] poster.

JF: These were both fairly grand gestures. They're not the result of conceptual analysis so much as the result of a kind of free emotion that just poured out. When you see it from a distance, the TDC poster clearly spells out the *T*, *D*, and *C*, but when you get up close, you realize there's a lot of detail going on.

KE: Every part of it is crafted, right down to the typeface that's used on the small text, so that there's entertainment on all levels. Hierarchy is important to us. We wanted to make sure that it works just as well close-up as from a distance.

JF: The Elsewhere poster was a similar kind of animal. We had Von's illustration to work with, and then the challenge was to find an expression for the typography. Rather than focus on the title "Elsewhere," we decided to use his name, "Von," as the commanding word. What followed is an experiment in baroque typography, a modern version of an embellished display typeface that we simply overprinted in copper metallic ink. Again, the smaller supporting typeface is custom made.

————And the Mordknull book?

KE: This is essentially a short text written by a Norwegian author and comedian that is in part funny and in part quite dark. We wanted the design to contrast with the darkness of the content. We wanted to make it beautiful but slightly difficult to access, so that you really have to sit down and look closely at the words in order to decode them. Some words were pushed to the fore, making them bigger and quite easy to read, but these were always the friendlier, less disturbing parts of the content. So the book shows itself as something quite innocent, but when you actually read all the text, it has a much darker side. In order to do this, we had to set every letter of every word by itself, which ended up being a massive labor of love.

————Jon, how did you feel about working on a book in a foreign language?

JF: I did get an English transcript of the text, but it doesn't do justice to the original Norwegian. There's an awful lot of subtlety in the native tongue that gets lost in a literal translation. But for me, when I'm handed a page to play with, I'm looking at it as pure form from the outset. And then Kjell will come along and say, "That word needs to be a little bit easier to read," or "This is really the word that should be emphasized." It wasn't until near the very end that we decided to print it with the text white out of black pages. As a result, we had to thicken up a lot of the thinner lines, which was a lot of work. But worth it. Of course, not only is the cover black, with the title blind debossed into the front, but we also printed the edges of the pages black too, so the text itself really jumps out of the darkness.

————What comes to mind when you hear the word "beauty"?

JF: What interests me about beauty is the idea of transience. You can regard something as beautiful one day, and then the next day, something else is beautiful. There wouldn't be a fashion industry if there weren't, at any given moment, the most beautiful way to wear a pair of pants, and that the pants that we wore five years ago weren't beautiful anymore. And presumably, five years from now, there'll be an even more beautiful way to wear pants. Perceptions of beauty seem so clear at any given moment, but they're constantly changing.

KE: Beauty obviously has more to do with the heart than the head. I mean, there can be beautiful ideas, obviously, but beauty as form sits more in your gut. It's a gut reaction to something. An emotional response.

————What is the most beautiful time of day?

KE: That would be a winter morning, around 6:30 a.m., and being out on cross-country skis. That would certainly be the best way to start any day.

JF: I'm not an early-morning person, myself. I like the afternoon. Actually, right now, in the autumn, when the leaves have fallen and the sun's hanging low—that's beautiful. I like autumn. I like decay. And I like the sun going down rather than coming up.

————What is the most beautiful place you've visited?

KE: I think Tokyo is the most beautiful place, for all its craziness. I love it as a city. It's not traditionally beautiful the whole way through. It's just so fascinating that I find it beautiful.

JF: I like Tokyo, too, but I think, despite being someone who spends his whole day immersed in contemporary, edgy stuff, I really like Venice. Oh, and Lake Como, and Italy in general. My spiritual home is Italy. Venice is magical; it really is. It's one of those places where, if it disappeared, if it were removed from the face of the Earth and had never existed, no one would think to dream it up. It's just crazy. It doesn't make any sense. That's beautiful.

KE: It's one of those places where everyone just drifts around. Wherever you go in Venice, there will be somebody standing there looking around, wondering where the hell they are. It's like the whole place is just full of people drifting.

— INTERVIEW WITH SUVI SALONIEMI

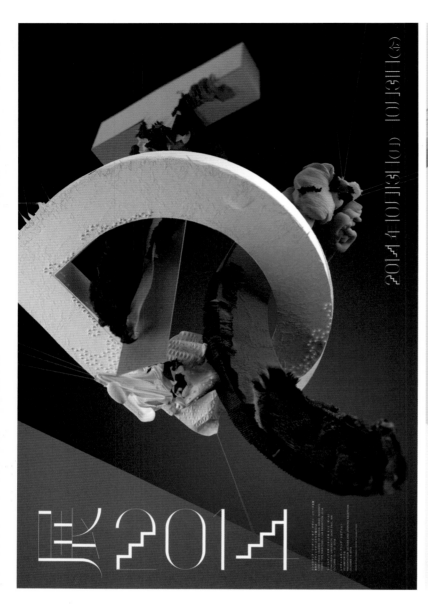

TOP, LEFT AND RIGHT: Posters, Tokyo Type Directors Club exhibition, 2014; Offset lithograph; 100 × 70.7 cm (39⅜ × 27¹³⁄₁₆ in.)

OPPOSITE: Non-Format with Illustration by Von; Poster, *Elsewhere* exhibition, KK Outlet gallery, London, 2014; Silkscreen printed in black and bronze ink; 70 × 50 cm (27⁹⁄₁₆ × 19¹¹⁄₁₆ in.)

ELSEWHERE BY VON IN COLLABORATION WITH JENS BUILY
KK. BUTLER GALLERY, LONDON

1—31 MAY 2014

Kustaa Saksi

—FINNISH, ACTIVE IN NETHERLANDS, B. 1975—

Lost somewhere between the dream world and the state of awakening is where one finds the surrealistic works of Kustaa Saksi. This pattern designer and textile artist mixes the sinuous lines of art nouveau with the psychedelic colors of pop art to create designs inspired by his memories of growing up in Kouvola, Finland. Trained in graphic design at the Lahti Institute of Design and Fine Arts, Saksi has applied his vision to textiles, patterns, spaces, and objects. He experimented with Jacquard weaving techniques to create Reveille (2015), a series of wool tapestries that visualize awakening—that blurred state of consciousness leading out of sleep where one may hazily encounter moths, bats, or celestial constellations. The textiles blend rubber, acrylic, lurex, and phosphorescent yarn with mohair and cashmere wool. Saksi moved to Paris in 2004 and now works in Amsterdam, where his studio occupies an old cigar factory. — JUSTIN ZHUANG

————Please describe your current way of working.

Some years ago, I had a chance to work with wool, designing a collection for an Italian cashmere knitwear manufacturer, Gentry Portofino. I was completely hooked with the softness, detail, and overall feel of the material. I loved the third dimension that textiles gave to my patterns. Two years ago, I started experimenting at the weavery at Tilburg's TextielMuseum [Netherlands]. There's a great heritage of tapestry making in this area between Belgium and Holland. That's where I started to experiment with Jacquard weaving technique, named after the French inventor Joseph Marie Jacquard [1752–1834]. His automated loom made it possible to weave complex, mechanically patterned silk fabrics, revolutionizing the textile-manufacturing industry around the world.

Weaving patterns definitely has its limitations as compared to printing, but it opens up a completely new world of possibilities, especially in detailing. In my artworks, I'm using the Jacquard weaving technique for its magnificent control over detailing and color and material combinations. I'm especially keen on using natural fibers like mohair, alpaca wool, cotton, and linen, and contrasting them with synthetic, high-tech materials such as glow-in-the-dark phosphoric and metallic acrylic threads. I'm producing my designs and artworks in small editions to keep them exclusive and at the highest possible quality.

I've always been into exploring new techniques, pushing myself away from my comfort zone, and experimenting with new

algorithms. A good example is a project for a pavilion we designed together with architect Gert Wingårdh [2013] for the Stockholm Furniture & Light Fair. I researched hundreds of old ceiling paintings and tried to capture the essence of that heritage, while Wingårdh took responsibility for the structural design of the cathedral-like pavilion. The structure resembled an otherworldly Darwinistic evolution—a work in progress that was constantly on the move. The design suggested a church interior, with rows of high tables in front of an "altar," where panels held sway. The tabletops were made of a mirror laminate balanced on stacks of A3 paper sheets—13,000 in total. The entire dome-like structure consisted of stacks of paper sheets that hung from the roof in a Venetian blind–like construction. The lowest sheet in each stack carried part of a gigantic illustration that formed the dome-shaped ceiling.

My shapes and characters tend to have a science-meets-imagination feeling, with a lot of texture and dimension. I still think back to my childhood skiing holidays in the snowy woods by the frozen sea, and I remember the shapes and characters your imagination molds out of the trees, rocks, and islands covered with snow and ice, and the flashes of northern lights in the sky. There was (and still is) something magical and mystical in that Finnish landscape. I know it's a cliché for a Finn to say, "I'm inspired by our nature," but that's a fact. Going into the forest, and smelling it, still means a lot to me, and I miss it sometimes in the urban environment where I live now.

————Tell me about current and upcoming projects, and something about the projected tapestries.

Currently, I'm dividing my time between commissioned projects and my own designs and artworks. I'm just finishing an animated video project for Salvatore Ferragamo, and, at the same time, drawing my new collection of tapestries. My collection for Finnish fashion and textile manufacturer Marimekko will be coming out in 2015. I've designed prints and patterns for their home textile, tableware, and clothing collections.

————What comes to mind when you hear the word "beauty"?

To me, beauty is an everyday phenomenon. I think everyone is aiming for beauty, even in their small, everyday habits: for example, covering the table with nice tableware, or cleaning up the house. As an artist, I am conscious of the dangers of too much beauty, which will lead to kitsch. Nature never creates kitsch. Its patterns, shapes, and colors always manage to stay well balanced. For me, beauty always has a fracture, an error, or a crack—and that makes it interesting. Perfection is not beautiful anymore.

————What is the most beautiful time of day?

In Amsterdam, my favorite time of the day is the evening or night, which changes the city into something more mysterious.

————What is the most beautiful place you've visited?

It must be the fairy tale–like, castle-filled hilltop town of Sintra, in Portugal. There, the Quinta da Regaleira palace is a strange mix of Gothic, Roman, and Renaissance, from its outer structure to its ornate interior. The palace has a mysterious park that could keep me wandering for days. It's got fascinating labyrinths of gardens, full of hidden tunnels, with wells that drop hundreds of meters into the ground, and secret passageways to explore.

— INTERVIEW WITH SUVI SALONIEMI

Nightless Night, from Reveille series, 2015;
Jacquard-woven mohair and rubber;
232 × 166 cm (7 ft. 7 9/16 in. × 5 ft. 5 3/8 in.)

Universal Egg, from Reveille series, 2015;
Jacquard-woven cashmere, mohair, acryl,
lurex, and phosphorescent yarn; 224 × 166 cm
(7 ft. 4 3/16 in. × 5 ft. 5 3/8 in.)

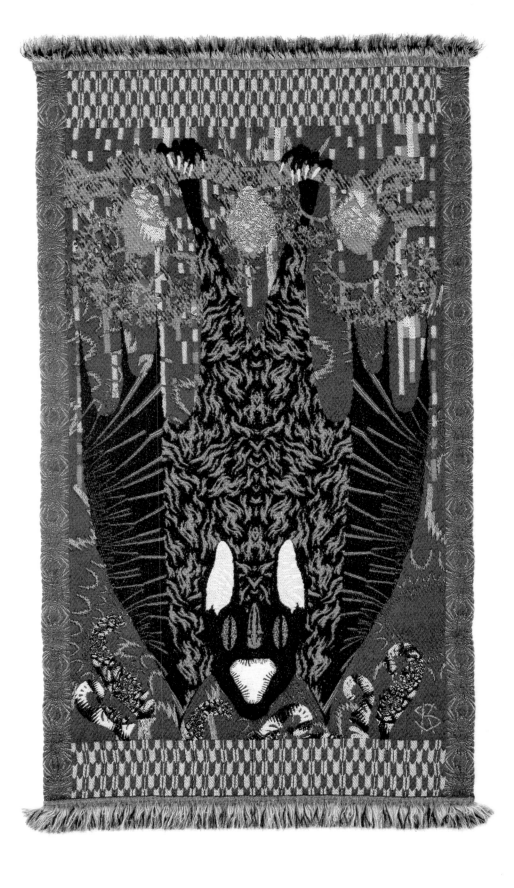

Hanging Loose, from Reveille series, 2015;
Jacquard-woven mohair, acryl, and lurex;
168 × 86 cm (5 ft. 6⅛ in. × 3 ft. 3⅞ in.)

Studio Job for NLXL, art direction by Job
Smeets; Alt Deutsch wallpaper, from Archives
Wallpaper collection, 2014; Shown with
cabinet by Studio Job for Moooi and Lounge
Cahri S13 by Alfred Hendrickx for Belform

OVERLEAF: Studio Job for NLXL; Wallpaper
designs, from Archives Wallpaper collection,
2014; Non-woven wallpaper, matte finish;
Each roll: 900 × 49 cm (29½ ft. × 19¼ in.)

Studio Job

—ANTWERP, BELGIUM, AND AMSTERDAM, NETHERLANDS, FOUNDED 2000—

Studio Job's work is based on iconography. Animal skeletons and gas masks, cooling towers and insects, kitchen utensils and Russian dolls, hands folded in prayer, crowns, candy, peace signs, syringes: Studio Job references are historical and contemporary, bizarre and banal. No motif is off-limits, and any surface becomes a canvas. Since the year 2000, husband-and-wife founders Nynke Tynagel (Dutch, b. 1977) and Job Smeets (Belgian, b. 1970) have applied their extreme ornamentation as marquetry on cabinets, in relief on porcelain tableware, as stained-glass windows, and on textiles, rugs, tiles, and much more. Studio Job's pattern archive became the inspiration for its Archives Wallpaper collection (2014) for Dutch company NLXL. Six distinct wallpaper designs reprise the iconography that has appeared in Studio Job's work since its founding. Running over 29 feet (9 meters) in length without repeat, the designs for each wallpaper revel in complexity to saturate the interior. The outcome is intricate, immersive, opulent, and at times sardonic. Very Studio Job. — ANDREA LIPPS

————How would you describe yourself as a designer?

JOB SMEETS: I would describe myself as a designer who never should have been one. I'm interested in many topics such as music and art, but not really in industrial design. The contradiction, meanwhile, is the inspiration: the struggle between who you want to be and who you are.

————What is your current way of working?

JS: I would classify us as applied artists who work following a Northern European sixteenth-century tradition of extreme crafts and crazy madness.

————How do you and Nynke work together? What is your process?

JS: Normally it starts by inspiration of a topic or theme—which can be "big," like landmark-based sculptures, or can be "light," like a pattern of banana leaves for a hand-knotted rug. The inspiration appears from the abyss. I just start sketching and leveling with Nynke, like a writer who asks his partner to evaluate his new novel. It also works vice versa, like the Godiva Chocolatier Valentine identity campaign and packaging. Nynke developed a series of graphics, which she designed on the computer (as she always does), and she showed me for feedback. The result is—ninety-nine percent of the time—a creative collaboration between two soul mates.

————How do you arrive at the type of iconography seen in your work?

NYNKE TYNAGEL: The Bavaria pattern, for example, we did based on a trip to the National Museum in Nuremberg in 2009. There, we saw the most beautiful collection of Bavarian hand-painted cupboards. Farmers made the furniture, while their wives hand-painted them. The cabinets were made in winter, when there was less work to do on the land. This way of processing inspired us to develop our own Bavaria furniture. Farmers are often an inspiration in our work. We feel connected.

————Tell me about the Archives wallpaper collection.

NT: The collection is a carefully curated selection from our archive of graphical patterns we designed the last decade. Each pattern has a status and function. For example, Withered Flowers is inspired on the genius of William Morris's famous flower patterns. But then, of course, the flowers are withered. A historical context inside a contemporary twist. *Alt Deutsch* comes from the pattern on a hand-painted furniture series called AltDeutsche Furniture, which was later distributed by Moooi.

————What comes to mind when you hear the word "beauty"?

JS: To me, beauty is context. Aesthetic beauty is often overrated and related to materialism. It is programmed by the industries that beauty is lifestyle; beauty is status. We are all addicted to it, me included. But I do my best not to get involved too much.

The world should dematerialize, of course. So the beauty I try to obtain in my daily life, whether it's a painting or a classic car, as well as the beauty in our work, needs to be related to durability. In a way that the "owner" becomes a conservator who passes the object on to further generations. It has nothing to do with the use of ecological materials, nor with functionality.

————What is the most beautiful time of day?

NT: Early morning. Up at 5:30!

————What is the most beautiful place you have visited?

JS: The Green Vault in Dresden.

— INTERVIEW WITH SUVI SALONIEMI

Hans Tan
—SINGAPOREAN, B. 1980—

Brought up with the Asian values of practicality and schooled in Dutch conceptual design, designer Hans Tan creates objects that efficiently communicate ideas of heritage, consumption, and materiality. Tan studied industrial design at the National University of Singapore, followed by the master's course at the Design Academy Eindhoven. Many of his works deform familiar objects to invoke fresh perspectives on material culture. Spotted Nyonya (2011–ongoing) makes use of traditional porcelain wares of the Chinese Peranakans, a mixed-race community native to Southeast Asia. Using a batik-inspired technique, Tan masks the porcelain's surface glaze with a dotted motif, which he then sandblasts. The protected decoration is preserved, while the white porcelain beneath is revealed, transforming these traditional vessels with a modern, graphic surface treatment. Striped Ming (2015–ongoing) is a continuation of the series, in which Tan transforms castaway Ming vases by sandblasting intricate striped patterns onto the surface. Both collections renew the aesthetic experience of otherwise traditional vessels. — JUSTIN ZHUANG

————Tell us about your approach to design.
I see design as a medium—a language that a designer or artist can use to communicate ideas to people, either through the marketplace, in museums, or in the virtual world. My works usually make use of utility as a pretext; explore ideas concerning heritage and consumption; and draw on notions pertaining to the materiality of one's imagination.

————Where did this approach originate?
My design approach has dual origins: Having done my master's in Eindhoven, the Dutch notions of design influence the focus on cultural context in my work. And being Asian, I am very influenced by notions of efficiency and practicality. So for me, communicating is one thing, but it's also about efficiency of communication—using the most direct but subtle manner to communicate.

————A lot of your works give a twist to familiar forms and objects. Why do you work this way?
I use archetypes as the starting point because it represents the preconception of the audience or user. The familiar form, object, or material serves as the canvas for deformation, so as to present a new idea or perspective. I like my works, whenever possible, to have one hand in the past and one hand in the future. If this is successfully attained, then a bridge is formed between times.

On the other hand, I subscribe heavily to [French philosopher] Gaston Bachelard—he asserts that imagination, rather than helping us form images, actually deforms our perception and frees us from existing images. This concept of deformation as imagination influences my design process and my teaching methods.

————How did Spotted Nyonya come about?
It started with my limitations as a designer who did not have much skill as a potter or ceramist, but had the desire to delve into it. I had a commission from the Economic Development Board of Singapore to produce a set of gifts, so I proposed applying the batik method of resist-dyeing textiles onto porcelain using industrial means. Since then, I have expanded the Spotted Nyonya series to create the Striped Ming series, in which I apply the technique on porcelain Ming vessels sourced from old shops in Singapore that largely regard them as dead stock.

————How did Spotted Nyonya lead to Striped Ming?

Hans Tan sandblasts the Striped Ming No. 1 porcelain vessel.

OPPOSITE, LEFT TO RIGHT: Original porcelain vessel; Vinyl stickers are applied prior to sandblasting; The final sandblasted vessel.

While researching and sourcing for appropriate porcelain vessels for Spotted Nyonya, I came across many old shops in Singapore selling out-of-date vases or porcelain wares. I thought of developing a pattern to reinvigorate these vases. Compared to the Spotted Nyonya, I buy the Ming vases for really, really cheap prices. The idea was to transform them visually to increase not only the value, but also their meaning, so they have a place in contemporary design culture.

————Many would regard the vessels for Spotted Nyonya as traditional objects of beauty. Isn't your design an act of defacement?
It certainly is. When I first presented the work, I got some negative reactions toward the dishonorable treatment of Peranakan wares. Although I don't use actual antiques, the vessels I use are essentially authentic productions from the same region in China as in the past.

For me, the idea of defacement—or erasure, as I prefer to call it—is very important. Instead of creating or ornamenting by the usual additive means, I wanted to create a new aesthetic by the act of erasure (a form of deformation). I don't think I've performed plastic surgery on the original Peranakan vessels. They are beautiful in their own way, and the ones I spotted have been transformed to suggest a new, perhaps more contemporary aesthetic.

————Works like Spotted Nyonya are born out of particular contexts. Do you also consider how they are received by outside audiences unfamiliar with them?
With most of my work, I am aware that, though the medium is particular, the concept should be universal. Even if one did not recognize the Spotted Nyonya vessels as traditionally Peranakan and that they were essentially defaced, the work still captured the fundamental concept of layering, and in this case, the physical aesthetic effect of subtractive layering where a geometric pattern is overlaid on a traditional-looking one. The main criterion while experimenting with the technique was the size and intensity of the dots. I wanted the viewer to perceive both the new and old patterns at the same time, and that one should not overpower the other. I believe that thinking global while acting local brings out the authenticity of ideas.

————What do you mean by "thinking global while acting local"?
After doing my master's, I returned to Singapore because I think it is very interesting to use medium and locality as a context for design. Spotted Nyonya is a very good example of this. When I exhibited Spotted Nyonya in Europe, [viewers] were drawn by its visceral and visual effect at first, but when they learned the process and the story behind the pieces, they were inevitably exposed to the Peranakan culture, too. So just by using something local, I could actually communicate broader ideas.

————What comes to mind when you hear the word "beauty"?
Beauty is commanding a good opinion. It is not just about a surface treatment, but more about having a good opinion about a piece of work, which can also come from the idea and concept behind it. Beauty can be visceral, intangible, and also fleeting.

————What is the most beautiful time of day?
When I receive something good I don't deserve.

————What is the most beautiful place you've visited?
Having traveled for work and holiday, to both natural and man-made constructs that are visually and atmospherically stunning, these places and buildings pale in comparison with the physical and emotional sensations I get when I return home to my family every evening after work. Home. It's the most beautiful place for me, and in my opinion, it's delivered by memory, familiarity, security, and joy, through people I love (my wife and my son) in an invariable place.

— INTERVIEW WITH JUSTIN ZHUANG

Vessel with Cover XL, from Spotted Nyonya
series, 2015; Sandblasted porcelain; 25 × 19 ×
19 cm (9¾₆ × 7½ × 7½ in.)

Warmer, from Spotted Nyonya series, 2015;
Sandblasted porcelain; 17 × 15 × 15 cm
(6 ¹¹⁄₁₆ × 5 ¹⁵⁄₁₆ × 5 ¹⁵⁄₁₆ in.)

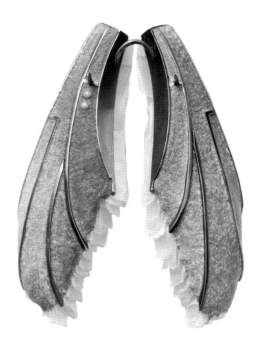

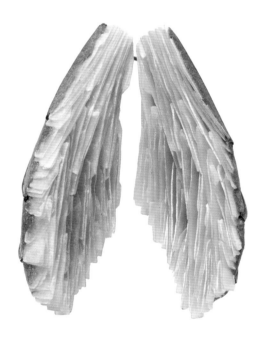

Wings brooch (back and front), from Curiosity
Collection, 2013; Mother-of-pearl, cement,
silver, wood; 8 × 6 × 3 cm (3⅛ × 2⅜ × 1¹³⁄₁₆ in.);
Courtesy of Rotasa Collection Trust

Terhi Tolvanen

——FINNISH, ACTIVE IN FRANCE, B. 1968——

Dialogue is essential to the work of jewelry designer Terhi Tolvanen—between materials, human and nature, harmony and discord, control and freedom. Tolvanen was born and raised in Helsinki, Finland, and studied silversmithing at the Lahti Institute of Design and Fine Arts. She moved to Amsterdam in 1993 to attend the Gerrit Rietveld Academy and the Sandberg Instituut, from which she graduated with a master's degree in 1999. Though she began with silver, Tolvanen later began to make sculptural jewelry using unconventional materials, including polyester, silk, cement, and many types of wood, from pear to pecan to willow. This has produced an eclectic but unified oeuvre, often inspired by nature and always with Tolvanen's signature impulse to highlight the beauty and complexity of the materials. For instance, the Jungle Scenery 1 necklace (2014) from her Jungle series pairs gnarled heather-wood branches with faceted and painted pearls. The Wings brooch (2013) from her Curiosity Collection sees mother-of-pearl flakes mounted in cement to resemble insect wings. Tolvanen often emphasizes the connections of her pieces and continues to maintain a rigorous dedication to creating textural, experimental, and highly wearable jewelry. — JUSTIN ZHUANG

——Tell us about yourself.

I was born in 1968, in Helsinki. I'm a city girl. After high school, I graduated as a silversmith from Lahti Design Institute. I thought of looking for a possibility to go abroad to study design for one year more, because at the time in Finland, it was not possible to continue. I ended, a little bit by accident, in Amsterdam. Via somebody I know, I heard about the Gerrit Rietveld Academy in Amsterdam. I started there thinking that I would stay one year. But I liked the school so much that I decided to stay another year. Then I did another two years. After those four years, I also did the master's degree.

——What did you study?

I was in the Jewelry Department. At that time, it was not really my main interest, but I thought, I will be able to apply what I am learning to other things. I did a lot of body-related things.

When school ended, I did a few little projects; there was a gallery in Amsterdam that was interested in what I was doing. That more or less decided my destiny. I started concentrating more on making jewelry. It was very exciting in Amsterdam because there were galleries; there were colleagues; there were all events around the contemporary art jewelry, so I stayed. After twenty years there, I moved at the beginning of 2014 away from Amsterdam to the French countryside, about one hour by car from Poitiers. It's very good for working. But I'm lucky to travel regularly. I need to get away from all this nature regularly to some big cities, meet people, and hear some noise.

——Tell me about your practice as a jewelry designer.

I have a strict system for working, with a daily timetable. When I'm in a good flow, I get up very early. When I'm really enthusiastic, I'm very impatient to see what the result will be.

——How do you start designing? How long does it take to make one piece of jewelry?

I don't really know. There is one piece I made in 2013 where I was able to keep track of the time, because it required time every morning and evening of gluing/work for a month. I was able to count that it took me one hundred hours to make it. Not every piece, of course, has this many hours, and there may be pieces that require even more hours.

The theme I am working on now, "Greenhouse," is a theme I was thinking about, five years ago, maybe even six or seven years ago. Now, it's ripe enough to really work with it.

I don't make sketches, but make notes about forms or ideas. I would rather sketch it directly in materials.

My main theme is the relationship between nature and human. The actions between the two, like an endless dialogue.

The work starts by collecting materials. I'm constantly collecting wood, because it needs to dry at least six months. With the minerals, I can buy stock at the fairs, normally only twice a year. The materials are really important. They are very related to what I do, what is my theme. I spend time to find solutions in my work that will best suit the materials. For example, now I'm working with amethyst. I cut it to separate all these little crystals.

Then, I rearrange them in my way. I find that the material is very suitable to do that. I have to also adapt to the color, to add something that brings up my material. The shape, that comes from my theme.

——You use a lot of wood in your jewelry, and I have noticed that in the recent collection you used pearls. What is your role as a designer working with two natural but different materials?

I'm the mixer in between. I work a lot on contrast, natural against artificial—organic against more strict in shape—but I'm not always the human part in it. Sometimes I'm on the other side. My task is to show in my pieces the beauty of the materials.

There are fantastic minerals, and wood that has fantastic shape, but it is not very visible. My task is to take it into another context and build a story around it so that it highlights the beauty of this particular piece of wood, the shape of the branches, the color of the mineral or the combination of several materials.

——What comes to mind when you hear the word "beauty"?

There is beauty in harmony, symmetry. But harmony and symmetry get interesting when they are disturbed.

——What is the most beautiful time of day?

It's the blue moment, the blue light just before it gets dark in Finland. I got a Christmas card from somebody where it was fantastically blue, a cottage in the snow. In the winter, the blue light, it's very visible because of the snow.

——What is the most beautiful place you've visited?

I'd say it's my family's summer cottage on the lake. When there's no wind at all, everything is mirrored on the water. Then there is this quietness.

— INTERVIEW WITH SUVI SALONIEMI

Jungle Plate Nr. 01 brooch, from Jungle collection, 2014; Amber, grapewood, silver, paint; 12 × 14 × 6 cm (4¾ × 5½ × 2⅜ in.); Courtesy of Marion Fulk and Ornamentum Gallery

Parrot Tulip brooch, from Curiosity Collection, 2012; Thuja wood, paint, silver, reconstructed opal; 12 × 14 × 6 cm (4¾ × 5½ × 2⅜ in.); Courtesy of Rotasa Collection Trust

Jungle Scenery 1 necklace, from Jungle collection, 2014; Heather wood, silver, faceted and painted pearls; 6.4 × 20 cm (2½ × 7⅞ in.); Courtesy of Rotasa Collection Trust and Ornamentum Gallery

Vlisco

—HELMOND, NETHERLANDS, FOUNDED 1846—

Vlisco specializes in Dutch wax prints, the brightly colored and elaborately patterned cotton textiles popular in West and Central Africa. Made using an industrialized version of the hand-printed, Indonesian batik process, Vlisco's wax fabrics were initially intended for the Indonesian market but soon found favor in Africa. The vibrant and colorful prints have been adapted to local preferences through a continued collaboration between Dutch designers and African traders: The local women traders who sell the fabrics often suggest colorways or themes, and many even name the designs, making them resonate within the local culture. Traditionally sold in open-air markets by these local traders, the wax fabrics are fashioned into bespoke dresses and suits by local tailors. Contrasting or complementary designs are intended to be mix-and-matched in the creation of personalized garments. For many, Vlisco fabrics remain a symbol of West and Central African fashion and culture. — ANDREA LIPPS

————What have been the important milestones in Vlisco's history?
ROGER GERARDS (VLISCO CREATIVE DIRECTOR): Vlisco has been in existence almost 170 years, and while we took part in the international textile trade, we also participated in an international design exchange. We use the Indonesian design style and technique—batik—to make interpretations in the factory studio in Holland and sell these products worldwide, especially to West Africa. Vlisco still has this long relation between the consumer in West Africa and the production and design department in Holland. But for the last eight years, we have been making a big shift to fashion and design globally. We are slowly working to get more and more relevancy outside West Africa. What we do now is develop ready-to-wear for the West African market, but sometimes it also finds its way outside. We also do a lot of collaborations with brands.

————What collaborations?
One collaboration is with the Belgian and Dutch company Studio Job. We found each other in the very expression of what we make. We both have a bold design DNA. Also we collaborate with Woolrich and with Eastpak, and most recently with Viktor & Rolf for their Spring 2015 couture collection.

It's not just brands that we've got, but design specialists for our in-house design team, like the Dutch graphic designer Michiel Schuurman, who has an independent career in communication design. Another important collaboration has been with a designer from Lagos, Lanre Da Silva Ajayi.

————You mention your in-house design team. Do you change your in-house design team with each collection, or are they all working long-term?
It takes one or two years for a designer to understand our technique, our way of designing. We have a team of fifteen textile designers, of which some already have a design career outside Vlisco. This design team needs to fit the design philosophy of the brand, the DNA of the brand, but on the other hand, we select people because of their signature and individual design sensibilities.

We make four concepts a year, and we choose designers for each. Our design departments even physically look like a fine-art atelier. It is a kind of meeting place per season, who's doing what on what level to challenge each other and really take effort in every print design we make. Every print design takes one month to develop, which is, for the print-design world, a long time. We really need to take time to make good design.

————Then you have the Tailor Academy, which you arranged for different countries in Africa. Can you talk about this?
The key of the West African fashion system is that we launch a lot of textiles and produce together with tailors and designers to make a bespoke design for each person. That means that, as a company, we sell a design process because people are inspired by our textile design, and from that, they make their own product. We have a kind of atelier relationship with companies or with tailors or other designers. In West Africa, we take a lot of effort to talk with tailors and stylists.

In a way we are creating fashion facilitation platforms. We allow other people to design products within their context, within their wishes. In the big cities in West Africa, some of them have 10,000 tailors who make fashion out of the textiles. The whole fashion system is totally different than in Europe or the States. We want to inspire the tailors by giving them courses or workshops about how to design, how to work with the print industry, how to finish the work, how to do measurements. So we also improve in the whole process—the expertise or the quality.

————What has been the feedback of this Tailor Academy?
People love that we take the business of tailoring and fashion that seriously: we create opportunities for talented tailors to acquire more fashion education and to let them be fully integrated in the African fashion industry. I did a presentation in Lagos to three hundred tailors. And after three hours, all these tailors started discussions about their jobs and about their expertise. And they said, "Well, maybe we should start a union or a school." And that's exactly what Vlisco wants. We want to have this dialogue about designing clothes.

We also had a presentation in a Dutch department store. The consumers were allowed to choose their own fashion style, and then, based upon their measurements, we made clothing for them with our prints, with our textiles. So we take this West African fashion system over to Europe. You get a kind of couture at a very commercial rate.

————It almost sounds like you have an ideology. . . .
Design is more than just nice things. Design is also having relationships with industry and consumers and companies everywhere. Africa is experiencing such a big change now that we want to jump on that train in a way that we empower all the partners we are working with. As a design company, you are always in the middle of culture, even in Europe.

————I read that you want to inspire women to bend, shake, and break the rules of fashion.
Well, it's true. We are aware that women, powerful women, buy our product and make a couture dress for one event to show who they are, their importance. And it's also about African identity, of course. Fashion is always about breaking the rules. We are trying to empower who you are by *showing* who you are. African fashion is about communicating your own identity.

————What comes to mind when you hear the word "beauty"?
Beauty is a personally perceived concept, and means empowerment. Beauty is a very proactive activity to our key consumers. And I think that African beauty is much more about empowerment and being somebody than the more passive beauty, which is about the woman who is beautiful for other people.

————What is the most beautiful time of day?
The first second that my eyes open. I love the moment always. Not because I survived the night, but because I always like to get awake.

————What is the most beautiful place you've visited?
Despite the tourists, I visit Venice once or twice a year. To feel history that strong always affects me. Or, I saw the British pavilion in the World Expo Shanghai—Thomas Heatherwick's Seed Pavilion—I had never seen a building like that before. It was stunning.
— INTERVIEW WITH SUVI SALONIEMI

Vlisco; Designed by Jac van Hoof; Textile, VL061834.06 Java, from the Think collection, 2015; Cotton, rotation and java resist printed on plain weave; 120 × 91.4 cm (47¼ × 36 in.)

Vlisco; Designed by Francesca Franceschi; Textile, 5246/RW/3 Java, from the Think collection, 2015; Cotton, rotation and java resist printed on plain weave; 120 × 91.4 cm (47¼ × 36 in.)

Vlisco; Designed by Jac van Hoof; Textile, VL061831.06 Java, from the Think collection, 2015; Cotton, rotation and java resist printed on plain weave; 120 × 91.4 cm (47¼ × 36 in.)

Dress and cape made using Vlisco textiles 5246/
RW/3 Java, VL061831.06 Java, and VL061834.06
Java, from the Think collection, 2015.

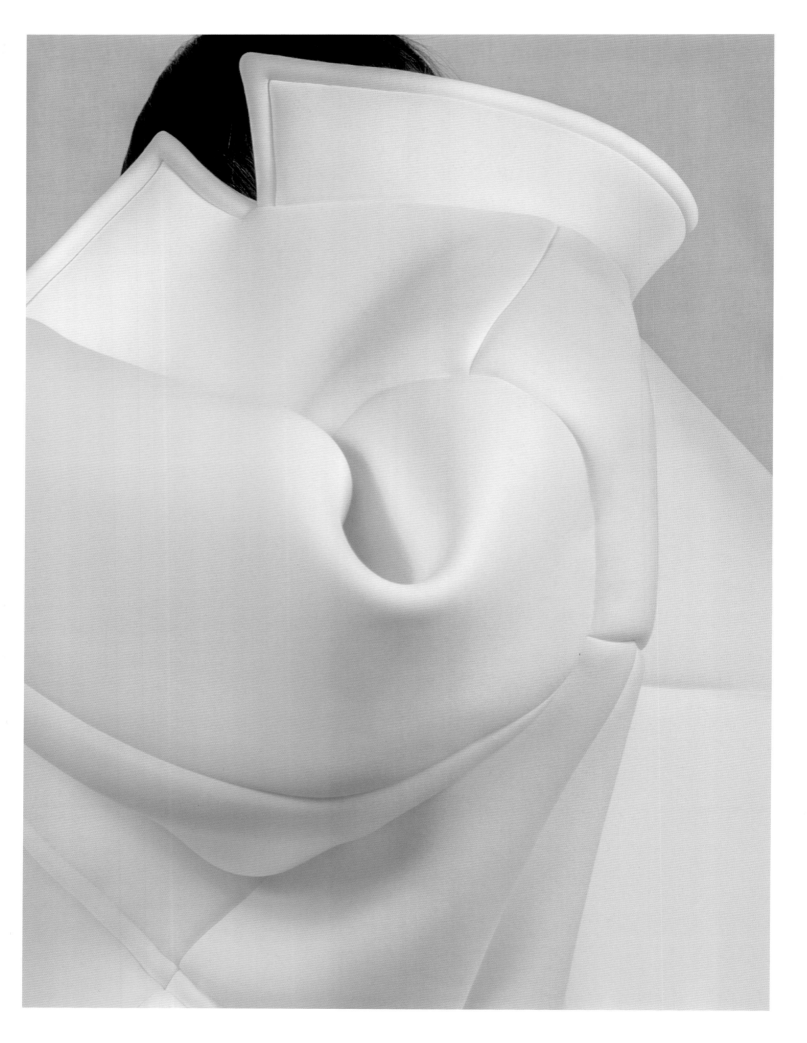

Transformative

Melitta Baumeister
Dokter and Misses
Elastic
Jantje Fleischhut
Francesco Franchi
Götz Gramlich
Brunno Jahara
Max Lamb
Laduma Ngxokolo
Scholten & Baijings
Brynjar Sigurðarson
Kris Sowersby
TheUnseen

Beauty mutates, shifts, and erases its own certainties. Familiar materials, vocabularies, and forms assume new and surprising identities. A powerful process of change takes place as sculpted surfaces reshape the body, found materials become precious things, or objects and images tell stories that unfold over time.

"The distance between a flat drawing and a real garment was always too far for me. Either the drawing can't reach the garment or the garment can't reach the drawing. I need to see it instantly on the body. Basically, I sculpt garments around a body."

——————————————————————— Melitta Baumeister

Melitta Baumeister

—GERMAN, ACTIVE IN USA, B. 1986—

Since her launch at New York Fashion Week in 2014, Melitta Baumeister quickly earned attention for her distinct approach to fashion. Interested in the sculptural quality of clothing, Baumeister exaggerates volume and plays with silhouette, often using rigid materials and experimental techniques. Garments are cast in silicone from molds of existing cable-knit sweaters and button-down shirts. Oversize proportions of neoprene or bonded velvet jackets generate a protective enclosure around a wearer. Padded paper dresses are sculpted to float on the body. The palette is largely monochromatic: either black or white. Baumeister's push to defy textile construction and silhouette is perhaps not surprising given her background. Born into a family of tailors, she has been familiar with making clothes since a young age. Baumeister attended a tailoring school in Germany before studying fashion at Germany's Pforzheim University School of Design, where she began exploring her own design language. In 2011, Baumeister moved to New York, where she is currently based, graduating with an MFA in fashion design from Parsons in 2013. — ANDREA LIPPS

————What is your aesthetic and approach for making garments?
The garments I make have this sculptural feel, and basically the body is not something that is necessary to shape the garment. The garment, on its own, already has a shape. I also include a lot of processes or materials that are uncommon. I try to question what is the making of clothes. Why are things made in that way? How could the processes of making clothing be challenged? So my first work was cast clothing. I poured silicon into a mold, and what happens is that the garment is not made anymore like we used to with a sewing machine, but it's liquid poured into a mold that looks like a garment or reminds us of a garment. It's another way of 3D printing. 3D printing technology is too slow to sometimes work with fashion, because fashion is so fast, and we can't keep up with the cycle almost. And that was my way of challenging the making. It's not that that would be the optimum way to produce the garment, but it raises the question about what other materials to use and causes us to ask, why has fashion been done for so many years in the same way?

————So, more toward experimental, conceptual, and speculative fashion.
Yes, it can possibly be seen that way.

————Do you think it's important that it's still wearable?
I think so. Because I don't want to have this extremely shocking effect. I still think of clothing as something that is worn on a body and that is worn on the street. That's where clothes are most important because that's something we will always need. But I don't think of clothing as purely art. It's an artistic approach, but I want still the connection to the body.

————How does the design process start? What is your whole process like?
I do not sketch anymore, actually. I always enjoyed drawing, but I felt that the distance between a flat drawing and a real garment was always too far for me. Either the drawing can't reach the garment or the garment can't reach the drawing. I need to see it instantly on the body. Basically, I sculpt garments around a body. For me, it's more an instant intuition of shape.

————You sculpt it—to become visible?
Yes. And this also guides my choice of materials. Sometimes fabrics are so frustrating to me because they collapse, and I just want to have more weight or something that has more structure. That's why I try always to kind of influence my fabrics so that they become more structured and hold in shape basically.

————What comes to mind when you hear the word "beauty"?
"Beauty," the word itself, has been so overly used. Still, as a designer or as a creator you always try to reach beauty with something that's pleasing for the eye or something that gives you a certain feeling. I think always when I work on shapes, I try to reach something that is beautiful. Maybe not in the very obvious way. I think it's a constant search.

————What is the most beautiful time of day?
I really enjoy those in-between moments. It's either very early when I feel nobody has woken up yet and you kind of feel that nothing is happening yet. Or at night, when it's kind of over but not really.

————What is the most beautiful place you've visited?
It's more a small moment when you see something surprising. That's when time is at a little bit of a standstill or doesn't go so fast—that moment lasts longer when you see something or experience something. I think experience is also something that can be very beautiful because it's something that is new. This kind of newness is what I enjoy. It can be a place, or it can be an object, or it can be a situation.

— INTERVIEW WITH SUVI SALONIEMI

Tank top, from Fall/Winter 2014 Ready-to-Wear collection, 2014; Cast silicone

SECTION OPENER: Jacket (detail), from Fall/Winter 2014 Ready-to-Wear collection, 2014; Neoprene

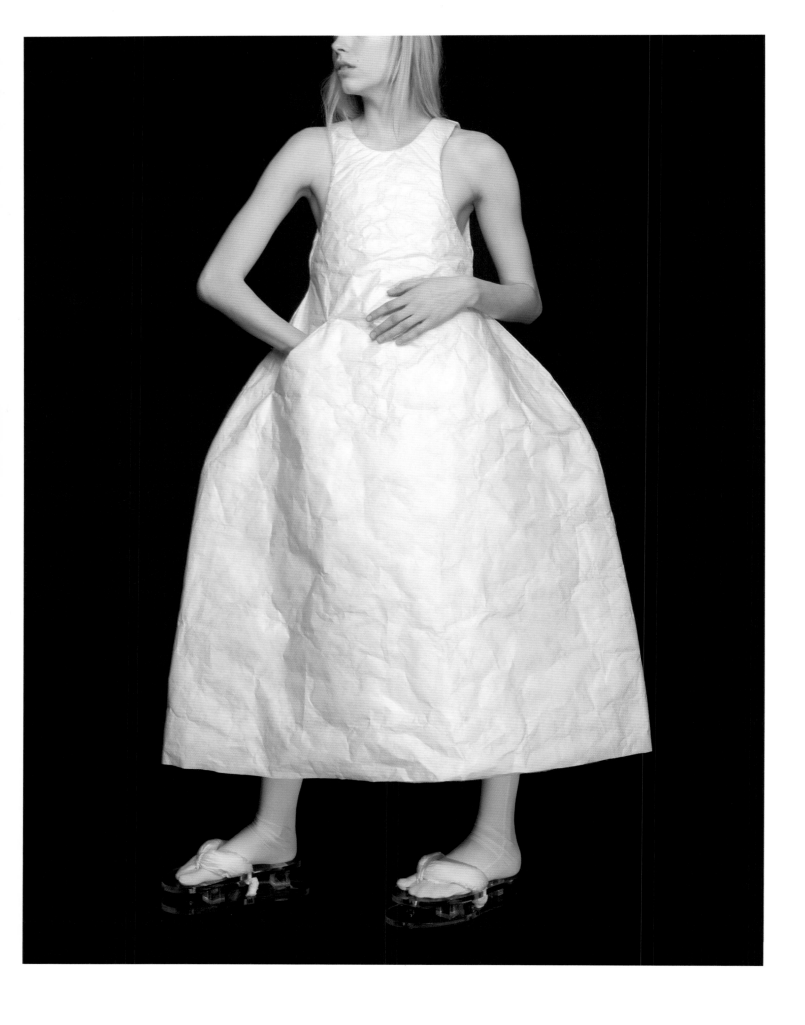

Dress, from Fall / Winter 2015 Ready-to-Wear
collection, 2015; Padded Tyvek

Jacket and culotte, from Fall / Winter 2015
Ready-to-Wear collection, 2015; Bonded velvet

Dokter and Misses

— JOHANNESBURG, SOUTH AFRICA, FOUNDED 2007 —

He trained as an industrial designer. She studied graphic design. Adriaan Hugo (South African, b. 1982) and Katy Taplin (South African, b. 1982) founded Dokter and Misses in 2007 in Johannesburg. The duo is best known for furniture, objects, and lighting inspired by, among other things, the culture of their continent. While their earlier works displayed bold lines and forms associated with South Africa's modernist architecture, Dokter and Misses's more recent Kassena series (2015) takes its inspiration from the intricately painted adobe homes of the Kassena people of northern Ghana and Burkina Faso. The original Kassena Server (2013) has an edition of fifteen, produced in one shape that incorporates assorted drawer configurations. The Kassena series has grown to include an upright cupboard, a bench, a light, and other pieces, all featuring disparate openings, drawers, cupboards, and secret compartments. The pieces group together to form a town or village, each one representing an architectural edifice in an urban drama— from a house, temple, and liquor store to a man who drives a fast car. Designed in the round with no front side or back side, each Kassena piece seamlessly combines graphic surfaces with three-dimensional form. — JUSTIN ZHUANG

——How did you get into making collectible pieces?

KATY TAPLIN: We got into this area about five years ago, when Trevyn and Julian McGowan, who run the Southern Guild gallery, started inviting African designers to conceive a piece of their own inspiration for exhibition at an annual event. These shows became stand-alone events, and Southern Guild started showing at international design fairs in Dubai, Basel, and Miami.

——What is the role of function in your collectible pieces?

ADRIAAN HUGO: The function is sometimes the aesthetic value of the piece, or its impact in the space. The Kassenas make a big impact because they are large-scale and intricately hand-painted on all visible surfaces. But both the function and the look change when you open the drawers. Every little detail of the drawer was designed according to its purpose; at the same time, all these openings contribute to the form's personality.

Some of our other products need to be functional as useful, everyday pieces. Function was paramount when we designed work desks for a university, although we still wanted the design to be as aesthetically pleasing as possible within the boundaries of its practical purpose.

——What is the role of craft in your work?

KT: Craft or handmade production processes open up new avenues. Currently, we're working with Gone Rural, a nonprofit cooperative enterprise from Swaziland, who weave using indigenous grass. We've developed a range of distinctive woven screens to serve as room or office dividers. This has allowed us to make a graphic, lightweight screen— which we couldn't have done using any of the production processes available to us at the time. Similarly, the process of hand-painting our cabinets accomplishes something that an industrial process could not. Neither craft nor mechanical processes are more or less important to us—they simply allow us to achieve different results.

——Tell me about the Kassena Server and its background.

KT: About two years ago, Adriaan came across some striking images of hand-painted African homes in adobe; they had small windows, and their exterior walls were hand-painted in intricate and delicate patterns. The structures were really solid, with beautifully rounded edges and interesting sloping side profiles. My sister, who is an art historian, told us these buildings are made by the Kassena people of northern Ghana and Burkina Faso. So this was how we were inspired to develop the Kassena piece in wood, with painted graphics. It was our first one hundred percent wood construction. Before this, we'd worked mainly in steel, or steel with some wood.

AH: Using wood instead of steel would suggest the soft solidity and warmth reminiscent of adobe. We've always been stimulated by architecture. To a certain extent, even our earlier work was inspired by modernist buildings in South Africa from the seventies, eighties, and nineties. As with the Kassena images, the photographic images of these buildings don't express their scale. So it's easy to picture them in the much smaller dimensions of a furniture piece.

KT: The interplay of graphics and architecture is big for us.

AH: In the past, we made similarly bold, graphic pieces, which were decorated using different processes by patterning a surface with a matrix of CNC-milled acrylic plastic pieces or by screen-printing on it. We've found that when a graphic is successfully integrated, the piece has a graphic and structural unity. Way back, while we were both still at university, our very first design venture was a cardboard carrier bag or purse. We were already combining our training and focus then— while I was making the object, Katy was designing the final graphic patterns to be printed on the object.

Shortly after making our first Kassena Server, we were invited to join Design Network Africa (DNA). This was a major change in focus for us: although we lived in Africa, our university training had focused on European design for guidance on aesthetics. Meeting other African designers got us thinking about how to make things that belong to where we come from.

——What comes to mind when you hear the word "beauty"?

KT: Often, I'm attracted to something that's not typically considered beautiful—that's a bit weird, or unusually big, or small, or just different. A beautiful thing is beneficially stimulating. You stop and pay attention to it, and you feel good. It moves you.

AH: If something works well, it should be beautiful because the function and engineering work. Some music sounds beautiful the first time, but not the third time. Later—say, the tenth time—you might be pleasantly surprised to discover new depths or levels. A complex object should have a lasting beauty that can reveal itself slowly.

——What is the most beautiful time of day? And what is the most beautiful place you've visited?

AH: The most beautiful time of day for me is just before sunset. The most beautiful place, I would say, is the Magaliesberg mountain wilderness in South Africa. I always feel at home there, in spite of its prehistoric geology.

KT: I have to agree about the time of day— just before sunset. The most beautiful place would probably be the wide-open plains of the Central Kalahari in Botswana. This vast sweep of flat grassland is very peaceful but full of life, and the air is fresh. And you're alone.

— INTERVIEW WITH SUVI SALONIEMI

Kassena buildings at Tiebele village, Burkina
Faso, 2009

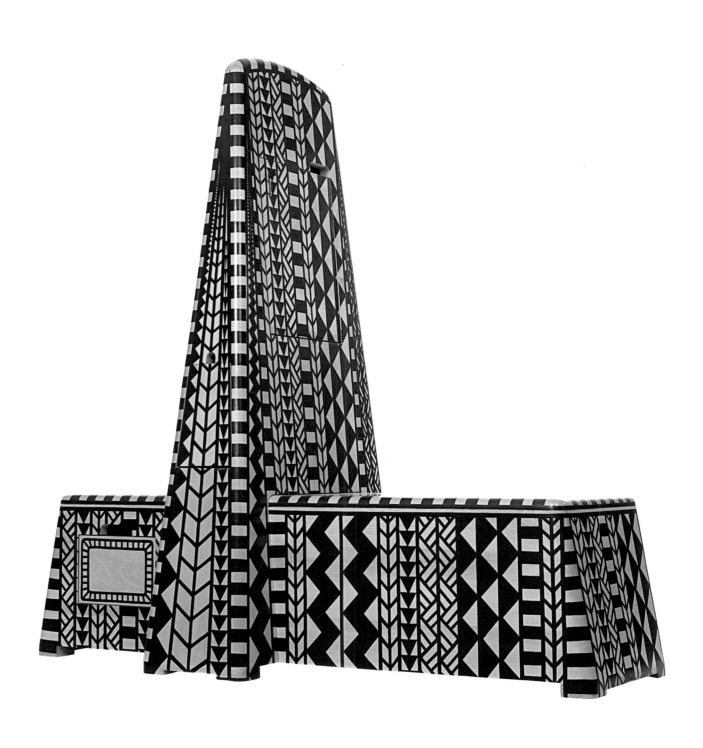

Horseman bench, from Kassena Town series, 2015; Hand-painted white beech, mild steel interior hinges and fasteners; 165 × 83 × 165 cm (5 ft. 4 ¹⁵⁄₁₆ in. × 32 ¹¹⁄₁₆ in. × 5 ft. 4 ¹⁵⁄₁₆ in.)

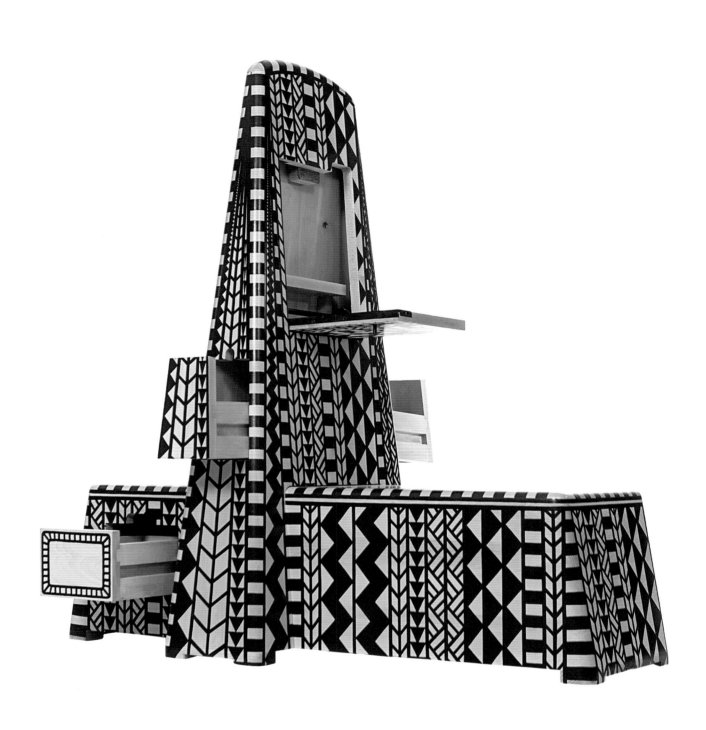

Elastic

—SANTA MONICA, CALIFORNIA, USA, FOUNDED 2008—

The visual culture of the late twentieth century infuses the main title sequences for *Masters of Sex*, *The Americans*, *Halt and Catch Fire*, and *True Detective*. The creative force driving this remarkable body of work is Elastic, the Santa Monica–based studio that also created the main titles for *Game of Thrones* (2011). In the opening sequence for *Masters of Sex* (2013), a mushroom grows, a flower blooms, and a rocket blasts off. Art directed by Leanne Dare (American, b. 1980), each shot delivers a payload of erotic innuendo, embodying the bottled-up sexuality of midcentury America. *Halt and Catch Fire* (2013) explores the birth of the personal computer industry in the early 1980s. The main titles, directed by Patrick Clair (Australian, b. 1982), track a shimmering white signal across a pixelated landscape bathed in the red glow of an LED bulb. Clair also directed the main titles for HBO's *True Detective* (2014). The first season is a Southern gothic tale of murder and conspiracy that shuttles in time between the 1990s and the present day. Large-scale portraits become translucent frames for oil fields and truck stops along the Louisiana Gulf Coast. The dark mood of the title sequence underscores a drama preoccupied with ritual sacrifice and inner demons. — ELLEN LUPTON

———Your work is largely about setting the mood or the tone of the piece. Where do you get your ideas and inspiration?
PATRICK CLAIR (CREATIVE DIRECTOR FOR *HALT AND CATCH FIRE* AND *TRUE DETECTIVE*): For me, the most critical aspect of a title sequence's success is whether it captures the essence of the story. When we're looking for inspiration, we really dig into the world of the show. Understanding the vision of the showrunner, producers, and writing team is at the heart of any solution. Beyond that, we try to cast a wide net—looking to sources outside of motion design to find evocative and powerful symbolic imagery. Photographers, architects, and contemporary artists are all people that we look to for inspiration, because their work is so often driven by conceptual concerns (rather than just pure aesthetics). In the end, it's about finding something that strikes the right balance between beautiful and meaningful. The titles must be simple enough to be elegant, and complex enough to watch week after week.

———How do the various aspects— typography, camera work, animations, music—come together to form a larger, cohesive sequence?
We try to start with a strong structure that's built around a narrative arc. That might be quite abstract with many sequences, but the narrative structure gives us guiding principles as we make decisions about small or specific aspects of the execution. No single element should overwhelm the central concept. Every element should serve the idea at the heart of the story. When all those elements come together, it's very exciting—the pictures work with the pace of the edit and music, and the typography and animation guide the audience's eye through the sequence.

———What does a typical team look like?
Early in the process, we work with designers (usually digital artists, who create "style frames" in Photoshop to explore looks and concepts), but we often also collaborate with storyboard artists, illustrators, and visual researchers. We compile "treatment" documents that define the concept and the progression of the sequence. These might be rough sketches, polished frames, or just eclectic collections of images. Combining these with text, we search for the most powerful and succinct way to distill our idea into a clear concept. Once we start production, the team often expands. Each team is built in a bespoke way to suit the creative execution required, led by a talented cluster of lead artists and technical directors who coordinate this complex process to serve the director's vision.

———This line of work blends art and film and graphic design. How did you find yourself in this world?
I like projects that combine many disciplines and challenges. Animation/filmmaking is very creative, but it also requires managing resources and logistical problem solving, not to mention technological innovation. That mix is really exciting to me. I think I'd be lost making pure art—I'll leave that to people driven by a more unique vision of philosophy and aesthetics. I want to tell stories, and I want to make people feel something emotional. Creating a piece of work that does that requires the coordination of many people, ideas, and practical limitations. I find that process thrilling.

———What are some of the challenges?
Collaboration is always the most complex part of any job. When collaboration goes right, it is magical, but when it goes wrong, it can become a nightmare, and worst, a waste. I hate wasting time and resources—whether it's my client's time, my team's time, or my own. I want everyone to be happy and get what they want. That sounds good in theory, but when there are many voices on a job—from directors, writers, and producers to designers and technical artists—the process can become chaotic and unproductive very quickly. The best jobs are the ones where everyone works hard to find a successful way forward.

———Are there any opening sequences that have made a particular impression on you?
There are some classic sequences that perfectly capture the heart of a show. The ideas are focused; the executions are elegant; and the aesthetic is varied. They sound so simple as one-liners—a man making breakfast, an executive in free fall, a body prepared for burial, a montage of Southern gothic. The sequences for *Dexter*, *Mad Men*, *Six Feet Under*, and *True Blood* are sublime. I think of them every time I sit down to crack a new brief. They are fantastic examples of the genre.

———Elastic's work is quite experimental, allowing for innovation in what a main title can be and how it can serve the story. What do you see for the future of the medium? Where would you like to see the field heading?
Main title sequences have no inherent right to exist. No show "needs" them—they are commissioned at the whim of the show's creators, and are only worth crafting if they enhance the story. There's no point making these sequences if we play them safe, or retread old ground. Each sequence must strive to distill the show it introduces in a way that is daring, creative, surprising, and engaging. That's what I love about titles. People bring passion to them, and they encourage exploration. As long as we can keep pushing the limits of how we tell stories, then I'm excited to keep working in the field.

———What comes to mind when you hear the word "beauty"?
Beauty is a surprising combination of elements that stirs something emotional inside you. Whether it's traditional beauty —like a pretty girl or a mountain vista—or a striking photo of an industrial car park or a powerful piece of art, beauty is not about being aesthetically pleasing, but about having an indefinable quality that moves you.

———What is the most beautiful place you've visited? Time of day?
Sydney, the dawn after a dust storm. The world turned red for two hours, and we couldn't see into the distance. Everything familiar was strange, for just a moment. It was magic.
— INTERVIEW WITH TIFFANY LAMBERT

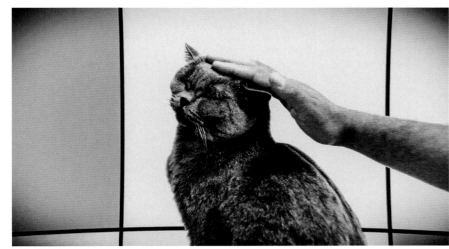

Elastic; Directed by Leanne Dare; Still from title
sequence, *Masters of Sex*, 2013

Elastic; Directed by Patrick Clair; Stills from
title sequence, *True Detective*, Season 1, 2014

Elastic; Directed by Patrick Clair; Stills from
title sequence, *True Detective*, Season 2, 2015

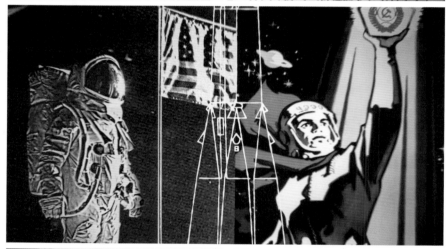

Elastic; Directed by Angus Wall; Stills from title sequence, *The Americans*, 2013

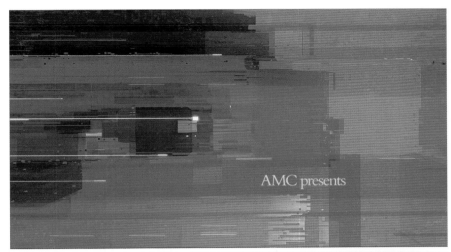

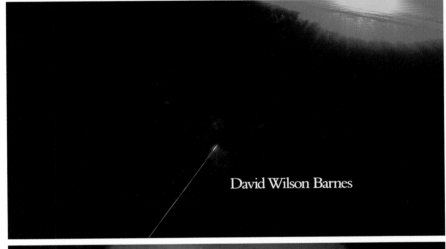

Elastic; Directed by Patrick Clair; Stills from title
sequence, *Halt and Catch Fire*, 2014

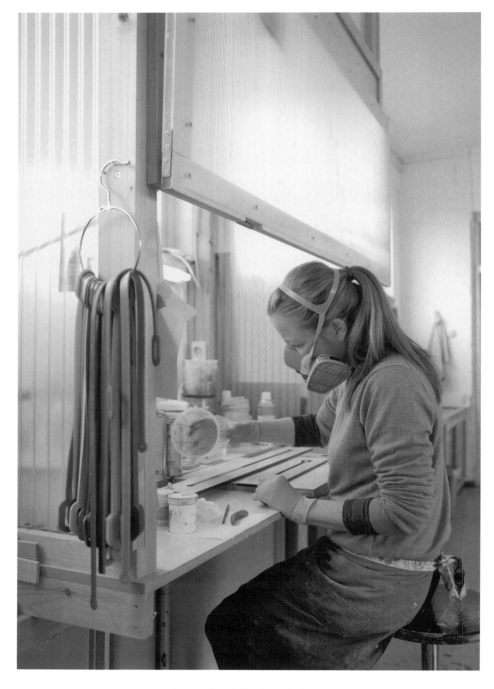

Jantje Fleischhut

—GERMAN, ACTIVE IN NETHERLANDS, B. 1972—

Silver, sponge, resin, foam, aluminum, found plastic: the work of Jantje Fleischhut conjures a winter picnic served along a postindustrial seaside. Judiciously mixing precious and nonprecious materials, Fleischhut honors a piece of plastic picked up on the beach with the same care and consideration she might bestow upon a chunk of amethyst or topaz. A luminous pink orb of fiberglass and resin is inspired by the bleached tones of plastic faded by the sea and sun. Aluminum facets reflect light against slabs of rock and sponge. Trained as a goldsmith in Pforzheim and Hamburg, Germany, Fleischhut expanded her vision as an artist and designer at the Gerrit Rietveld Academy and the Sandberg Institute, both in the Netherlands, where she developed a designer's eye for complex materiality, a sculptor's sense of scale, and an alchemist's drive to explore the universe by unlocking the secrets of the earth. —ELLEN LUPTON

————You've described your studio as resembling a laboratory. What do you mean by that?

My experience and background [in Germany] in watch design led to a very precise way of working. I have combined the typical goldsmith's bench with an experimental way of working at the fume hood [for ventilating toxic materials]. My fascination with plastic material has led to permanent research in this field. I spend a huge part of my time in the studio with gloves and breathing protection handling toxic substances. A new collection of jewelry needs the company of materials research and experiments with 3D modeling. A project might involve exploring the behavior of fiberglass and epoxy, or the process of rotation casting. These discoveries suit the visual outcome.

————Can you reflect on your development as a designer? How has your work evolved?

During my first years in the jewelry field in Hamburg, I experienced a straight product-design direction, working in series and designing watches—form and function. My education in the Netherlands added artistic content and a conceptual way of working. There is constant change and variation in my work, from one-offs to multiples and the other way around. Thinking about multiples still attracts me as much as creating one-off pieces, with my fascination with stars and the universe as a reference. The one-offs as well as the multiples are handmade in my studio. I will pay attention to both in the future. I would like to get the multiples even one step further, into production.

————When you work with stones and gems, do you have any preference for specific cuts?

Oh, no. For a unique piece, I choose the elements very intuitively, regarding form and color. During a residency in Idar-Oberstein at Villa Bengel, I worked on raw stones and made several cuts by myself, which was very exciting, and I used them in various pieces, but the classical cuts and facets always appeal to me. I do like to combine something unknown and nonprecious with something regarded as precious and known. The best facets are elaborated to the most extreme brightness in precious stones. The forms are known, and the refined sparkle is esteemed. I use this quality in the series 0,5 ring. Amethysts, topaz, and aquamarine—as well as the setting and band—are radically cut through lengthwise. Thus, the classical golden ring with a stone exists here merely in half.

————Is the weight of your pieces something you consider?

There is a difference between the unique one-off and the multiple pieces. The multiple pieces are very easy to wear; they are meant for daily use. I keep weight and size in consideration as I develop the product. For the gallery collection, the artistic idea and content are more central; weight and size can sometimes lead to a more unwearable piece.

Fleischhut at work in her studio.

──── You give the same care and attention to precious metal as you give to plastic. With this approach to materials, are you questioning concepts like luxury and consumerism?

The use of plastic materials—such as resin and rubber—in my studio is very crafted. A great range of subtle color nuances is reached with pigments; these are colors you cannot find in industry. While plastic items are normally associated with industrial mass production, here the colors, touch, and quality hunch for something else.

The jewel reveals a completely new facet of plastic; the material becomes highly precious. A discolored piece of plastic found on the beach can been seen as garbage, but in my studio, found plastic is sorted by color. Each one is a unique piece—when using it in a piece of jewelry, I have to be very sure where and how to cut it. Gold or silver, I can just order again.

Jewelry will always be a luxury to purchase. It does not really matter what kind of material is used. An audience that is not familiar with contemporary art jewelry needs more explanation about the materials and the ways of making; this explains the price.

──── You write wonderful, arresting narratives for each collection. Could you talk about how you develop those? When did you begin this practice?

I do like to switch the medium from word to drawing to 3D object while developing new work. Waard Schrijver writes most of the texts accompanying my works; one is by Ulrike Möntmann (2002).

──── Your website intersperses images that have inspired a collection with documentation of your own work. I'm thinking particularly of Neighbourhood (2005), which includes pictures of buildings and stacked shipping containers. Are these associations embedded in the ultimate forms?

Yes, indeed. While developing the collection Neighbourhood, I was inspired by my very close surroundings—buildings, architecture, constructions, all the small details I pass by with the bike.

──── There is quite a lot of interesting work taking place at Redlight Design in Amsterdam. Could you speak to your involvement? How and when did it get started?

Droog, Community Amsterdam, and Ymere [housing cooperation] coordinated and established the project 1012 Red Light Design. It started in 2008 after Red Light Fashion and was followed by Red Light Art. The contract we had with our cooperation was for only one and a half years. For the locations around the Old Church, six international jewelry designers were invited to work and live in spaces that where formerly used by prostitutes. My complete studio moved for that time to number thirty on the Oudekerksplein; my assistant during that time, Sarah Mesritz, lived on the top floor. We worked next door to three girls from South America—an environment and surrounding to get used to. The window display was changed every six to eight weeks. On a blog I created for this location, people from outside Amsterdam could follow what happened behind my windows.

Together with all six jewelry designers, we founded the group Delux to organize events and present our works. We invested a lot of our time on the project. We invited Dutch Designers to our ground-floor spaces to design a new environment for prostitutes, and we worked with photographers to show our jewels worn on the body. Huge prints of 2 x 3 meters [6½ × 10 ft.] were hanging in the Old Church later. It was a great opportunity to be public in an unusual spot.

──── Who does your jewelry tend to appeal to?

The one-offs as well as the multiples are shown in the contemporary jewelry galleries —their clients like and appreciate my work. Design admirers, as well, are attracted by several of my works. The multiple collections—Precious Plastics refer to stereotypes of jewelry—are shown in museums and design shops, where a younger audience responds positively to the works.

──── What comes to mind when you hear the word "beauty"?

I am fascinated with the magnificence of the infinite heavens: overwhelmingly beautiful, irrationally ominous, forever in motion, the dynamics of the universe. But beauty can be simply present in a weird color combination, in a discolored piece of plastic at the beach, in a landscape, in clothes from Prada, or in a bike ride in the early morning.

──── What is the most beautiful time of day?

The early morning in Amsterdam on the bike—no rain!

──── What is the most beautiful place you've visited?

I do like the seaside very much: the enormous wide view and the horizon. It clears your mind and makes you think of nothing. Luckily, Amsterdam is located very close to the seaside, and a twenty-minute train trip helps to recharge the battery.

— INTERVIEW WITH TIFFANY LAMBERT

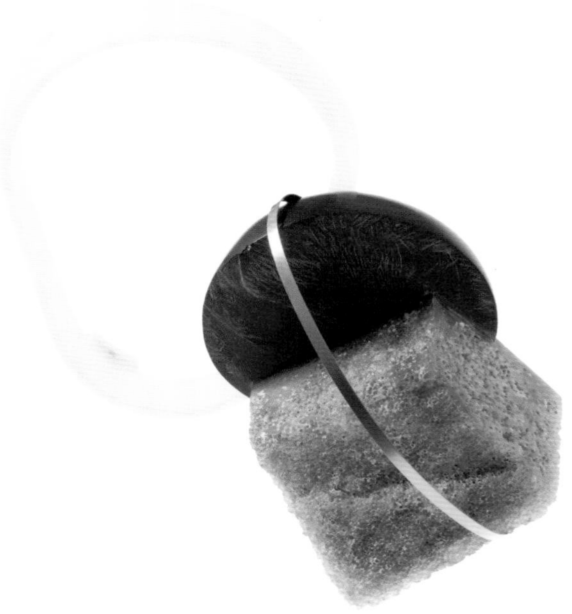

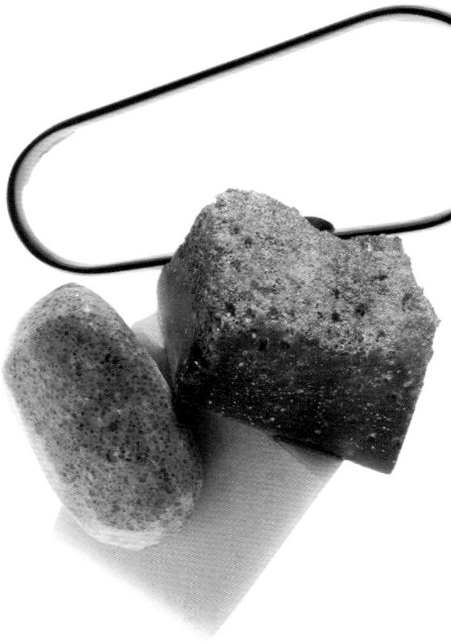

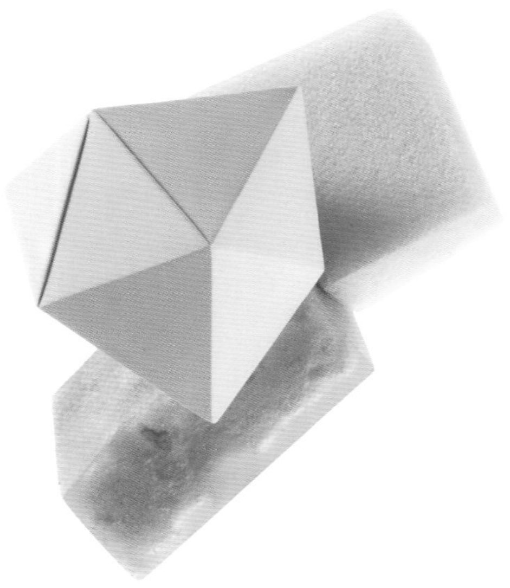

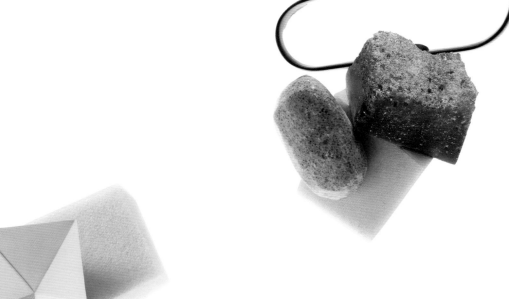

Brooch, no. 1, from How Long Is Now collection, 2014; Matte translucent plastic, copper-bronze, silver, resin, sponge; 6 × 11 × 9.5 cm (2⅖ × 4⅒ × 3 7/10 in.); Courtesy of Gallery Rob Koudijs

Brooch, no. 8, from How Long Is Now collection, 2014; Polyamide, Ytong aerated concrete block, sponge, resin, foam; 7 × 9 × 9 cm (2⅘ × 3½ × 3½ in.); Courtesy of Gallery Rob Koudijs

Brooch, no. 10, from How Long Is Now collection, 2014; Sponge, resin, foam, aluminum; 6.5 × 8 × 7 cm (2⅗ × 3⅒ × 2⅘ in.); Courtesy of Ornamentum Gallery

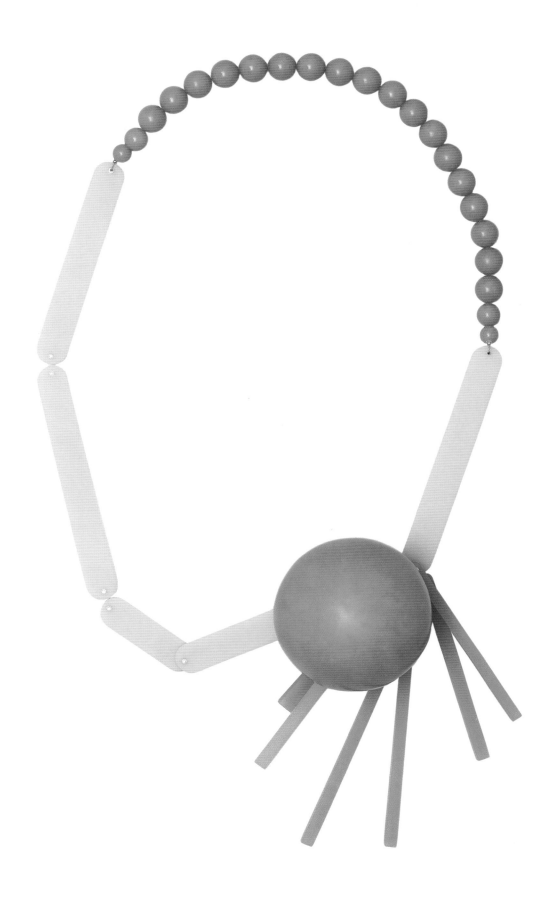

Pink Pearl, from Synthetic Delight collection, 2013; Silver, corian, fiberglass, found plastic, resin, thread; 60 cm (23⅜ in.); Courtesy of Ornamentum Gallery

Francesco Franchi

—ITALIAN, B. 1982—

In print media, it is not enough for a project to be only informative or only well designed. In Francesco Franchi's world, every layout and illustration must walk the line between journalism and graphic design. Franchi studied industrial design at the Politecnico of Milan and completed an ERASMUS exchange at the London Metropolitan University. He currently works as art director of *IL* (Ideas and Lifestyles), a monthly magazine that supplements Italy's leading economics newspaper, *Il Sole 24 Ore*. Today, data, graphics, and illustration are merging into print and digital presentations to tell a story. Widely known around the world for his innovative work as an editorial designer, Franchi is the author of *Designing News: Changing the World of Editorial Design and Information Graphics* (2013). Franchi's intricately detailed digital print Memory Palace, commissioned by the Victoria and Albert Museum, London, maps the history of memory techniques used to access information in the mind before the age of print. Above all else, Franchi's work balances artistic and utilitarian function. — LAUREN SCIARAPPA

———How did you become both a graphic designer and a journalist?

The magazine *IL* is similar to the *New York Times Magazine*—fashion, culture, and news. I have a contract with the newspaper as a journalist. In Italy, when you have this contract, you work exclusively for one newspaper or news company. To become a professional journalist, you take an exam, and if you pass, you enter into the community of journalists. I also do freelance projects, but I have to ask permission from my editor in chief.

———Tell me about your process.

The process I use to design comes from studies at the Politecnico of Milan. I start every project with analysis, taking inspiration from around me or from the past. Then I begin thinking and sketching; I always do sketches before I start working in front of the computer. At the university, we did some design projects for newspapers and magazines, especially during my first job in a design studio in Milan, where I started working while I was at the university. That's when I learned how the newsroom worked, and I realized that sometimes design was just the last step of the process. The design was only an aesthetic solution. My final dissertation was called "The RE-Designer." *Re* in Italian means "king," and redesign means to rethink, to redraw something. The designer can play an important role in the redesign, in the rethinking, of a newspaper or magazine. In my book *Designing News*,

I connected this idea from my dissertation to my own professional experience, and I collected case studies from the *New York Times*, *Bloomberg Businessweek*, and *The Guardian*, where the designer plays an important role in the process. Today, editors and publishers are trying to make sense in the digital world, so it's an interesting moment to be a designer in the newspaper field.

———What changes are taking place in journalism?

Design is taking on a new role in the newspaper. New forms of visual journalism are connecting and embracing different languages, such as data, illustration, and news analysis. Even the technology of writing is undergoing a change. Designers and writers are combining different languages. We are merging data and digital illustration with graphics and layout. The designer is becoming a journalist because he's doing research and selecting content and information. Designers are working across different channels, across different devices and media. We are also designing the workflow, the process of working among the designers and journalists and editors.

———How would you describe your own style as a designer? What is important to you?

I really like the Swiss school. My work has always been based on a grid. In the magazine, every layout is inspired by a grid designed by Karl Gerstner in 1962. We design a square in the page, and the page is composed of fifty-eight units, and fifty-eight is a number that can be divided into two, three, four, five,

and six columns, always keeping two units between the column. Even my infographics are all based on a grid. When you're following rules, you are able to break the rules, but in an intelligent way. Even when you're presenting a simple chart, like a bar chart, you can add something clever. You can add an idea.

———What comes to mind when you hear the word "beauty"?

Beauty happens when an object is working. Beauty is linked to the daily function of the object. In information design, beauty is a balance between the utilitarian aspects —or the information aspects—and the artistic aspect. On one side of the spectrum, we have information, communication. This side is utilitarian. On the other side, we have the aesthetics, the arty side. What we need is a balance. If we stay too close to the content, we can create cold pages, cold graphics. If we go too close to the arty side, we can create graphics that are nice to see but lack content. And, of course, beauty in a magazine is related to the quality of the paper, the quality of the print.

———What is the most beautiful time of day?

Early morning and late evening. These are the quietest moments, when you can concentrate. Early morning is when you start work. If an idea occurred to you during the night, you start working with that idea, and you are more productive. Or the late evening, because you work all afternoon, and in the late evening it is quiet again. You can concentrate more, and you can maybe get an idea that works.

———What is the most beautiful place you've visited?

When I went to Japan last summer, I was fascinated by the attention to every detail. Before getting a train, I got a bento box in the station, a box of sushi. Opening up this box was like opening a product designed by Apple. Inside the box, the sushi was perfectly arranged and was covered by leaves. It was hot outside, but the sushi was wrapped inside leaves from a tree, and it was fresh.

— INTERVIEW WITH SUVI SALONIEMI

Poster, Memory Palace, for *Sky Arts Ignition: Memory Palace* exhibition, Victoria and Albert Museum, 2013

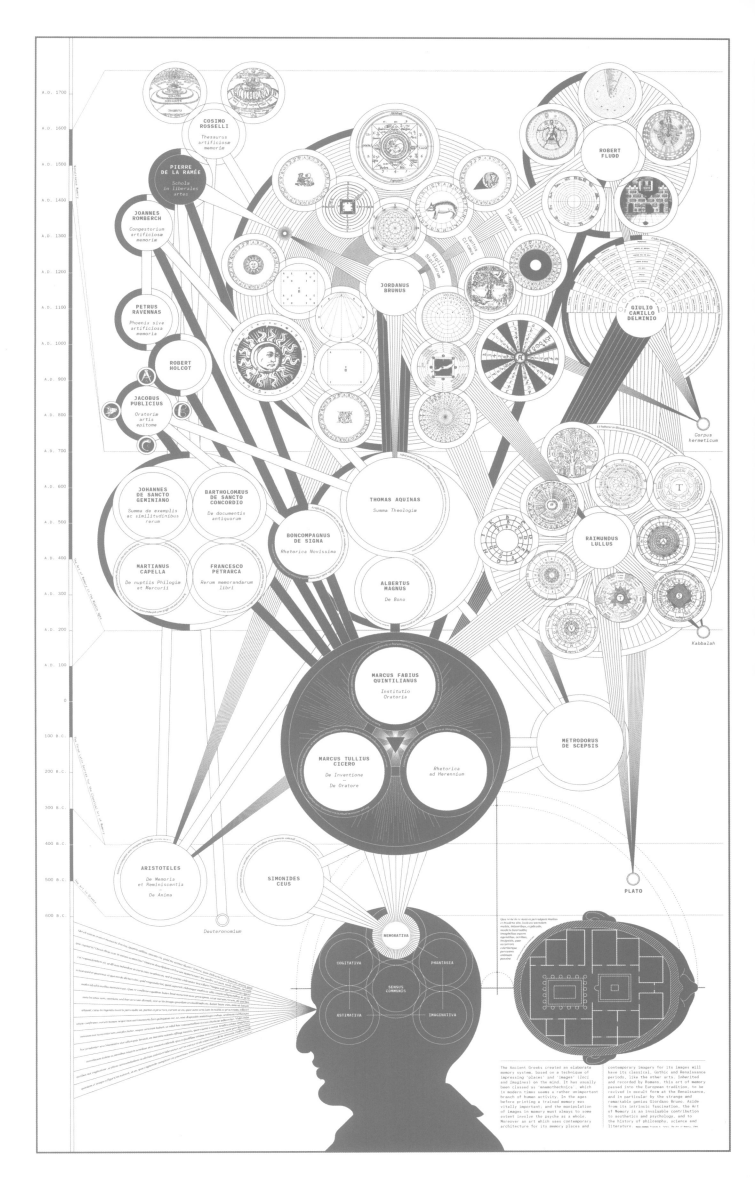

The Ancient Greeks created an elaborate memory system, based on a technique of impressing 'places' and 'images' (loci and imagines) on the mind. It has usually been classed as 'mnemothechnics', which in modern times seems a rather unimportant branch of human activity. In the ages before printing a trained memory was vitally important; and the manipulation of images in memory must always to some extent involve the psyche as a whole. Moreover an art which uses contemporary architecture for its memory places and contemporary imagery for its images will have its classical, Gothic and Renaissance periods, like the other arts. Inherited and recorded by Romans, this art of memory passed into the European tradition, to be revived in occult form at the Renaissance, and in particular by the strange and remarkable genius Giordano Bruno. Aside from its intrinsic fascination, the Art of Memory is an invaluable contribution to aesthetics and psychology, and to the history of philosophy, science and literature.

5 | Ultimo step: protagonismo politico

DIPLOMAZIA DI NICCHIA

Paese piccolo significa nessun peso politico/diplomatico. Così almeno in dottrina. La **"NICHE DIPLOMACY"** è la via che il Qatar ha scelto per contare di più. Dapprima attraverso la politica del **"FRIENDS TO ALL"**, abbastanza simile alla "zero problems" turca, in grado di posizionare l'Emirato al centro di numerose dispute mediorientali e del Golfo. Trovare la propria nicchia diplomatica, attraverso l'equidistanza – o supposta tale – nei confronti dei propri vicini sembra aver funzionato abbastanza bene. Il peso diplomatico di Doha è aumentato a dismisura, arrivando a lambire questioni teoricamente distanti (Afghanistan/talebani, solo per fare un esempio)

IL PIGMEO DAL PUGNO DI GIGANTE

Da "amico di tutti" il Qatar è stato protagonista di tre mediazioni importanti: Yemen (fallita), Sudan e Libano (con qualche risultato). L'Emirato è intervenuto anche nella questione israelo/palestinese, nella Libia di Gheddafi in caduta e nel conflitto siriano. Ma è in generale con le "primavere arabe" che Doha ha mutato atteggiamento diplomatico: da equidistanza a velata partecipazione, come dimostrano l'appoggio ai ribelli sia in Egitto sia in Siria. L'obiettivo è quello di aumentare la propria sfera di influenza regionale e meritarsi il titolo di "pigmeo dal pugno di gigante" datogli dall'Economist

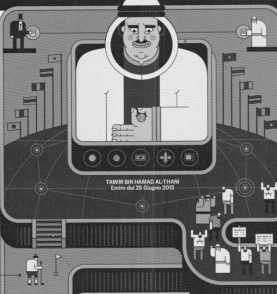

TAMIM BIN HAMAD AL-THANI
Emiro dal 25 Giugno 2013

4 | Boom della finanza velata

CASH! | *LE CASSEFORTI* | **CASH!**

Qatar Investment Authority

È il braccio armato dell'Emirato: il fondo sovrano che gestisce acquisizioni e dismissioni interne e sul mercato estero. Fondato nel 2005 per gestire i surplus del settore degli idrocarburi, si stima detenga asset per oltre 60 miliardi di dollari

QATAR HOLDING

Sussidiaria di Qatar Investment Authority, ha gestito acquisizioni importanti come quella del 100 per cento dei grandi magazzini Harrods e del 10 per cento (poi cresciuto al 13 per cento) di Barclays

La SCALATA al MONDO

2008	
BARCLAYS	10%
CEGELEC	100%
J SAINSBURY	17,9%
2009	
VOLKSWAGEN	12,5%
2010	
AGRICULTURAL BANK OF CHINA	2,1%
BANCO SANTANDER BRASIL	5%
HARRODS	100%
2011	
IBERDROLA	6,2%
2012	
CREDIT SUISSE	6%
LVMH	1%

Qatar *Capitale dello Sport*

A TENNIS E GOLF Il Qatar ExxonMobil Open di tennis e il Master del Qatar di Golf sono tra le manifestazioni sportive che vantano i più alti montepremi per gli atleti

B QATAR INTERNATIONAL RALLY Si tratta di una manifestazione a suo modo storica, essendo la prima edizione risalente addirittura agli anni Settanta

C 2022 WORLD CUP Il Qatar ospiterà la Coppa del Mondo di calcio nel 2022. Previste spese da record per realizzare gli stadi: si parla di 200 miliardi di dollari

D FC BARCELONA Da molti considerata la migliore squadra di calcio al mondo, dopo una lunga tradizione di maglie senza sponsor è capitolata a favore dell'Emirato

Foto: LaPresse (2)

Qatar *Capitale Culturale*

E QATAR FOUNDATION È l'organizzazione non profit guidata dalla moglie dell'ex emiro, Sheika Mozah bint Nasser al Missned. Tre i pilastri: istruzione, ricerca e scienza

F FANAR La più grande moschea dell'Emirato ospita il Centro culturale islamico più importante del Paese con corsi, speech e letture di prominenti studiosi

G MUSEO D'ARTE ISLAMICA Progettato dall'architetto sino-americano Leoh Ming Pei, la struttura è nata per mostrare le connessioni storico-culturali del mondo islamico

H EDUCATION CITY Progetto faraonico, contiene le sezioni distaccate di sei università americane, una britannica e una francese. Occupa una superficie di 14 chilometri quadrati

Fonti: J.E. Peterson, "Qatar and the World: Branding for a Micro-State", Gina Granado, "Strong Small State Diplomacy: A Case Study of How Qatar Used Power Well", Qatar Airways

UNA FLOTTA IN CRESCITA
2015 — 117
2013 — 110
2011 — 100
2006 — 50
2003 — 28
1997 — 4

3 | La rivoluzione è nei cieli

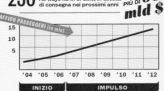

I Migliori Qatar Airways vincitrice come "Miglior Compagnia Aerea del Mondo" nel 2011 e nel 2012 e "Miglior Business Class del Mondo" nel 2013, agli Skytrax World Airline Awards. Cinque stelle per il suo straordinario servizio di bordo e l'eccellenza operativa

250 Gli aerei che la compagnia Qatar Airways ha in ordine, in attesa di consegna nei prossimi anni — PIÙ DI **50** *mld* $

TRAFFICO PASSEGGERI *(in mln)*
15 / 10 / 5
'04 '05 '06 '07 '08 '09 '10 '11 '12
INIZIO | IMPULSO

الجزيرة

13

Airbus A380
Il aereo più grande del mondo per numero di passeggeri, in consegna dal 2014

1996
L'emiro lancia Al Jazeera investendo
150 mln $

Dall'hub di Doha fino a **125 DESTINAZIONI**

EUROPA – Austria, Azerbaigian, Belgio, Bulgaria, Croazia, Danimarca, Francia, Georgia, Germania (3 destinazioni), Grecia, Italia (3), Norvegia, Polonia, Regno Unito (2), Romania, Russia, Serbia, Spagna (2), Svezia, Svizzera (2), Turchia (2), Ungheria
MEDIO ORIENTE E AFRICA – Algeria, Arabia Saudita (5), Bahrein, Egitto (3), Emirati Arabi Uniti (2), Giordania, Iran (3), Iraq (4), Kenya, Kuwait, Libano, Libia (2), Marocco, Mozambico, Nigeria, Oman (2), Ruanda, Qatar, Siria (2), Sudafrica (2), Sudan, Tanzania (2), Tunisia, Uganda, Yemen
ASIA MERIDIONALE -- Bangladesh, India (12), Nepal, Pakistan (4), Sri Lanka
OCEANO INDIANO -- Maldive, Seychelles
ASIA/PACIFICO -- Australia (2), Birmania, Cambogia, Cina (5), Corea del Sud, Filippine, Giappone (2), Indonesia (2), Malesia, Singapore, Thailandia (2), Vietnam (2)
NORD AMERICA -- Canada, Stati Uniti (4)
SUD AMERICA -- Argentina, Brasile

40-50 milioni
Media degli spettatori di cui
uomini donne
66% 34%

HAMAD BIN KHALIFA AL-THANI
Emiro dal 1995 al 2013

2 | Espansione nell'etere

POTENZA *ASSOLUTA*

Secondo uno studio di Brandchannel, Al Jazeera è tra i cinque più importanti brand al mondo, al pari di Apple, Google, Ikea e Starbucks. Più riconosciuta anche di Coca-Cola, Virgin e Yahoo!

NON SOLO TV

Dalla sua fondazione, il ruolo di Al Jazeera è aumentato enormemente, diventando la "voce" degli arabi e musulmani. Per questo è spesso accusata di essere una sorta di "braccio politico" dell'Emirato

L'ESPANSIONE
DELL'OFFERTA DI
Al Jazeera

- **AL JAZEERA Sport (2003)** Trasmette diversi importanti eventi sportivi come le manifestazioni UEFA e le Olimpiadi
- **AL JAZEERA Mobasher (2005)** Canale live di politica e fatti di interesse pubblico con focus esclusivo sul mondo arabo
- **AL JAZEERA English (2006)** In Italia ricevibile via satellite Hotbird, e anche su Sky, Tivù Sat e Alice Home TV oppure in streaming

KHALIFA BIN HAMAD AL-THANI
Emiro dal 1972 al 1995

1 | Dalle perle all'oro nero

QATAR PIL — Pro Capite
103.900 $ — NUMERO 1 AL MONDO

TUTTO È NATO DA QUI ... UN PAESE DI PESCATORI DI PERLE

Fino a quando non fu scoperto il petrolio, nel 1939, le perle sono state una delle principali fonti di reddito del Paese a partire dalla civiltà mesopotamica, attorno al 2000 a.C.

Tabloid presenta

Benvenuti a
QATARTICA

Come si crea una potenza mondiale in 5 *mosse*

di **Alessandro Giberti**, infografica a cura di **Laura Cantadori**, illustrazioni di **Giacomo Gambineri**

Infografica realizzata con la collaborazione degli studenti del workshop del **Master in Brand Design** dell'**IED** di Milano

Le riserve di *Gas naturale* e di *Petrolio*

GAS NATURALE
Il Qatar è il terzo Paese al mondo per riserve di gas naturale dietro Iran e Russia, per un ammontare di 25.400 miliardi di metri cubi

12° AL MONDO — **PETROLIO**
L'Emirato è anche il dodicesimo Paese al mondo per riserve di petrolio (25 miliardi di barili)

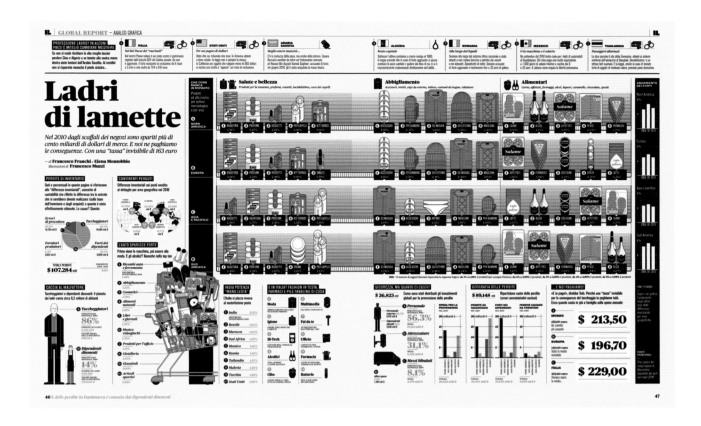

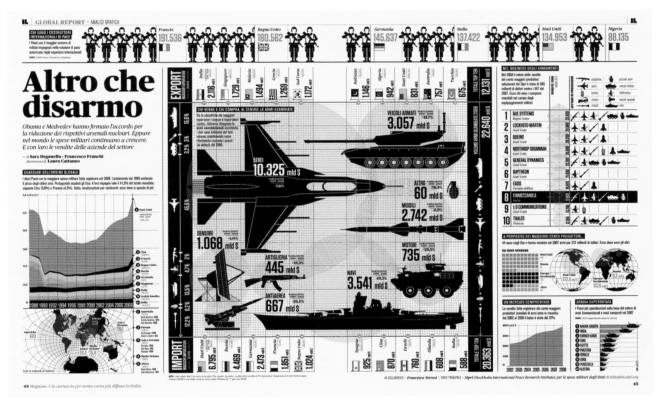

Francesco Franchi for *Il Sole 24 ORE*;
Illustration by Francesco Muzzi; Edited
by Elena Montobbio; Magazine layout,
Ladri di lamette (Thieves Strip), from
IL, No. 29, April 2011

Francesco Franchi for *Il Sole 24 ORE*;
Illustration by Laura Cattaneo; Edited by
Sara Deganello; Magazine layout, Altro
che disarmo (Other Than Disarmament),
from *IL*, No. 20, May 2010

OPPOSITE: Francesco Franchi and Laura
Cantadori for *Il Sole 24 ORE*; Illustrated by
Giacomo Gambineri; Edited by Alessandro
Giberti; Magazine layout, Benvenuti a
Qatartica, from *IL*, no. 53, September 2013

Götz Gramlich

—GERMAN, B. 1974—

Götz Gramlich was born in Heidelberg, where he currently lives and works. While studying design in Darmstadt, he came across the work of legendary Swiss designer Niklaus Troxler, who founded the Jazz Festival Willislau and for many decades created striking posters for the annual festival. Gramlich contacted Troxler and landed a place as an intern in his studio. He stayed there to work for several years before receiving his diploma in 2005. Gramlich now runs his own small studio, gggrafik design, where he designs communications in a range of media, including an ongoing exploration of the origins and future of the poster. In addition to animated digital posters and numerous posters in print, he designed a campaign for local political party Generation Heidelberg, a series of three printed posters that were placed on the streets over a period of time. The posters are printed so that they look like as if they are being torn, revealing a new message beneath the bland, smiling face of a politician. — ELLEN LUPTON

————Politics and graphics used to be heavily intertwined, but they are not so connected nowadays. Do you have some ideas about bringing back the history of posters and politics?

Generation Heidelberg is a small political party in my hometown. It was a pleasure to work with them, and was a pleasure to try to change some stuff in the political scene with graphic means. As graphic designers, we have been trained to compress complex processes into a very simple picture. We should use this talent or ability to bring some good stuff to the people. Right now, I'm organizing a poster competition with some other guys called "Mut zur Wut" [Courage to Anger]. We are collecting posters about social issues and bringing them to the streets. If we can get just a few people to think about some social issues in new directions, we will have achieved a lot.

————How do you work? How do you start? What is your process?

I start by just thinking about the problem. How do I communicate? What's the issue I want to communicate? And how do I find a picture or a visual approach or a visual language to communicate this issue in a fresh or new or curious way? It's good to make people curious, to stop them in their hectic life and get them to take a look at the stuff you're presenting. If you make them curious, you kind of have them on the hook. So my work approach is thinking, doing research, and

thinking again, and making some scribbles. Sometimes I have a brilliant idea in a minute, but normally I need some days to think about it. It feels like being "brain pregnant." When I get an idea, I am usually not in front of the computer—I'm out with my dog or going swimming or something like that. After that, I'm just working to bring the idea to paper.

————Describe your process with the Generation Heidelberg posters.

Nowadays you have lots of posters during election times, but usually you see only faces of model-looking people. There is no content about the aims of the party. It's just about looking good and looking furious and looking confident. So the idea was to build a typical politician. I browsed the Internet, and I found five or six pictures of typical political guys, and then I merged them in Photoshop, and then I printed out this newborn guy. I created ten or twenty different variations until I got the perfect three. Then I scanned them and put them on the typographical background as a layout.

The campaign is called Generation Vielfalt (2014), which means "diversity". They have lots of different cultures in the party. I wanted to work with colors because colors communicate diversity in a simple, straightforward way. I wrote the word "Vielfalt" on the back of the poster, and I multiplied it, so the cultures are mixing and giving impulses to one another. I wanted to show that our party doesn't have typical politicians, and we don't

communicate by showing just faces. The posters were shown in three phases: first, with just the politician's face; then, with most of the face torn away; and finally, with the colorful poster behind the face fully revealed.

————What else are you doing to reinvent the poster?

I'm experimenting with digital posters. When I go to cities like Paris or Berlin, I see giant screens, and they always seem to have TV ads on them. Instead of making a small movie or a TV ad, we could use intelligent animation to underline the idea of a poster. I did an animation for Shanghai, which was shown on the world's biggest LED screen. It's a whole side of a big skyscraper. I am also trying to animate some of my printed posters to share on the Web.

————What comes into your mind when you hear the word "beauty"?

Of course, beauty lies in the eyes of the recipient, but personally, for me, beauty, in one word, is nature. That's pure beauty for me.

————What is the most beautiful time of day?

I like the early morning hours, when we get fog on the river. It's beautiful. And actually, I have a lot of early mornings because I have a small kid.

————What is the most beautiful place you've visited?

Always places in nature, like standing on top of a mountain, where I can enjoy beauty and silence. Just three weeks ago, I was in China, and I was in the Gobi Desert, and it was just beautiful. One of my beautiful places is in India, the Hanuman Temple. It is a small city, a pilgrimage place. You have to go up some one thousand steps to the top of the mountain, and there's a small temple, and you have a fantastic view over the whole landscape. But of course, I also love my hometown.

— INTERVIEW WITH SUVI SALONIEMI

The Generation Vielfalt poster on a street corner in Heidelberg, Germany, 2014.

gggrafik design for Generation Heidelberg;
Posters, Generation Vielfalt, 2014; Offset print;
86.3 × 61.7 cm (34 × 24⁵⁄₁₆ in.)

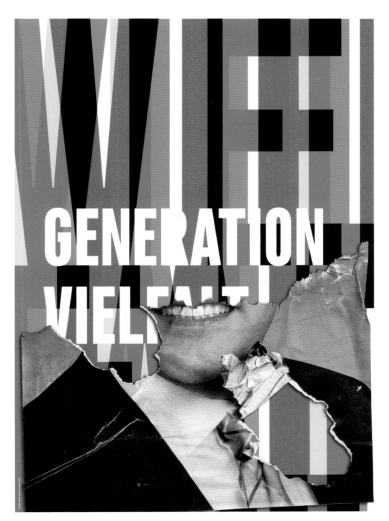

Brunno Jahara

—BRAZILIAN, B. 1979—

Brunno Jahara's objects delight the senses and provoke reflection. He transforms abandoned newspapers into delicate light fixtures, and he turns aluminum into colorful vases, lamps, and bowls. Jahara's ongoing collection Multiplastica Domestica began in 2012 with a trip to a recycling center located near his studio. Astonished by the center's ready supply of barely used plastic containers, Jahara began experimenting with this nearly virgin material, devising a way to connect the objects with a central metal spine in order to make spectacular bowls, lamps, fruit trays, and serving dishes. Born in Rio de Janeiro, Jahara studied industrial design at the University of Brasília and Venice University of Architecture. He worked for Fabrica in Treviso as well as several studios across Europe before establishing Jahara Studio in São Paulo in 2008. The studio designs production pieces for various manufacturers and makes original objects from locally sourced materials. — ELLEN LUPTON

————Tell me something about your current way of working.

I'm interested in researching sustainable materials and developing a Brazilian way of practicing design, a more tropical and warm style of making things. The studio is sometimes like an atelier, in a sense that we make the pieces, but most of our work is coming from companies. We develop porcelain collections for Vista Alegre in Portugal, and we're making pots and pans, and appliances with Tefal. In my personal research, I am trying to find some innovation in design in a way that is friendly to consumers and helps them understand a little bit of the design process.

————What is the source of your ideas?

Multiplastica Domestica is made from plastic that has been thrown away. Close to our studio, there is a recycling center. We collect materials and bring them back. We sterilize and clean all the pieces. We separate them by colors, and then we start making the different objects, like fruit trays, or lamps. We play a lot with the shapes and the colors. The material is practically new, reflecting a big investment in tooling, injection, and production. I work with either cold colors or warm colors to mix and make the shape of objects. It is a series in which every piece becomes unique. There is no repetition. It's not really industrial; it's in between craft and design. That's very much how you manage to do design in Brazil, because manufacturers still don't have all the structure of European factories that would put a mass amount of products to the market.

————How did you get interested in recycled materials?

When I came back to Brazil, I started a collection that is made of aluminum. Here in Brazil, the percentage of aluminum that is recycled is very high because people who live in the streets can sell cans for money. So, you don't really see aluminum trash in the street. I started to think about how aluminum is a soft material, and wondered how I could give that sensation through objects. We make vases, lamps, and trays from hammered aluminum; a process of dyeing makes the material stronger and also colorful.

————What comes to mind when you hear the word "beauty"?

The function of design is to please the eye and the senses of the user. Beauty is relative because something beautiful for me may not be beautiful for you. We know people have different tastes, but the idea of beauty has existed all over the history of humankind. Beauty is a simple thing. Beauty doesn't have to be complicated. I think any person who sees a beautiful object will be attracted to it immediately.

————What is the most beautiful time of the day?

My favorite time of the day is actually the night.

————What is the most beautiful place you've visited?

I've lived in different cities like Rio, Brasília, and Venice; these are all beautiful cities. Rio has natural mountains and beaches, and it's very vibrant, but Brasília is beautiful because it was created by architects and designers. It was designed and thought about in this way, to be a beautiful city for the future. And Venice is a magical city— beautiful by the water—with an amazing history and amazing art.

— INTERVIEW WITH SUVI SALONIEMI

Fruit bowl, from Multiplastica Domestica collection, 2012; Plastic and aluminum; 60 × 35 cm diam. (23⅝ × 13¾ in.)

OPPOSITE: Hanging lights, from Multiplastica Domestica collection, 2014; Plastic and aluminum; Sizes vary, up to 70 × 9 cm diam. (27⁹⁄₁₆ × 3⁹⁄₁₆ in.)

Max Lamb
—BRITISH, B. 1980—

Max Lamb digs, pours, carves, burns, hacks, saws, and casts in his quest to unearth forms. Much of his work is made by hand, forging objects from raw materials. For the designer, the process is as important as the final object. Lamb's pieces have a rough, tactile quality, illuminating his often primal, elemental, and transformative material explorations and techniques. The Scrap Poly Pastel Rainbow chair and table (2014) are carved from polystyrene offcuts and coated in rubber. The pieces maintain a visual density while retaining the material's lightness. The Copper Chair (2014) is made using an electro-deposition process to build nanocrystalline copper (similar to electroplating) onto a sculpted wax form, which is then melted away. The Pewter stool (2014) is crafted with a primitive sand-casting technique. A form is dug in sand at the beach, into which melted pewter is poured. Once the pewter dries, the table is excavated from the ground. Lamb graduated with a bachelor's degree in 3D design from Northumbria University in 2003 and, in 2006, with a master's in design products from the Royal College of Art. He established his eponymous studio in 2007. — ANDREA LIPPS

————Tell me about your background. What led you to design?
I was born and raised in Cornwall, England. My mother was a teacher and my father a survival instructor in the Royal Air Force. Both were—and continue to be—a great inspiration to me. They have always been supportive, and always incredibly active and energetic. We moved to a different part of the country every couple of years and once to Germany due to my father's job, so I got a good taste of travel and cultural variety, and learned very quickly to be versatile.

My grandfather is a scientist, builder, and farmer, and his farm in Yorkshire was probably my favorite place to spend holidays as a child, tinkering with machinery and generally getting up to mischief. I'm an inquisitive, curious type, and probably stubborn. I prefer to find things out for myself rather than be told.

I didn't like school besides sport, art, woodwork, and the playground. In these subjects, I formed good relationships with the teachers, which certainly helped my enthusiasm and concentration. When I was fourteen, my grandfather bought me a swivel lounge chair from a car-boot sale for £4 [$6.25], which turned out to be a first-series Eames Aluminium Group Lounge Chair.

When I was fifteen, he bought me a black plastic "hairdresser's" trolley that he thought would be useful to keep my "art stuff" in, which turned out to be a Boby Trolley by Joe Colombo. Both items he bought because they looked good and were made well. When I was seventeen, I visited the Design Museum in London, where they had on display a line of iconic chairs visitors were allowed to sit on—which I did—such as Rietveld's Red Blue Chair, Bertoia's Diamond Chair, a Mackintosh Argyle Chair, a Ponti Superleggera, and an Antelope Chair by Ernest Race. In the shop, I bought the newly published *1000 Chairs* book, from which point I was hooked.

————What are the fundamentals of your studio practice?
Physicality, materiality, industriousness, economy of means, efficiency of process, expediency, human capacity, man-made, independence.

————What does functionality in design mean to you?
To work. To be appropriate. To be beautiful. To be fit for purpose for as long as possible, with grace.

————What narratives or histories are important in your work?
Human's ability to transform the raw materials nature provides. The power of nature. Geology, geography.

————What comes to mind when you hear the word "beauty"?
Balance, grace, poise, function, pertinence, place, peace.

————What is the most beautiful time of day?
There is no rule or consistency to the most beautiful time of day. It is simply when I am most conscious of my actions and surroundings.

————What is the most beautiful place you've visited?
The beauty of a place is related to time, context, and consciousness.

— INTERVIEW WITH SUVI SALONIEMI

Sand-casting pewter furniture for the Pewter series, 2014.

Stool, 30 Triangles, from Pewter series, 2014;
Pewter poured into molded sand; 40 × 55 ×
50 cm (15¾ × 21⅝ × 19¹¹⁄₁₆ in.); Courtesy of
Johnson Trading Gallery

Chair, from Copper series, 2014; Nanocrystalline
copper; 86 × 46 × 47 cm (33⅞ × 18⅛ × 18½ in.);
Courtesy of Almine Rech Gallery

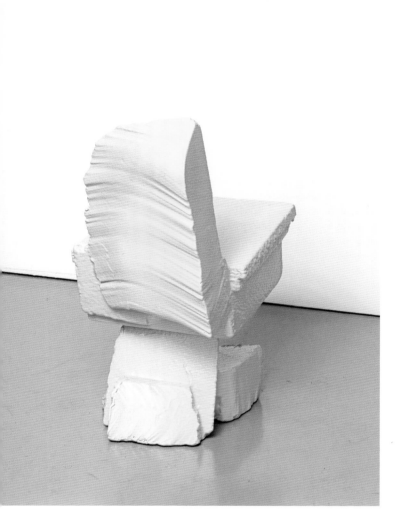

Chair (back and front), from Scrap Poly Pastel
series, 2014; Polystyrene, polyurethane rubber;
68 × 36 × 48 cm (26¾ × 14³⁄₁₆ × 18⅞ in.);
Courtesy of Kate MacGarry Gallery

CLOCKWISE: S'cangci III, Jacquard medium-weight knit sleeveless cardigan, from Buyel'mbo collection, 2014; Merino wool, kid mohair

Bomvane, Jacquard medium-weight knit crewneck, from Buyel'mbo collection, 2014; Merino wool, kid mohair

Nkonde, Jacquard medium-weight knit cape, from Buyel'mbo collection, 2014; Merino wool, kid mohair

Dyasi'yedabi II, Jacquard medium-weight knit varsity jacket, from Buyel'mbo collection, 2014; Merino wool, kid mohair

Laduma Ngxokolo

—SOUTH AFRICAN, B. 1986—

Laduma Ngxokolo has taken the traditions and arts of his native South African Xhosa culture and reimagined them as striking and elegant high-fashion statements. Starting with his belief that Western-styled clothing should not be used in the context of Xhosa rituals, he struck on the idea of making modern knitwear based on the extraordinary traditional beadwork of his people, using locally sourced mohair. His colorful, patterned sweaters and vests for men—and now the jackets and skirts in his women's wear line, as well as the blankets in his interiors offshoot—reflect the intricacy and precision of those handicrafts. In 2010 he started his knitwear brand with the support of his alma mater, the Nelson Mandela Metropolitan University in Port Elizabeth, South Africa, and subsequently launched his brand, MaXhosa, in early 2011. Though he is still in training—he won a scholarship to the prestigious Central Saint Martins in London, where he will be studying for his master's—his designs have graced runways in Paris, Oslo, and Johannesburg and been featured in fashion editorials. Ngxokolo was awarded *Vogue*'s inaugural Scouting for Africa prize in early 2015. — PENNY WOLFSON

————Tell me about your background and entry into design.

I was born in Port Elizabeth, which is the smallest city of South Africa. My late mother taught me how to use a sewing machine when I was about sixteen years old. Sadly, she passed away a year after, but I managed to learn the basics of how to use the machine. I am a curious and enthusiastic person, so I continued from there. I chose to do design subjects in high school—like textile design and fine art—and had the opportunity to blend all of that by specializing in textile design and technology at the Nelson Mandela Metropolitan University. I graduated with a BA in 2010. That is when I established my knitwear project, which I call today MaXhosa by Laduma, based on a concept of developing a collection of sweaters inspired by traditional Xhosa beadwork. The collection is a response to my personal experience as a Xhosa initiate, a tradition of Xhosa people from the Eastern Cape in South Africa.

When we are aged between eighteen and twenty-five, we have to go through a circumcision ritual and dress in new, dignified clothes following the initiation. I felt that the clothes that we wore after the ritual had no cultural resemblance of where we come from because we only have Western-styled clothing that is available to purchase on the market. So I went to explore patterns that are inspired by traditional Xhosa beadwork, and that is how I came up with the project, which is something that I am still continuing today, translated into a fashion brand.

————Could you tell us what future projects you're working with?

I'm taking a new journey. I have just started studying at Central Saint Martins doing a course, which is more futuristic compared to what I'm doing now [with MaXhosa by Laduma]. It is based on anticipating what future needs will be. I am planning to do exhibitions here in the UK and in the Netherlands and South Africa with my current work, and hoping that it will also carry the same spirit as the collections that I've launched since I started. I'd say I'm very excited about the future more than anything else.

————So what is your most important milestone to date?

Achieving a scholarship from Central Saint Martins. I value education more than any other thing, because for me it means accumulating knowledge that I can preserve forever. It is the opportunity to learn new things and to teach others back home what I have learned.

Besides that, getting to move to another country was quite a big milestone for me because I'm learning a lot of things from the fashion capital, London. It is a great opportunity for me to move to other territories from here. I also value the achievements that I got from South Africa, like winning the Emerging Designer of the Year Award [in 2014] from African Fashion International, and a few others that I got from South Africa. But I think where I'm at right now is one of the most important milestones.

————What comes to mind when you hear the word "beauty"?

Beauty for me is a very dynamic term to interpret. In terms of human senses, beauty is a feeling that one reflects when they see something they adore and are not restricted by barriers. For instance, living in the world that we're living in today, we are exposed to various other cultures that are expressed in different languages. We are exposed to various aesthetics, which are influenced by other cultures, but the common aspect that we share is beauty. I think that beauty is an international language. I think beauty is a definable term that a lot of people relate to globally.

————What is the most beautiful time of day?

From twelve to three in the morning. Things are more relaxed. I don't get distracted at that time because a lot of people are sleeping, and I often take advantage of that time because I think I get more focused than I do during the day. That is my golden time of the day.

————What is the most beautiful place you've visited?

The most beautiful place I've visited is the Eastern Cape, which is specifically at the rural areas of the Transkei. It carries a lot of profound history that hasn't been told. For me it means a lot to get to see that type of environment and see how humble it is. To someone else who is from another country, it could mean something very different, but I just love the environment. And I guess as a Xhosa person, I understand why Nelson Mandela chose to be buried in his homeland because he feels connected to it. He saw it in a way that nobody else does. He understood the environment.

— INTERVIEW WITH KATHLEEN BOMANI

Scholten & Baijings

— AMSTERDAM, NETHERLANDS, FOUNDED 2000 —

For Stefan Scholten (Dutch, b. 1972) and Carole Baijings (Dutch, b. 1973), the husband-and-wife team behind design studio Scholten & Baijings, the mark of beauty resides in a personal design signature. Over the last fifteen years, they have successfully created their own signature centered on elegant, minimal form punctuated with rich color, layering, and graphic lines. They marry an artisanal design approach with industrial partnerships for the likes of Danish furniture maker HAY and German auto manufacturer MINI. In particular, the Colour Porcelain (2012) tableware series for Japanese porcelain manufacturer 1616 / Arita Japan showcases the studio's refined sensibility for local craft and industry. Analyzing traditional porcelain decoration in Arita's archive, Scholten & Baijings recontextualized the Arita color spectrum into a distinct palette applied in different textures and shades of glaze to highly resolved porcelain forms. The result is a layered collection of covetable objects that is at once contemporary and timeless. — ANDREA LIPPS

————Tell me about how you approach design.

CAROLE BAIJINGS: The way we work in our workshop is special. By making paper models, we arrive at new forms. We call this "constructive thinking." In fact, we've been teaching this way of working from 2006 until 2011 at the Design Academy Eindhoven, in the "Atelier" department. In our design process, we combine this method with color, material, texture, and tactility. People now refer to this as typically Scholten & Baijings.

STEFAN SCHOLTEN: We care about skills. Working by hand provides very direct feedback. The handle on a cup that looks right in the design drawing might not be in proportion on a cardboard model. You can see that right off. We're not concerned with a glorified notion of "handicraft," but rather with the surprising results that can emerge only during the process of making the object.

————Can you tell me more about how you develop your own materials?

CB: We endlessly develop new materials, colors, color gradations, variations on patterns in our studio. Together with our team, we work with spools of thread, markers, glue, knives, paper, and cardboard. Then we put together books full of "recipes" that accurately describe the ingredients and techniques we have used.

SS: Our method is traditional at every level. We don't just invent forms and then find the right materials and the right producer. First, we dive into the process ourselves. This means that we remain open to the surprises that can occur while we're experimenting with materials.

CB: We don't consider design a cerebral process. Many ideas emerge through the process of working with materials. This harks back to the "Atelier-way-of-working" we mentioned earlier.

A good illustration is the Paper Porcelain (2009) collection, which initially was to consist of round shapes. Because we made scale models in cardboard, we were forced to come up with solutions for making the curves, which we did by cutting through the cardboard and then bending it. The result was a series of polygonal shapes that turned out to be particularly appealing. This sort of thing can't be worked out mentally in advance; it emerges while you experiment with materials and shapes. We thought those angular shapes were finished and decided to translate them into porcelain cups.

————What is your approach to color?

CB: To us, color is as important as form. For a long time, color was not even addressed in design. At one point, almost all interiors were virginal white, yet color can add so much to the quality of life. We think in color—it is definitely not a choice we make afterward.

As the forms are quite minimalistic, color alongside grids and layering gives the products an extra level of detailing. Color emerges from the way we design. We immediately see an object in color.

SS: It's interesting in that regard that color has no grammar. Using the rules of language, you can combine words into sentences, with which you can ultimately tell a story. That's not the case with color. We use music as our model for this purpose. In music, you can create combinations that transgress those laws and rules and yet are works of genius. We formulate our own "grammar of color." And then violate it entirely!

————What comes to mind when you hear the word "beauty"? How is it related with your practice?

CB: We see beauty as a complement to the final result of a meticulous design process. To us, beauty is therefore layered, actually an amalgamation of design ingredients where every layer of the product has to be right and contribute to the appearance of the product. Natural beauty is the way in which the basic material, function, form, texture, and, of course, color coalesce into one unique end product.

Our signature, in key words, consists of color, rich detail, layers, and transparency, coupled with hand-drawn illustrations and the combination of different materials.

SS: We use these elements to transcend anonymous mass production. That's one of the most essential features of our style. There's a need for a personal imprint. Objects that stand the test of time are always those in which you can see a story, a way of working, or a personal expression. The story of design begins with the prehistoric axe head. The caveman who made that object was already working with design. Long before our era, he cared about more than mere functionality. He'd carve in an extra line for decoration, or adjust the shape for a better grip. So in that sense, design is really in our DNA.

CB: In our work, the emphasis is not only on the conceptual statement. We do start from a concept—an idea—but we go a step further by engaging in collaborations with industry. We attach great importance to the quality of the execution. That quality lies in the attention to the detailing of the materials and the techniques we choose, the manner in which we make our compositions, the colors, the layering. These are qualities that do not shout at you, but rather whisper.

————What is the most beautiful time of day?

CB: Our studio is like a glass box with views of the Amsterdam IJ River and the famous, beautiful Dutch skies. We never imagined that these views could have such an impact on our way of working.

Since everything we do can be observed from the outside, we started to concentrate even more on the essence of our work. By this we mean that each step in the design process has become a "work" in itself. Because of our glass studio, we are closely connected to the elements. This is important for our intuition and perception of the spirit of the times.

————What is the most beautiful place you've visited?

SS: We were in Costa Rica showering under a waterfall when there were these blue— almost fluorescent blue—butterflies fluttering around us. That's where we noticed that the beauty of nature is overwhelming, and it's this beauty that we strive for in the colors of our own products. Nature is always perfect in its balance, and that's a great inspiration to us. How can we achieve the same balance within what we design?

— INTERVIEW WITH SUVI SALONIEMI

Sketches and scale models of DOT Chair for HAY.

Scholten & Baijings for 1616 / Arita Japan; Colour Porcelain series, 2012; Porcelain

CLOCKWISE: Sugar and milk set, or soy and ginger set, on platter; Sizes vary, up to 2.5 × 18 cm diam. (1 × 7 ¹⁄₁₀ in.)

Deep plates with espresso cup; Sizes vary, up to 2.5 × 18 cm diam. (1 × 7 ¹⁄₁₀ in.)

Platter with bowl and container for tea; Sizes vary, up to 3 × 25 cm diam. (1 ⅛ × 9 ⅝ in.)

Scholten & Baijings for Verreum; Carafe and tumbler, from Chromos series, 2014; Hand-blown, colored glass with metallic coating; 24.8 × 11.7 cm diam. (9 ¾ × 4 ⅝ in.) and 7.5 × 8.1 cm diam. (2 ¹⁵⁄₁₆ × 3 ³⁄₁₆ in.)

High Shelf (detail), from The Silent Village
Collection, 2013; Ash wood, metal, Krion,
ropes, nylon strings, feathers, fur, leather,
printed fabrics, chains, and hooks; 240 ×
85 × 57 cm (7 ft. 10½ in. × 33⅞₆ in. × 22⅞₆ in.);
Courtesy of Galerie Kreo

Brynjar Sigurðarson

—ICELANDIC, B. 1986—

Working like an anthropologist, Brynjar Sigurðarson studies cultures and environments in order to express a place and its people through objects. Sigurðarson's Silent Village Collection (2014) began with a trip to Vopnafjörður, a tiny Icelandic fishing village, where a shark hunter taught him a technique of creating nets. Using their traditional tools and methods, Sigurðarson then crafted his own collection of furniture pieces. These culturally rich works reflect Sigurðarson's education in design. After obtaining a bachelor's degree in product design from The Iceland Academy of the Arts, he enrolled in ECAL (University of Art and Design) in Lausanne, Switzerland, and went on to teach there for several years. Sigurðarson believes that the function of an object's decorative and sculptural elements can be utilitarian, intellectual, or emotional. Currently based in Lausanne and Berlin, Sigurðarson credits his years of living abroad with expanding his understanding of beauty, including a renewed appreciation for his home country, Iceland. — JUSTIN ZHUANG

———Tell me how your background has inspired your work.

For my diploma project in Iceland, I left the environment of the school and the city and went to a small rural area in the northeast of Iceland called Vopnafjörður. I stayed in this tiny little fishing village for one month. After three weeks, I met a man who hunts sharks in the ocean, which we eat in Iceland. He was preparing nets for a hundred-day lumpfish season. He was using an interesting wooden tool called a netting needle to tie together nets. I stayed with him in his workshop for a couple of days, and I learned his method of using this netting needle. He was using it for a very functional goal: to tie together string to make nets, so he could hunt this specific fish. I started to experiment, and I found that this needle has a variety of aesthetic uses. From there, I started to experiment with materials and methods from the fishing harbor environment. I felt that I had found an authentic Icelandic craft in the workshop of the fisherman. That project set the guidelines for my practice today.

———Tell me about the role of anthropology and archeology in your work.

Anthropology is the study of cultures and people, and our goal as designers is to create something that will be part of our culture and is for people. Archeologists are basically scientists of objects. They study cultures and societies of the past through objects. After doing research in this fishing village in the northeast of Iceland, I figured out that I was using similar tools as anthropologists. The anthropologist goes to a culture or a place that's foreign or exotic in order to learn more about his own culture. In the end, I'm translating what I'm seeing and experiencing in this fishing village into an object that is part of my own culture or environment.

Anthropologists use tools, drawings, audio recordings, interviews, and even sketches, but they often end up in the shape of text. They tell stories about what they are looking at. I'm sort of trying to make objects that speak the language of the fishing village. I see my studio as a laboratory, or a place where I'm looking for some sort of magic in materials and objects.

———What is the role of function in The Silent Village Collection? What is the relationship between art and design?

All these things are meant to be used and be part of a home. I also give myself a bit of freedom to think about the balance between functionality and sculptural value. All these ropes and knots and details are an integral part of the furniture. You can hang your coat on my coat hanger, but the piece speaks more the language of sculpture, and it references the harbor environment in the fishing village. I'm not really interested in the distinction between art and design, or graphics and filmmaking. It's more about subjects for me. I'm interested in the harbor environment, and there are not many designers I'm able to speak to about this precise subject. Therefore I meet fishermen, people living in that environment. I meet rope makers who can tell me something about what they do.

———What comes to mind when you hear the word "beauty"?

After I moved away from Iceland, I started to be intrigued by all sorts of situations within the urban environment, such as where a plastic tube runs into the bottom of a wall and you don't have a clue where it's going or what it's for. I find these random situations to be very beautiful.

Then I always find nice things when I go back to Iceland. During the summer, I go and stay in my family's summerhouse. Walking on the beaches around Iceland, you find beautiful scraps of plastic that have been polished by the ocean for years, or you find crab shells in the sand. I don't find the crab shell as beautiful if I see it in a shop or a natural history museum. So I guess the experience and the situations have a lot to do with my personal perception of beauty.

———What is the most beautiful time of day?

I find mornings really beautiful. In Iceland, morning is never the same because we have such an extreme difference between winter and summer. The summer is light more or less the whole twenty-four hours, and the opposite during the wintertime. But early morning I find really nice.

———What is the most beautiful place you've visited?

I went this summer to a place in the west of Iceland called Snæfellsjökull, and we camped underneath a small, beautiful glacier. Since I moved away from Iceland, I really like to be a tourist and to go on glacier hikes, which I never did when I was living there in Iceland, and to go on whale-watching tours and drive around the island and camp in random valleys. I experienced a lot of beauty in Iceland after I moved away from Iceland. That's giving things that you take for granted a second chance.

— INTERVIEW WITH SUVI SALONIEMI

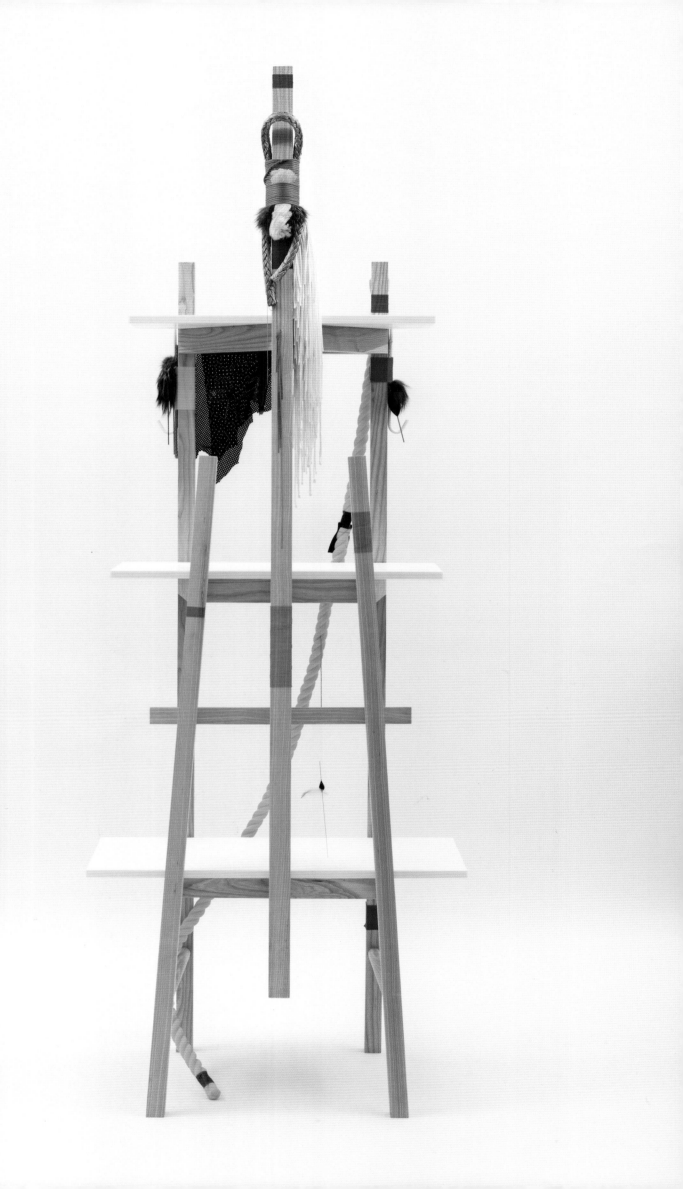

High Shelf, from The Silent Village Collection, 2013; Ash wood, metal, Krion, ropes, nylon strings, feathers, fur, leather, printed fabrics, chains, and hooks; 240 × 85 × 57 cm (7 ft. 10½ in. × 33⁷⁄₁₆ in. × 22⁷⁄₁₆ in.); Courtesy of Galerie Kreo

Kris Sowersby

—NEW ZEALANDER, B. 1981—

A typeface is a collection of characters related to one another through form, line, proportion, and details. Typefaces with multiple weights and styles, such as Kris Sowersby's Domaine family (2013), contain thousands of characters, becoming robust systems capable of meeting a vast range of communications challenges. Domaine's combination of lyrical elegance and surprising mass has made it a sought-after typeface among graphic designers around the world. Sowersby completed his studies at Whanganui School of Design in New Zealand in 2003. He founded the Klim Type Foundry in Wellington, New Zealand, in 2005. While Domaine revels in voluptuous delicacy, Sowersby has explored other sides of typography as well; Manuka (2014) is blunt, unpretentious, grotesque, while Maelstrom is a display face whose reverse-stress construction flirts with typographic profanity. — ELLEN LUPTON

————Tell me how you approach typeface design.

If I'm commissioned to make a typeface for a client, then I need a clear brief. What does the client intend to do with the typeface? How do they want to use it, and what style or atmosphere or feeling do they need?

Another situation is making typefaces for retail rather than for a specific client. Here, it's just me drawing letters and following an idea and seeing if things work. I might be flicking through old type specimens or see a letter somewhere and I'll think, "Oh, maybe that could work as an entire typeface." I'll make some test letters and test prints. I then leave it alone and come back to see what's worth keeping and what isn't. Sometimes it's all rubbish and I throw it away, but sometimes there's something useful there. At the moment, I'm working on a Garamond typeface [inspired by the types of sixteenth-century printer Claude Garamond]. This project has been bubbling away in the background for six or seven years, on and off. It's only last year that it finally found its voice and became something worthwhile. The typeface looks completely different now from what it did when it started.

————Would you say you have a particular style that is identifiable?

I'm fairly sure that I have a style, but I can't see it myself. Sometimes I can feel it, like when I'm walking through the street or in a shop, I'll see a book cover, and it feels familiar, like it's speaking or reading in a familiar voice. I look at it closer and see that it is indeed my typeface. I may open a page of a book, and I'll feel that maybe this is my typeface, and then upon closer inspection, I find that it actually is. I can't tell you exactly what my style is, but I can feel it.

————You said that when you're doing your retail fonts, you tend to look at old specimens for inspiration. Is there any particular period you're looking at?

I'm interested in what various countries have done over the years, which typefaces have fallen out of fashion, which ones have stayed in fashion, and how they've changed with the different methods of production. Old specimens are nice to look at because there's care in their production. Typically, the typefaces themselves are no longer being used. Looking at the original source material of these historical forms is like a musician going back and listening to, say, Lead Belly. Imagine if you could listen to him directly rather than listening to recordings that have been passed down, transmitted and deteriorated over the ages.

Looking at old specimens is like looking at the originals. For example, I never really understood Helvetica, because my experience of it has only ever been digital and maybe a few phototype settings. But when I saw some of the original typeface specimens of Helvetica, I immediately understood what Helvetica really was, which is quite different from the digital typefaces we use today. If I had been a designer in the fifties or sixties and that Helvetica specimen landed on my desk, it would have blown me away. I look at old specimens in order to understand what these typefaces were like before they were readapted and changed and reproduced and all the rest of it.

————What makes typography beautiful?

I know I apply rules and criteria to what I do, but I couldn't properly articulate them. I started using Pinterest to help articulate this. I started pinning things that I liked. I didn't think about it too much. I'd just flick through and pin it. Patterns emerged. When I go back over the last year or so, I see two broad categories: things that I like and things that I do. The things I like are different from the things that

I actually make. The things I like are on the cusp of being undesigned, especially typographically. I like single-word letterpress and large wood type pieces that aren't produced professionally. I like things that aren't overly considered, that are raw and speak to you on a gut level. They're just simple things that don't use all the nice fine details like old-style numerals and small caps. They haven't been fussed over. It's like a direct, raw, unmediated hit of typography. That's the stuff I like.

————But when it comes to your typography, you're obsessed with the details.

All designers are into details. I read a post by [Erik] Spiekermann about this just yesterday. The details are the design. Obsession with details is not really obsession—it's just doing the thing properly. In my own stuff, I spend so much time and effort fiddling around and doing all those fine adjustments. A piece of under-designed typography is just the opposite. It's a relief. You could be sitting out in the hot weather and you're all sweaty, and then you jump into an icy cold pool. That's the effect. It's the visual equivalent of that.

————Has being in New Zealand and away from the main design capitals influenced how you see design?

What are the main design capitals?

————Let's say New York or London, where there are so many design activities going on. Coming from New Zealand, do you see design and concepts of beauty differently from the rest of the world?

Once upon a time, geographic distance was a problem, but not anymore. Everybody can see what everybody else is doing on the Internet. But living in the culture is another thing altogether. New York is nice, but I couldn't live there. It's not where I grew up. It's not my culture.

You and I could look at the same piece of design. I could look at it, and all I'm going to see is the things that I'm accustomed to seeing and interpreting. You'd look at it through your eyes and see what you're accustomed to seeing, and someone in Indonesia would see something entirely different again. For example, I did a typeface for House Industries in the US. It is called Exotique (2009). It is a digitization of an inline typeface with large ball terminals on the end of all the strokes. New Zealand designers started asking me about my "koru typeface." I'm like, "What are you talking about?" They show me, and I say, "Oh, that's Exotique from House Industries." For New Zealanders, the koru is a very traditional motif in Māori design, carving, and art. Nobody else sees it like that, but that's how we see it.

106——TRANSFORMATIVE Kris Sowersby

I'm redrawing National (2010) at the moment, because there are some parts of it that I'm not happy with. I'm expanding it to different widths and weights. But in general, if you try and just have one small, simple idea, like the Garamond, and you stick to that, there will be a point—really hard to define—when you're drawing, and the typeface just snaps into focus. It becomes right. From there, it's just a matter of filling out the character set and making sure the letters all work together. For me, once it feels right, it's not that hard to finish it. Sometimes it takes ages to get to that point. This Garamond thing's been taking bloody ages. Other things happen quite quickly, like Pitch (2012), for instance. I smashed that out really quickly because I was kerning Metric (2012) and Calibre (2012), and I just needed a break. I made a few sketches and didn't think about it too hard. I managed to do Pitch in a few months. Some things are quick, and some are slow. That's just the nature of it.

————When you design a typeface, do you start with certain letters first?

I start with some of the lowercase letters, like the *n* and *o*. From there, you can make an *h*, *l*, *i*, *m*, and *u*. Then with the *o*, you can move on and make a *p*. You can make a *b* and a *d* and a *q*, and then just throw in a *v* for a bit of interest. From there, all the letters inform other letters. I use a good tool called adhesion-text. You type in some letters, and it throws out a bunch of random words with just those letters. If it's holding together there, you make a few more letters. You make some uppercase letters, and then you test and test, and then move on from there. There is some structure to it, but how it happens is quite intuitive.

————Do you design on the screen, or do you draw things out?

Always on the screen. I do some thumbnail sketches, but they're just rubbishy things, just to quickly figure out an idea. I never draw a thing out and then digitize it. It's always straight on the computer because it's much easier to manipulate.

————Are you concerned about how people use your typefaces? Does how you use it determine whether it is beautiful or not?

That's one of the best parts. That's the only part to it, actually. Up until the typeface is used, it kind of doesn't exist. If I design a typeface and display it on my website, that's just the typeface advertising itself. It's not until someone licenses it, and uses it for print or a website or an app or whatever, that it comes alive. It's like a knife just sitting in a knife block. Until it starts chopping things, it's

bloody useless. I love seeing what people do with a typeface, because you can never predict that. It's always interesting. It's not always beautiful, but that doesn't matter. There are a lot of typefaces out there. That somebody has taken the time to look at it, select it, purchase it, and work with it for several hours, get it through the client meetings—that's quite a long, involved process.

————What comes to mind when you hear the word "beauty"?

Beauty is a state of being. It's not fixed. It fluctuates from person to person and throughout the ages. It's a nebulous thing. It's more of a concept. It's not really concrete. Beauty can be nice, but it can also be dangerous. It's nasty, I think. Yeah, that's what I reckon. That's, I suppose, what I think of beauty.

————What is the most beautiful time of the day?

Dusk, because the day's almost over and it's a good time to think. It looks good. You get long shadows. There's a warmth about the atmosphere, and you will probably have a beer. That's a good thing as well.

————What is the most beautiful place you've visited?

The South Island of New Zealand. It's the landscape and the amount of natural bush on the west coast. It has long, dry plains in the middle, Central Otago. It has rugged cliffs and huge mountains. It's got big lakes, beautifully clear lakes. The color of the water, you just can't believe it. It is definitely the most beautiful place.

— INTERVIEW WITH JUSTIN ZHUANG

"B" specimen, Domaine Sans typeface, 2014

Marquette

Assyrtiko ✓

Nerkarat

Garnatxa

Merzling ✓

Sylvaner ✓

www.klim.co.nz

Specimen, Domaine Display typeface, 2013

RIZLING

GANZIN

MORRO

GARCIA

OLIVER

www.klim.co.nz

  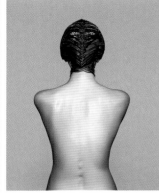

TheUnseen

—LONDON, ENGLAND, UNITED KINGDOM, FOUNDED 2012—

Lauren Bowker (British, b. 1985) founded TheUnseen as a creative house to explore the application of biological and chemical technology to wearable materials. Bowker studied chemistry and textiles at the Manchester School of Art and received a master's in printed textiles from the Royal College of Art, where she developed color-changing inks that respond to environmental conditions. Applying these inks and compounds to fashion enables wearers, and those around them, to visualize otherwise invisible phenomena. The AIR collection (2014), for example, includes wind-reactive ink—which changes color based on movement and turbulence in the air around it—applied to a finned leather jacket. The Swarovski headpiece (2014) is made from black spinel gemstones infused with a compound that changes color in response to varying energy levels in the brain. The technology could enable communication with those who are unable to do so by any other means. — ANDREA LIPPS

——You are a self-described alchemist and designer. What led you to this line of work?

LAUREN BOWKER: As a child, I wanted to show creative collections at High Fashion Week, to be a fashion designer. And I was always interested in formulating different concoctions, working with them creatively rather than technically. I started studying in the textiles industry, but got quite ill and had to spend a lot of time in the hospital. As an eighteen-year-old, I quickly burned out with the systems in place to record my pain and to analyze what conditions I was going through. The procedures that I had to endure just to learn what was causing my pain were quite bad. I didn't feel they were human-oriented. And it seemed quite alien to be an eighteen-year-old girl treated and diagnosed like an eighty-year-old patient.

I still have this condition in my spine, which means that every six months I am in hospital again. So that's this real anchor point for a lot of our research. The ultimate solution is to create a surface or a textile that's able to track different pain levels in a human, an early-warning indicator system to give myself an easier life, to give a language to everything that my body's going through. The human brain doesn't always let you know

exactly what's going on. You might have a pain in your arm, but it's coming from your back. And so I try to use creativity and science to make my everyday a bit easier.

——Wow, what an incredible driver. One sees that in your work—it proposes a new mode of visual communication with inks that render invisible conditions into visual cues.

Yes, but it comes from research. The AIR collection, for example, came from a commission we did for Formula One to track the aerodynamics around a car. But with TheUnseen, we're focused on the human, and so we wanted to bring that technology to how a human interacts in their environment. It is about using color and form to express these different worlds beyond the eye, the ear, and the nose, beyond what we as humans see. It's being aware of that, and creating materials and pieces so people don't have to think about it. They just see it.

——What is your starting point for a new project or technology?

Everything's been an evolution of the last thing. We don't clean the slate and start again. We are just discovering the world.

Our material selection for each garment becomes a creative and technical process. For the Air collection, we knew we needed

a material that would absorb the pigments we were developing and [that] would be quite porous. We also wanted it to react in an aerodynamic way, so we needed something thin that could become layered as a structure around the body.

——How does aesthetic beauty factor alongside the material's technology?

I think the aesthetic beauty naturally comes out in the shapes that we always go for. With the Air collection, there's a technical angle as to why they're shaped the way they are, so they trip the wind. I like using one material and tessellating it over and over and over again, so then it naturally has its own form and shape. It silhouettes whatever space you're working with, but it's always one repeated pattern. There's never really a starting point for our aesthetic. We just keep building on it.

——What are the possible applications for the material technologies that you develop?

Everyone we have been approached by seems to have their own idea, from a car seat that changes color to a toothpaste that lets you know where to clean your teeth. We are interested in creating materials that can be inserted into everyday life to improve it—a universal color code that is an early-warning indicator of an oncoming asthma attack, or a material to easily communicate the state of your body or health. It is a catalyst to create knowledge.

——What comes to mind when you hear the word "beauty"?

Beauty is in revealing something that you don't normally notice. It is seeing the unseen.

——What is the most beautiful time of day?

For me it's the time just before you fall asleep, when you're in between states of consciousness, and the mystical phase when the sun has set but the night hasn't quite drawn in.

——What is the most beautiful place you've visited?

It would have to be a moment in time. I was really ill and being taken out of the house on a stretcher. It was at dawn. The sunrise is the most beautiful coloring in the sky. It was all I could see. This time, I had been diagnosed with all sorts of illnesses, and I remember thinking, "Well, this has got to be it. This is like the last thing I'm ever going to do. If I come through this, I'm not going to live my life the way that I had been doing." That's been the memory that drags on. Even though it wasn't a beautiful time, it meant that everything that's happened now was because of that time. And for me, that's beautiful.

— INTERVIEW WITH ANDREA LIPPS

Lauren Bowker for Swarovski Gemstones; Headpiece, 2014; Black spinel gemstones

OPPOSITE AND OVERLEAF: Jacket, from the AIR collection, 2014; Leather, wind-reactive ink

Cooper Hewitt Design Triennial

Beauty

COOPER
HEWITT

Andrea Lipps and Ellen Lupton

COOPER HEWITT

Published by Cooper Hewitt,
Smithsonian Design Museum
2 East 91st Street
New York, NY 10128
USA
cooperhewitt.org

This book is published in conjunction with
the exhibition *Beauty—Cooper Hewitt Design
Triennial* at Cooper Hewitt, Smithsonian
Design Museum, February 12, 2016–August
21, 2016.

Beauty—Cooper Hewitt Design Triennial is
made possible by generous support from
Edward and Helen Hintz.

Additional funding is provided by Margery
and Edgar Masinter, May and Samuel Rudin
Family Foundation, Inc., and Rockwell Group.

ISBN 978-1-942303-11-4

2016 2017 2018 2019 /
10 9 8 7 6 5 4 3 2 1

Distributed Worldwide
by ARTBOOK | D.A.P.
155 Sixth Avenue, 2nd floor
New York, NY 10013
USA
artbook.com

Library of Congress
Cataloging-in-Publication Data

National Design Triennial
(5th : 2016 : New York, N.Y.)
Beauty—Cooper Hewitt Design Triennial/
Andrea Lipps, Ellen Lupton.
pages cm
"This book is published in conjunction with
the exhibition "Beauty—Cooper Hewitt Design
Triennial at Cooper Hewitt, Smithsonian
Design Museum," February 12, 2016–August
21, 2016."
Includes index.
ISBN 978-1-942303-11-4 -- ISBN 978-1-
942303-12-1 (epub) -- ISBN 978-1-942303-
13-8 (mobi) 1. Design--History--21st century-
-Exhibitions. 2. Aesthetics--Exhibitions. I.
Lipps, Andrea, author. II. Lupton, Ellen, author.
III. Cooper Hewitt Museum, host institution,
issuing body. IV. Title.

NK1397.N38 2015
701'.17--dc23

2015027031

Printed in China

For complimentary digital versions
of *Beauty—Cooper Hewitt Design
Triennial* in a variety of formats, visit
cooperhewitt.org/publications/
beauty-book

Head of Cross-Platform
Publishing—
Pamela Horn

Publishing and Image Rights
Associate—
Matthew Kennedy

Copy Editor—
Joelle Herr

Book Design—
Kimberly Varella,
Content Object Design Studio

Color—
Embassy Graphics

Printer—
Print Plus, Ltd.

Type—
Domaine (Kris Sowersby, Klim Type
Foundry), Graphik, and Union

Paper—
Daio, Munken, and Holographic
C1S Artboard

BELOW: In Kimberly Varella's studio
in Los Angeles; early cover
development for *Beauty—Cooper
Hewitt Design Triennial*

Contents

Foreword
Lens of the Senses

Cooper Hewitt, Smithsonian Design Museum established the Design Triennial series in 2000 in order to provide an ongoing critical review of contemporary design. Each Triennial explores a diverse range of practices by outstanding designers, placing emphasis on emerging careers. With the Triennial, Cooper Hewitt acts as a lens for viewing the broader field of design as it unfolds within the currency of our time. Over the years, the series has proven itself to be a prescient look at a wide array of the latest design ideas and examples.

For each Triennial, two or more curators examine the current state of the field in order to convey a distinct point of view. Some iterations of the Triennial have emphasized technology; others have stressed design for social and ecological responsibility. The 2016 Triennial—the fifth exhibition in the series—is focused on beauty. Assistant Curator Andrea Lipps and Senior Curator of Contemporary Design Ellen Lupton have celebrated design as a creative endeavor that engages the mind, body, and senses. With projects ranging from precious jewelry, singular prototypes, and one-of-a-kind objects to interactive games, digital typefaces, and architectural interventions, *Beauty* presents works of astonishing form and surprising function. I thank them both for their embrace of this intangible theme, and for their tireless pursuit of beauty over the last three years.

With *Beauty*, Cooper Hewitt shows that aesthetic innovation can drive change, whether materially, structurally, or ethically. *Beauty* celebrates objects and practices that are exuberant, ethereal, atmospheric, experiential, exceptional, or sublime. Objects of beauty provoke immediate reactions and demand judgment—asking us to redefine what is lovely or grotesque, formed or malformed, virtuous or subversive. As the curators explain in their essay, objects of beauty exalt experience as a living, unfolding exchange between people and things.

Cooper Hewitt is the only museum in the United States dedicated exclusively to historic and contemporary design. With the Triennial, we tell a history of the present, looking at new developments as they surface in studios, fairs, shops, galleries, and in digital media and publications around the world. As the nation's design museum, Cooper Hewitt celebrates the American experience within the context of a global conversation. For the first time, we engaged a panel of international curatorial advisors to assist us early in the project by identifying designers working in diverse fields worldwide, enriching our American perspective with their global vantage points. Suvi Saloniemi, Chief Curator at the Design Museum in Helsinki, Finland, conducted many of the interviews that form the core of this book. A pair of Mobius Fellowships, funded by the Finnish Cultural Institute, allowed Suvi to travel to New York City to work with Cooper Hewitt staff in 2014 and brought Andrea Lipps to the Design Museum in Helsinki in 2015. These exchanges have greatly enriched our understanding of design's global vocabulary.

Finally, this print publication befits the richness of its title. Book designer Kimberly Varella of the Los Angeles–based studio Content Object worked closely with the curators and our Head of Cross-Platform Publishing, Pamela Horn, to craft a book that stands out in its page composition and format. The exposed pink stitching and the reveal of the full-bleed foil upon opening the cover are only two of the numerous alluring surprises in *Beauty*. Many thanks for the innovative process and thoughtful design that give shape to this transcendent volume.

Beauty—Cooper Hewitt Design Triennial is made possible by generous support from Edward and Helen Hintz. Additional funding is provided by Margery and Edgar Masinter, May and Samuel Rudin Family Foundation, Inc., and Rockwell Group.

— Caroline Baumann, Director
  Cooper Hewitt, Smithsonian Design Museum

WHAT COMES
TO MIND
WHEN YOU
HEAR THE WORD
"BEAUTY"?

Delfina Delettrez: Beauty is not necessarily attractive, and ugliness is not always repulsive. Patrick Clair/Elastic: Whether it's traditional beauty—like a pretty girl or a mountain vista—or a striking photo of an industrial car park or a powerful piece of art, beauty is not about being aesthetically pleasing, but about having an indefinable quality that moves you. Simon Haas/The Haas Brothers: It is like finding a pattern among chaos. Hechizoo: When you see beauty, you have this moment of silence, of stillness. Brunno Jahara: Beauty is a simple thing. Beauty doesn't have to be complicated. I think any person who sees a beautiful object will be attracted to it immediately. Mary Katrantzou: [My] focus has always been about turning filtered beauty into applied design and design into function. Tuomas Markunpoika: There can be something in the object that renders it beautiful as soon as you know something about it, like a process or a history that makes you look at it in a very different way. Laduma Ngxokolo: Beauty is an international language. Richard Niessen: Beauty can be found in very well-worked-out concepts. Design becomes convincing, and beautiful, when it's worked out in a very consequential way. Jon Forss/Non-Format: There wouldn't be a fashion industry if there weren't, at any given moment, the most beautiful way to wear a pair of pants. Gareth Pugh: It's a constant and never-ending search. Jenny Sabin: For me, beauty is biological. Kustaa Saksi: Beauty always has a fracture, an error, or a crack. Stefan Scholten/Scholten & Baijings: Objects that stand the test of time are always those in which you can see a story, a way of working, or a personal expression. Kyuha Shim: For me, beauty emerges from a mixture of parameters. Simogo: When you really can't explain why something is beautiful, then maybe that is beauty? Job Smeets/Studio Job: The beauty . . . in our work needs to be related to durability. . . . The "owner" becomes a conservator who passes the object on to further generations. Lauren Bowker/TheUnseen: Beauty is in revealing something that you don't normally notice. It is seeing the unseen. Giambattista Valli: Beauty surprises you; it can make you dizzy or erode you like an obsession. Jolan van der Wiel: I always like to have beauty and ugly next to each other, so it's attraction and revulsion. Jean Yu: Beauty is like a design scheme to pave the way to where you want to go but didn't know existed.

Detail of vinyl stickers applied to Hans Tan's Striped Ming No. 1 porcelain vessel prior to sandblasting.

Preface
Heart of the Book

"Print isn't dead. It just smells funny."—Francesco Franchi

The previous rendition of Cooper Hewitt's Design Triennial series, which opened in 2010, asked *"Why Design Now?"* Looking at such fundamental human needs as energy, mobility, health, and communication, our curatorial team emphasized problems and solutions over aesthetic delight. The 2016 Triennial now turns its gaze elsewhere. Drawn to the glimmer of sensual invention, we decided to view contemporary practice through the lens of beauty, a concept that suggests ephemeral effects and carnal desires as well as cosmic truths and natural patterns of growth and change.

Why beauty now? Since the turn of the millennium, design's dominant discourse has moved away from objects and artifacts to focus on systems and services. As "design thinking" bubbled up in corporate meeting rooms and added zing to the start-up economy, new disciplines sprang forth to plan complex, interactive products. User experience became more important than physical things, and "design" grew into a broader, more encompassing activity. Yet the role of "the designer" was somehow diminished. In many areas of contemporary practice, the designer's role as visionary creator melted into a multidisciplinary taskscape.

Designers have continued, however, to invent objects, images, and environments that confront us both intellectually and sensually. Such works tell stories and ask questions. They tease the mind and please the senses by manipulating surface, structure, materials, and ideas. To create this book, we honored the voices of designers by conducting original interviews about their works and processes. Over the course of a year, a team of writers—Kathleen Bomani, Tiffany Lambert, Suvi Saloniemi, Lauren Sciarappa, Penny Wolfson, Justin Zhuang, and ourselves—talked with over sixty designers and teams and crafted brief appraisals of their work. Those conversations and texts form the body of this book.

Since the inception of Cooper Hewitt's Design Triennial over fifteen years ago, the museum has published a book with each exhibition in the series. That same period has witnessed the ravenous spread of the Internet, the rise of social media, and the invention of new formats and devices for displaying content. Despite the primacy of digital media in these fervent times, our printed Triennial books have already outlived the electronic presence of most previous Triennials. Pixel dust will drift away, but these books do stay with us.

Designed by Kimberly Varella, our book on Beauty is an object to be touched, smelled, and savored. In order to give breathing room to both text and image, Varella paired dense pages of dialogue with luxurious, open spreads of photographs. Each of the book's seven sections is printed with its own accent color. We hope you will enjoy the smell of the ink, the tooth of the paper, and the pleasure that Varella has taken with every detail.

A smaller signature of pages at the center of the book holds the project's curatorial DNA. This book-within-a-book contains the apparatus that editors and publishers call "front matter" and "back matter"—from the title page and foreword to the credits and index. You are here, in the heart of the book, which also contains our curatorial essay, "Beauty as User Experience."

Along our journey to contemplate beauty in contemporary design, we met with a team of international curatorial advisors who nominated designers for us to consider for inclusion: Adélia Borges from Brazil, Claire Catterall from England, Kenya Hara from Japan, Mugendi M'Rithaa from South Africa, Sarah Scaturro from the United States, and Annemartine van Kesteren from the Netherlands. We were later joined by Suvi Saloniemi from Finland. Our initial team gathered in New York City in February 2014, to share nominations and discuss emerging themes. That meeting resulted in a core list of designers. We went on to refine our list and group them into seven categories of beauty: ethereal, intricate, transformative, transgressive, elemental, emergent, and extravagant. We hope that these seven concepts, like the seven colors of the rainbow or John Ruskin's seven "lamps of architecture," will illuminate a diverse spectrum of contemporary design practice.

— Andrea Lipps and Ellen Lupton

WHAT IS THE MOST BEAUTIFUL TIME OF DAY?

Melitta Baumeister: Those in-between moments. It's either very early when I feel nobody has woken up yet. . . . Or at night, when it's kind of over but not really. Daniel Brown: Dusk, somewhere hot, such as Barcelona. Emma Aiston / Daniel Emma: [At five a.m.] there's a sense of achievement when you've been up already for four hours when some people are just rolling out of bed. Homa Delvaray: Afternoon. Sou Fujimoto: A silent evening. Emiliano Godoy: [My two-year-old son] rises up like the sun. . . . So morning is the most beautiful time of the day for me. Götz Gramlich: The early morning hours, when we get fog on the river. Pepe Heykoop: Sometimes I don't even know . . . if it's a Monday or a Friday. Kim Colin / Industrial Facility: Sunrise or sunset. . . . The light is so incredible at those times of day. Brunno Jahara: My favorite time of the day is actually the night. Pat McGrath: Watching the sunset overlooking the Hudson or against the trees in Hyde Park in the summertime. Neri Oxman: Evertime. Brynjar Sigurðarson: In Iceland, morning is never the same. Jing Liu / SO–IL: The most beautiful moments of the day can come to you at any given time. It's the air; it's the noise; it's the color; it's the inner voices. Kris Sowersby: [At dusk] you get long shadows. There's a warmth about the atmosphere, and you will probably have a beer. Hans Tan: When I receive something good I don't deserve. Sissel Tolaas: The early morning. My nose is smartest in the morning. Terhi Tolvanen: The blue light just before it gets dark in Finland. Hua Li / Trace Architecture Office (TAO): A slice of sunlight in early morning, the quietness of late afternoon, the stone path lit by the midnight moonlight. Olivier van Herpt: Buildings are different [at night]; lights dot the landscape; and the world changes. Shapes, shadows, and light are all more sculptural while being draped in peace. Roger Gerards / Vlisco: The first second that my eyes open. . . . Not because I survived the night, but because I always like to get awake. Ken Wong: In the dead of night, that's when my creativity works best. Naomi Yasuda: Before I go to bed, I get the most ideas. Noa Zilberman: The beginning of the evening, when you look on one side of the sky and see a very, very dark blue, and then when you look on the other side, to the east, and you see that it's already pitch-black.

Beauty as User Experience

Andrea Lipps and Ellen Lupton

Beauty: this intoxicating idea has been pondered by philosophers, pursued by artists, and bottled by the fashion and fragrance industries. Yet somehow, beauty remains just out of reach. In the words of designer Olivier van Herpt, "Beauty is a fleeting dream of an object, thought, or moment. An intangible impossible, an elusive, effervescent ultimate expression of a goal beyond the farthest reaches of our imagination and ability." Van Herpt works in clay, a material that starts out soft and pliable, and turns into a solid object capable of endless endurance. Van Herpt creates fluted ceramic vessels that pulse with idiosyncratic energy. Each one is made with a 3D printer that he built himself so that he could make human-scaled objects of lasting value, produced in a "noble and beautiful material."

Like clay, the concept of beauty speaks to both plasticity and permanence. Beauty is a flash of insight processed and absorbed by our overburdened sense receptors. Beauty also embodies our search for ideals and absolutes, for objects and concepts of lasting value. Experimenting with lava and glass, respectively, Formafantasma and

Olivier van Herpt with his 3D-printed ceramic cylinder vase from the Sediment collection.

Emiliano Godoy give shape to matter that quickly shifts from liquid to solid. The limbs of letters ebb and swell in the typography of Kris Sowersby and Non-Format, who impart a strange new elegance to the archetypal alphabet.

To talk about design and beauty is to talk of objects and materiality: a tapestry woven with phosphoric threads (Kustaa Saksi), a stool cast on the beach from molten metal (Max Lamb), or a ring made with diamonds and iron (Hemmerle). Beauty lives in the mind and in the body. Beauty is form; beauty is fantasy; and beauty is the stunning purity of mathematics and nature.

We spoke with dozens of designers in the process of creating this book and exhibition. Many of them described beauty as fugitive, relative, and unknowable. Perhaps beauty doesn't reside in physical things, but in our reactions to them. Ken Wong, who designed the game *Monument Valley*, leaves it up to users to interpret the value of his work: "At the end of the day, if people say that it's beautiful, then who am I to argue with them?" Inspired by the tessellated drawings of M. C. Escher, Wong designed isometric buildings based on the temples and monasteries of Spain, North Africa, and India, creating an interactive world rather than a typical contest of skill or chance. Simogo's game *Device 6* is a typographic map, a story that takes the reader over and across geographic space. Beauty belongs to the user, not to the thing itself. A game is only beautiful if it's played.

Aesthetics is the philosophy of beauty.[1] Immanuel Kant's *Critique of Judgment* (1790), considered the foundation of modern aesthetics, derided color and ornament as mere finery that detracts from the underlying form that is the "proper object" of our judgment. Valorizing line and structure over color and shadow, Kant rejected the transient effects of light in favor of a static, unchanging "design." Color and emotion, he argued, contribute to beauty only insofar as they draw our attention to that "proper object," embodied in a pure, unchanging, universal form. Devaluing the experience of light and color, Kant assigned such subjective phenomena to the realm of "play" (*spiel*), divorced from the higher plane of form (*gestalt*).[2]

Fueled by a similar mistrust for surfaces, modern designers embraced basic geometries and solid structures over fleeting sensations. Although designers overturned such orthodoxies decades ago, a distrust of surface, light, and feeling still riddles our thinking about form and function, ethics and morality. Articulating a postmodern theory of aesthetics, twentieth-century writers from Jacques Derrida to Roland Barthes reclaimed the dynamics of play. Barthes, explaining how readers actively produce meaning, wrote that the reader plays the text "as one plays a game" or performs a piece of music.[3] This project on beauty embraces the sensory appeal of light and color, of sound and scent that plays out in the experience of each user.

In our interviews, we asked designers to identify the time of day they find most beautiful. Resoundingly, their replies were about light, weighted toward dawn or dusk, when natural light enters the world or fades away. Light is a necessary condition of life and visibility. Like beauty, light is fleeting, relative, and ever changing. Colombian designer Jorge Lizarazo, founder of Hechizoo, loves the purple light that descends on Bogotá at dusk. In Brynjar Sigurðarson's native Iceland, with its extreme difference between winter and summer, morning is beautiful because it is never the same. American Aaron Koblin, who often works with projected light, enjoys the sun's angled rays at dawn, when color quickly yet gradually intensifies. Daniel Rybakken, who endures long, dark winters in his native Norway, created his Compendium lights as a tall, diffuse source aimed at the wall to mimic daylight entering through a window.

Many of the designers featured in these pages explore the passage of time and the transformation of materials and meaning. To honor his grandmother's failing memory, Tuomas Markunpoika welded small rings of steel around a hulking wardrobe and then burned away the wood, leaving behind a lacy shell of blackened metal. The piece "became like a naked memory, a physical memory of the furniture—kind of a smoky, shady, semitransparent memory of it." Nail artist Naomi Yasuda lavishes effort on embellishments that last only a few short weeks, and Lauren Bowker of TheUnseen invents materials that change color in response to currents in the air or energy levels in the brain. Playing with frames and double meaning, Elastic creates moody, transparent montages and sly visual puns, while graphic designer Theseus Chan assembles lo-fi collages that are "odd, imperfect, used, distressed, broken, handmade." In his native Heidelberg, Götz Gramlich created a political campaign in which a series of posters appeared to peel away over a period of weeks to reveal a hidden message.

Beauty is a reaction, a response. Beauty is the ultimate user experience. Beauty happens when we see, touch, smell, and otherwise activate what is before us. Sam Hecht and Kim Colin, founders of Industrial Facility, explain that beauty isn't a fixed attribute of objects. Wondering where beauty resides in a product, they ask, "Is it in its making, in its use, its form, the personal memory it may signify, or its cultural relevance? Or is beauty found in the equilibrium of all of these things?" Hecht and Colin designed Formwork (for Herman Miller), a series of desk organizers whose modular slots, shelves, and balconies fit together like the towers and bridges of Ken Wong's *Monument Valley*. Industrial design duo Daniel To and Emma Aiston of Daniel Emma also strip away extraneous elements, creating playful objects that answer to use. Their Cork Cone and Magnetic Tower look like solid volumes of cork or wood, but hidden magnets unexpectedly attract paper clips to their surfaces. Yeongkyu Yoo's World Clock rolls to display the time in all twenty-four time zones; the hands of the clock automatically recalibrate as the user rotates the object.

Beauty arises from interactions between people and things. Cypriot lighting designer Michael Anastassiades defines design as a conversation: "Beauty exists when making an object that people can relate to. Design, at the end of the day, is about communication. You design something because you want to start a dialogue with somebody, with an audience that is there." Anastassiades seeks elemental purity in his work—a sphere of glass perches on a slender stalk of brass, or a simple cone hangs from a weighted cable that activates the room around it. A polished brass sphere called Fairest reflects and distorts the surrounding space and its inhabitants. Affixed to the wall like a piece of jewelry, Fairest speaks to our anxieties about beauty, time, and vanity.

The experience of beauty is visceral and embodied, not just visual. For visionary makeup artist Pat McGrath, beauty "impacts the senses." Her embellished masks for Givenchy, and her masterful use of color, proportion, and dimension, are tantalizing embodiments of the sensorium. Beauty resides not only in the beholder's eye, but also in the ears, nose, mouth, and gut. Architecture firm SO–IL's proposal for the Greek

Pavilion at the 2014 Venice Biennale incorporates the sound of the wind into the building. Jean Yu, creator of delicate architectural underclothes, says, "When I see something beautiful, it's arresting. It hurts. I feel it in my body." Giambattista Valli, who dresses women in chromatic clouds of tulle, believes that beauty "touches the five senses, yes—you can almost say it strikes you—it can caress you, hit you right in the face, or worse, get you right in the stomach." Valli's candy-colored gowns beg to be touched and smelled, even tasted.

Rejecting traditional opulence, scent designer Sissel Tolaas wants to expand our tolerance for stimuli that society represses and overlooks. Tolaas is collecting smell molecules derived from thousands of physical sources, from diesel fumes and dead leaves to African shops and dusty bricks. By preserving these sources both mundane and exotic, she is building a vast physical archive and a new linguistic dictionary of scent, a vocabulary for naming what we smell. Tolaas believes that embracing olfactory diversity instead of masking it behind the sanitized aromas of fruits and flowers can move humanity toward a more tolerant coexistence.

Transgressing the norms of beauty allows us to accept otherness. Ana Rajcevic's Animal headpieces partly obscure the face of the wearer, creating a strange hybrid between art and personal adornment that blurs the boundary between humans and animals. Equally startling is Noa Zilberman's Wrinkles, a series of jewelry pieces that distribute lines of gold across the artist's face and cleavage, creating the uncanny appearance of a face in fast-forward. Made after the birth of her first child, Zilberman's pieces shocked people around her, including her husband: "When I made Wrinkles, I felt that I was making myself beautiful. It was beauty to me, but people that love me were very disturbed by it." Rad Hourani creates unisex clothing collections with the aim not to subvert gender roles, but to transcend them: "It doesn't make sense to me to limit things. It is about creating form that can be present at all times without fitting in any past categories."

The sublime is beauty's dark sister. Theorized by Edmund Burke and other philosophers in the eighteenth century, the sublime accounts for aesthetic experiences that overwhelm the intellect with their staggering scale or disruptive presence—the oceans, the Alps, the ruins of Rome. If beauty triggers delight and attraction, the sublime provokes feelings of shock, awe, and surprise—even horror and repulsion.[4] The sublime dissolves or obliterates form rather than perfecting it. The realm of fashion and jewelry is especially rich in efforts to subvert traditional notions of beauty. Jólan van der Wiel's gravity machine uses magnetic force to shape stools, shoes, garments, and other objects out of shards of material, yielding pieces that appear unformed or out of focus. Gareth Pugh's spectacular gowns, meticulously assembled from garbage bags or plastic drinking straws, overflow with materiality, while Melitta Baumeister casts garments instead of sewing them, defying our expectations of how clothing is made. The alarming hair constructions of Guido Palau and the prickly headpieces of Maiko Takeda turn users into seductively alien creatures. In Palau's words, "I find the grotesque can be beautiful. I find things that are disturbing beautiful. I like beauty to sometimes shock me." Several designers spoke to us about seeking errors and imperfection. Delfina Delettrez explains, "In Italian the word for mistake is *errore*, which also means to wonder," and Terhi Tolvanen says, "There is beauty in harmony, symmetry. But harmony and symmetry get interesting when they are disturbed." Both are jewelry designers who've found opportunity in miscalculation and disruption.

Detail of Terhi Tolvanen's Jungle Twins necklace from the Jungle collection, courtesy of Susan Beech and Ornamentum Gallery.

Whether confounding norms or embracing difference, beauty exists as a reaction in viewers. The Haas Brothers are creating fantastical beaded creatures in their Afreaks collection, made in collaboration with beaders from the Khayelitsha informal settlement outside Cape Town, South Africa. The brothers lovingly call their collaborators the Haas Sisters; these women are the inspiration, skill, and personality driving each expressive form. Simon Haas further developed beading algorithms based on natural phenomena, which the beaders follow to create hyperbolic beaded vegetation. The collection is deeply tied to the location from which it originates—the dusty roads, corrugated tin shacks, hand-painted signage, extreme poverty—to become colorful, weird expressions materialized from the imaginary.

The Haas Brothers with three of the Haas Sisters and Eyes-Ik Newton.

A beaded love letter from The Haas Sisters to the Haas Brothers.

Can a false flower be beautiful? Daniel Brown creates digital representations of blossoms whose beauty stems from their frank unreality. This computer-graphics pioneer is drawn to a "traditional, romanticized sense of aesthetics, inspired by flowers, painting, theater, even fashion." Brown's ongoing project On Growth and Form uses mathematical formulas to generate hyperreal blossoms. Since becoming paralyzed from the chest down after a spinal injury in 2003, Brown has employed adaptive technologies to continue growing as a designer and artist, working exclusively in typed lines of code rather than with his hands.

The convergence of natural and artificial life fuels the work of Jenny E. Sabin, Neri Oxman, and Alexandra Daisy Ginsberg, three visionary designers who are inventing new materials and crafting strange futures for the planet Earth and beyond. Inspired by the mechanisms of biological growth, Sabin creates knitted architectural structures that not only support weight and offer shelter, but also absorb and convey light. Oxman's Wanderers series consists of 3D-printed, wearable objects permeated with capillaries. She imagines seeding these capillaries with microorganisms that could digest biological waste and hydrocarbons, in principle enabling human survival on distant planets. Ginsberg's project Designing for the Sixth Extinction depicts genetically engineered creatures that could someday clean the air of toxins, neutralize acid in the soil, and collect and scatter seeds. Beneath Ginsberg's seemingly utopian proposals runs a dark commentary on the current state of Earth's ecosystems and the dangerous directions that biological modifications might take.

Structural elements and decorative marks accrete and multiply in the ethereal structures of Sou Fujimoto Architects, the intricately constructed textiles of Sandra Backlund, the code-generated letterforms of Kyuha Shim, the hyper-detailed infographics of Francesco Franchi, and the profusely patterned furniture of Dokter and Misses. In a project created by the firm Humans since 1982, dozens of analog clocks cluster together in a grid to create a giant digital timepiece whose elements align every sixty seconds to read out the time in a number font made of clock hands. Each of these practices traffics in redundancy. Graphic designer Richard Niessen tells us, "You can't measure beauty with an economical system. It's something in a work that is not directly functional. It's something extra." Niessen's Palace of Typographic Memory is a graphic toolkit of faceted visual elements that accumulate to crowd the surfaces of his posters.

Beauty enhances function in a world overrun with things. Beauty elevates objects in our daily lives, promoting durability over waste. Brunno Jahara creates tiered serving dishes from brightly colored plastic reclaimed from a recycling center near his studio in São Paulo. Pepe Heykoop collects scraps of leather and stitches them together around found objects, cloaking an old office chair or a discarded lamp inside an imperfect and uncanny simulacrum of itself. By making something precious out of discarded materials, Heykoop isn't saving the world: "What might happen to these pieces is that they inspire other people to think about waste and how can we look at waste. I think that impact is much bigger than the actual piece."

Design studio Scholten & Baijings creates everyday objects—glasses, plates, tea towels, bowls—that defy obsolescence by balancing color, form, and details. As Carole Baijings explains, "Pieces that have a personal, unique touch are the pieces that also touch you. It's so important to give detail to products, to give them an extra layering and touch so people will hold on to them instead of just throwing them in the garbage when something new comes along." The plates and bowls in their Colour Porcelain collection, designed for the Japanese manu-factory 1616/Arita, nestle one inside the other, their colors mixing and interacting. The collection's vivid, creamy hues may seem familiar. The designers excavated this palette from 1616/Arita's archives (1616 refers to the year the manufactory was founded): the blood red and soft pink come from hand-painted flower petals; the light blue was once the rolling sea; the gold derives from an ornamental detail. Extracted from their original context, these colors become an intense and evocative elixir. Studio Job creates patterns that appear traditional at first glance yet give way to a jarring iconography of the everyday— from gas masks and peace signs to syringes and kitchen tools. Such works resonate within both the history of ornament and the contemporary visual landscape.

In a similar way, Hans Tan's Spotted Nyonya series engages narratives of heritage, transformation, and a global mix of cultures. Tan defaces vividly painted porcelain vessels created by the Peranakan community, which inhabits Peninsular Malaysia and Singapore. He adheres a geometric pattern to the surface of each vessel and sandblasts away the existing decorations, leaving behind compressed layers of new and old ornament. Tan's process contemporizes the traditional painted surface while transmitting ideas about Peranakan life: "When I exhibited Spotted Nyonya in Europe, [visitors] were drawn by its visceral and visual effect at first, but . . . they were inevitably exposed to the Peranakan culture, too." Laduma Ngxokolo, a South African designer, has created a line of knitted sweaters for young men in South Africa's Xhosa community who have gone through the rite of circumcision. Ngxokolo's knits are inspired by traditional Xhosa beadwork. Homa Delvaray's posters employ typographic and architectural elements from Iranian visual culture to build intricate intersections of traditional and contemporary vocabularies. The Dutch company Vlisco produces wax-printed textiles for sale in West and Central Africa. The company consults with African tailors and traders to develop new fabric lines that express an African ideal of beauty, which is "more about empowerment and being somebody than the more passive beauty, which is about the woman who is beautiful for other people."

Dress made using Vlisco textiles ABC/
VL048913.06, VL0404614.06, and
VL061477.06 from the Think collection.

Beauty rewards close inspection. Celebrated for her digitally printed fabrics, Mary Katrantzou has recently turned to texture to augment the surface innovation associated with her work. A gown from her Spring Summer 2015 collection glistens from a distance but overflows with intimate detail up close. As Katrantzou explains, "Many of the details in the pieces are missed on the catwalk, so when people have the chance to see them up close they can see each tiny glitter flock, each embroidered panel and seam detail." Shapes break on the body like landmasses adrift at sea. A primordial form wriggles across the shoulder. A gown that initially appears to embody purity reveals its rich and primal concept: Pangaea, the earth's first continent.

The buildings of Trace Architecture Office (TAO) listen to the pulse of the earth: "The site, program, climate, technique, all these conditions that I call 'gravity,' will be confronted during the design process. It is gravity that makes my design specific and concrete." The quest for beauty leads us from the foundations of our planet to the outer cosmos. Jewelry designer Jantje Fleischhut shapes abstract compositions from precious materials and found objects, balancing coincidence and craft. Brooches from her How Long Is Now collection suggest asteroids and interstellar debris hurtling through space toward explosive collisions or endless orbit: "I am fascinated with the magnificence of the infinite heavens: overwhelmingly beautiful, irrationally ominous, forever in motion, the dynamics of the universe."

Construction of Trace Architecture Office's Tree Clubhouse, in Grand Canal Forest Park.

An initial encounter with an object of beauty can make one curious about the secrets it holds within. Such encounters kindle a glimmer of awareness that there is something valuable to learn, that our lives benefit from the object's presence. Beauty, as philosopher Alexander Nehamas says, broadens our vision: "To find something beautiful is, precisely, not yet to have finished with it, to think it has something further to offer."[5] Social theorist Elaine Scarry suggests that beholding beauty radically decenters us; beautiful things "act like small tears that pull us through to some vaster space."[6] Beauty drives fertility, reproduction, inspiration, creation, and replication.[7] Beauty suggests possibilities beyond, material and immaterial, sacred and erotic. It is about revelation, not just improvement.

Beauty is not a fixed thing or attribute, but an experience. Beauty is not tied to an abstract concept or physical material, as Kant suggests in his *Critique of Judgment*. Just because an object is made of gold does not mean it is beautiful.[8] Yet as an idea, beauty is difficult to articulate when not attached to something, such as a beautiful sky or a beautiful face. For centuries, philosophers have contemplated beauty or have elected to ignore it. It has been the root of deep division, politicization, ostracization. Beauty is vulnerable, subject to what Scarry calls the pendulum swing of preference.[9] But our attraction to beauty endures. It is both an aesthetic quality and a value, as art critic and philosopher Arthur C. Danto points out, like goodness or morality, that is deeply seated in the human condition.[10] A world without beauty is unfathomable. May we continue to seek out objects, images, places, and materials that touch the body and mind, change the way we think and feel, and pull us into the moment.

Endnotes
1. Leonard Koren, *Which "Aesthetics" Do You Mean? Ten Definitions* (Point Reyes, California: Imperfect Publishing, 2010).
2. Kant quoted in Jacques Derrida, *The Truth in Painting*, trans. Geoff Bennington and Ian McLeod (Chicago: University of Chicago Press, 1987), 52–3. See also Immanuel Kant, *Critique of Judgment*, trans. J. H. Bernard (New York: Hafner Press, 1951).
3. Roland Barthes, "From Work to Text," in *Image/Music/Text* (New York: Hill and Wang, 1977), 162.
4. Jeremy Gilbert-Rolfe, *Beauty and the Contemporary Sublime* (New York: Allworth Press, 1999).
5. Alexander Nehamas, "An Essay on Beauty and Judgment," *The Three Penny Review* 8 (Winter 2000), http://www.threepennyreview.com/samples/nehamas_w00.html.
6. Elaine Scarry, *On Beauty and Being Just* (Princeton, New Jersey: Princeton University Press, 1999): 111–12.
7. Scarry elaborates on this point: "[Beauty] seems to incite, even to require, the act of replication. Wittgenstein says that when the eye sees something beautiful, the hand wants to draw it. Beauty brings copies of itself into being. It makes us draw it, take photographs of it, or describe it to other people. Sometimes it gives rise to exact replication and other times to resemblances and still other times to things whose connection to the original site of inspiration is unrecognizable." *On Beauty and Being Just*, p. 3.
8. Nehamas, "An Essay on Beauty and Judgment."
9. Elaine Scarry presentation, October 11, 2012. School of Visual Arts.
10. Arthur C. Danto, *The Abuse of Beauty: Aesthetics and the Concept of Art* (Chicago: Open Court, 2003): 15.

WHAT IS
THE MOST
BEAUTIFUL
PLACE YOU'VE
VISITED?

Michael Anastassiades: Home. But not my place in London where I live. . . . Home is the place that I am able to feel comfortable. Sandra Backlund: The ocean. Bastian Bischoff/Humans since 1982: In the Alps between Milan and Zurich. . . . It's beautiful to see the contrast between the snowy mountains and the valleys. Theseus Chan: I was traveling in an old, yellow bus across this river. . . and underneath it is a forest with trees and plants of every kind. The place is unknown, but I know I have been a few times in my dreams. Katy Taplin/Dokter and Misses: The wide-open plains of the Central Kalahari in Botswana. This vast sweep of flat grassland is very peaceful but full of life. . . . And you're alone. Jantje Fleischhut: The enormous wide view and the horizon [at the seaside]. It clears your mind and makes you think of nothing. Formafantasma: We recently spent some time in a traditional *ryokan* in Japan. . . . The shadows of plants were on the [paper] windows. Francesco Franchi: I got a bento box in the station [in Japan]. . . . It was hot outside, but the sushi was wrapped inside leaves from a tree, and it was fresh. Alexandra Daisy Ginsberg: South Africa. (Where my family comes from!) The scale of the landscape is awe inspiring. Christian Hemmerle: Luxor in Egypt. It is a place with. . . amazing aesthetics that have remained untouched. Rad Hourani: We know so little about the inside of the ocean. Water is magical to me. Aaron Koblin: [Virtual reality] will allow us to simulate and create spaces that have a scale and have a sense of presence. Max Lamb: The beauty of a place is related to time, context, and consciousness. Neri Oxman: Neverland. Guido Palau: Greenland. . . . There were incredible big night skies and the aurora borealis, all those things you think you will never see. Ana Rajcevic: In my head. Deep, secret places, where no one has ever been before apart from me. Daniel Rybakken: Lysekil, on the west coast of Sweden. . . . We can walk out along the coastline and see almost 180 degrees of sky and water, so you feel that you're inside an enormous dome. Maiko Takeda: Somewhere up in a mountain in Japan. I was very small, and my parents took me and my sister to watch shooting stars. Yeongkyu Yoo: Yongnuni Oreum on Jeju Island . . . is a volcanic cone in my hometown. . . . Its smooth line from flatland to the hill naturally meets the sky.

Lava rock landscape after Mount Etna's eruption in November 2013, taken during Formafantasma's research for their De Natura Fossilium collection.

Acknowledgments

Many people touched this book and the exhibition it accompanies. The volume before you now is a textual and typographic meditation on beauty and its modalities. Its deliciousness of form and its unity of content were overseen by Pamela Horn, Cooper Hewitt's ingenious Head of Cross-Platform Publishing, assisted by the exacting and attentive Publications and Image Rights Associate Matthew Kennedy. Graphic designer Kimberly Varella created the book's tactile, inventive design, proving her unwavering love of process and professionalism from start to finish. Joelle Herr applied her scrupulous editorial eye to each and every page. As authors and curators, we have rarely found greater satisfaction in the creative teamwork that is publishing.

Sixty-two designers and firms participated in *Beauty*, sharing their work, ideas, and voices in the pages herein. We thank each of them, along with their teams, photographers, manufacturers, and gallerists, for their contributions. Their work is evidence of the beauty in design.

The exhibition was designed by Tsao & McKown Architects, whose keen eye and sensitivity have ensured that the exhibition design is every bit as beautiful as the objects on view. It has been a pleasure to work with the firm, especially Calvin Tsao, Allen Prusis, Richard Rhodes, and Justin Scurlock.

Dozens of professionals at Cooper Hewitt made *Beauty*—the book and exhibition—possible, including curators, conservators, digital-media producers, educators, registrars, development staff, and more. We are particularly grateful to Caroline Baumann, Director, who enthusiastically embraced the exhibition's theme and breadth from the start, and with each phase inspired and championed our process.

We thank Brooke Hodge, Deputy Director, and Cara McCarty, Curatorial Director, for pushing the exhibition staff and curatorial team to think rigorously and act creatively. Additional thanks to everyone on the museum's staff, including Shamus Adams, Julie Barnes, Laurie Bohlk, Helynsia Brown, Susannah Brown, Marites Chan, Seb Chan, Michelle Cheng, Perry Choe, Kimberly Cisneros, Andrew Coletti, Lucy Commoner, Kira Eng-Wilmot, Maria Fernanda Alves da Silva, Deborah Fitzgerald, Gregory Gestner, Yvonne Gomez-Durand, Kelly Gorman, Jocelyn Groom, Allison Hale, Annie Hall, Kimberly Hawkins, Halima Johnson, Kathleen Kane, Sarah Keefe, Amanda Kesner, Steve Langehough, Katherine Lewis, Matilda McQuaid, Antonia Moser, Matthew O'Connor, Caroline Payson, Chad Phillips, Kimberly Randall, Wendy Rogers, Larry Silver, Cynthia Smith, Ann Sunwoo, Mathew Weaver, and Paula Zamora. Curatorial Assistant Andrew Gardner's keen attention to detail, thorough organization, and untiring support kept the project running smoothly. Interns Danielle Charlap and Justin Zhuang provided indispensible assistance from the start of the project; as a contributing author, Justin shared his voice throughout this book.

Finally, we extend our deepest gratitude to our families. To Andrea's husband, Ryan Heiferman, and son, Luca, thank you for your enduring love and patience. To Ellen's husband, Abbott Miller, and wonderful children, Jay and Ruby Miller, much thanks for your love and patience.

— Andrea Lipps and Ellen Lupton

Index

Authors

Andrea Lipps joined Cooper Hewitt, Smithsonian Design Museum in 2008 and is an Assistant Curator focused on international contemporary design. Lipps has contributed to numerous books and exhibitions, including *Design with the Other 90%: CITIES* (2011), *Why Design Now?: National Design Triennial* (2010), and *Design for the Other 90%* (2007). In 2015, she was a Mobius Fellow in Helsinki, Finland. Before joining Cooper Hewitt, Lipps served in MoMA's Architecture and Design department, assisting on *Design and the Elastic Mind* (2008) and *Home Delivery: Fabricating the Modern Dwelling* (2008). Lipps publishes articles in leading design magazines, serves on international juries, and lectures in the MA program at Parsons/ Cooper Hewitt and the MFA program at the School of Visual Arts. She holds a master's degree in History of Decorative Arts and Design from Parsons/Cooper Hewitt (2008), and a bachelor's degree in French, Sociology, and Women's Studies from the University of Michigan (2000).

Ellen Lupton is a writer, curator, and designer. She is Senior Curator of Contemporary Design at Cooper Hewitt, Smithsonian Design Museum, where recent projects include *How Posters Work* (2015), *Beautiful Users* (2014), and *Graphic Design—Now in Production* (2011–14). Lupton also serves as director of the Graphic Design MFA Program at MICA (Maryland Institute College of Art) in Baltimore, where she has authored and edited numerous books on design processes, including *Graphic Design: The New Basics* (2015), *Type on Screen* (2014), *Graphic Design Thinking* (2011), *Exploring Materials* (2010), *Thinking with Type* (2010), *Indie Publishing* (2008), and *D.I.Y.: Design It Yourself* (2006). She co-authored *Design Your Life* (2009) and *D.I.Y. Kids* (2007) with Julia Lupton. She holds a BFA from The Cooper Union (1985) and a doctorate in Communication Design from University of Baltimore (2008). She received the AIGA Gold Medal for Lifetime Achievement in 2007. A frequent lecturer nationally and internationally, Lupton will speak about design to anyone who will listen.

Photography Credits

OVERLEAF: Delfina Delettrez; Single earring, from Infinity Spring/Summer 2013 collection, 2012; Gold, enamel, silver, pearl

Transgressive

Ana Rajcevic
Theseus Chan
Delfina Delettrez
The Haas Brothers
Pepe Heykoop
Rad Hourani
Gareth Pugh
Jólan van der Wiel
Noa Zilberman

These objects challenge normative standards of beauty, gender, genre, or behavior. Embracing androgyny, anti-form, the grotesque, the formless, and the fantastic, transgressive beauty blurs established boundaries and definitions, challenging us to see and live differently.

"What does it mean to be human today? What is 'able-bodied' in the twenty-first century? For me, the body is like the core, and I build layers, surfaces, and concepts on top of that. My practice explores the themes of mutation and evolution, relationships between the rational and the subconscious, the human and the animal. The body, for me, is a site of pleasure, eroticism, and exploration. It's all about the unknown and the atemporal. Everything that doesn't belong to a particular time or place."

—— Ana Rajcevic

Ana Rajcevic

—SERBIAN, ACTIVE IN UNITED KINGDOM AND GERMANY, B. 1983—

The uneasy border between humans and other creatures is a touch point for Ana Rajcevic's ANIMAL (2012) series. Constructed from metal, polymers, and leather, these elegant yet alarming headpieces challenge our views of fashion and personal adornment. Like the horns of an antelope, a rhinoceros, or a reptile, these pieces could serve as weapons of aggression and self-defense as well as displays of strength and fertility. Partially covering the human face, they also embrace the history of masks, suggesting hidden identities as well as situations of submission and confinement. Trained initially as an architect, Rajcevic went on to study fashion at London College of Fashion, where she won the LCF Best Design Award for her ANIMAL series in 2012. Designed both to be displayed as sculpture and to be worn on the body, these pieces suggest new directions for ornamental jewelry and protective headgear. They also make us wonder about future mutations of the human animal itself. — ELLEN LUPTON

————You originally studied architecture. What influence did this have on your practice?

I am still strongly influenced by my architecture background, and I enjoy shifting experiences from one field to another. I love envisioning a three-dimensional subject when I look at work, so I create three-dimensional objects, myself.

What always fascinated me is the interaction with a piece—the ability to walk into the sculpture, which was my approach while studying architecture, and the ability to wear a sculpture, or become a sculpture yourself, which is my approach now. I question what a sculpture is, the concept of sculpture, the process of making it.

Over the course of time, I changed the context of my work, moving from building to the body, but still keeping a very sculptural approach. I work with a body and around the body. I like to say that I moved from the architecture of the city to the architecture of the body.

————What is the most remarkable building you have seen?

I was always in love with Santiago Calatrava and his work, and I still am. I find his buildings innovative and beautiful—so different from the generative bold style of architecture that is so popular and overused today. His inspiration from natural and human forms, fused with his carefully chosen materials and play with light, creates perfect aesthetic harmony. Another architect I really love is Frank Gehry, his use of bold, postmodern shapes and unusual fabrications.

I must add Renzo Piano. The Auditorium Parco della Musica in Rome, the Jean-Marie Tjibaou Cultural Center, and Centre Pompidou in Paris are masterpieces for me.

————Where does your interest in exaggerated, mutated forms come from?

I see mutation as a permanent change, a form of reconstruction. My work is all about reconstructing the human figure, experiencing new forms and shapes, creating and reshaping our silhouette. It is about us. There's something so primal and immediate about seeing human bodies mutated. It calls into question our ideals about beauty and normality. What does it mean to be human today? What is "abled-body" in the twenty-first century?

For me, the body is like the core, and I build layers, surfaces, and concepts on top of that. My practice explores the themes of mutation and evolution, relationships between the rational and the subconscious, the human and the animal. The body, for me, is a site of pleasure, eroticism, and exploration. It's all about the unknown and the atemporal. Everything that doesn't belong to a particular time or place.

————You're known for using synthetic polymers, metal, and leather. What do these materials bring to your work?

I do predominantly figurative work. I love the labor-intensive part of making art—research, experiments, drawings, and craft. I love the "hands-on" approach to creativity, using my hands to frame and formulate my pieces. I believe that craftsmanship, materiality, and design should always work alongside one another.

Materials like rubber and resin are perfect materials for 3D object treatment because they offer a wide range of possibilities in crafting. They are contemporary materials, predominantly made for industrial usage, so when used in arts, they give the feel of unreal, everlasting perfection. They are, as well, mutants themselves and can imitate any form and finish you imagine. They can go from liquid to solid, and they can be bent, molded, or formed into any shape, be it rigid or flexible. This transformation of shape and materialization of their substance aligns with my own research and approach.

————There is a strong sense of personality in your work. Do you think there is room for the wearer? Is that important or irrelevant?

I believe that my work is the meeting point in the relationship between those who watch and those who perform. The pieces perform a double function: they exist as objects attached to the wearer, as well as separate artworks, exhibited in gallery spaces.

————Much of your work deals with questions of self-identity and evolution. What does the future look like?

Future is the element of the unknown, and as Alan Kay said, "The best way to predict the future is to invent it."

————The notion of transgressive work has strong historic ties to art and architecture. The idea of the avant-garde, for example, explored uncharted or forbidden territory. Can you identify any early influences on your work?

My appreciation and knowledge of art and what I consume changes over the years. I'm constantly changing my aesthetic appreciations. In general, I don't have role models. I try to create my own style without referencing other people or things. Of course, there are influences, but they are never direct and specific, and they change, because I change.

————You were born in 1983 in Serbia. Did you grow up there? Where are you living now?

I grew up in Belgrade, during the violent setting of war and instability of the 1990s. It was a childhood full of chaos and troubles. Growing up in that situation, my primary focus was to get out of it as soon as possible. I studied architecture at University of the Arts in Belgrade, and then I lived a bit in different places in Europe before getting a scholarship to do the master of arts at University of the Arts London. Since then, I have lived mostly in East London, in the areas of Shoreditch and Hackney. At the moment, I am actually between two cities, London and Berlin. These are opposite cities, almost contradictory to each other. I like that—I like contradictions. It's a good change. And as I said before, it is all about change.

————What is your ideal of beauty?

An ideal beauty is one that evolves and transforms. I am searching for perfection! I want to make the unbearable bearable, to provoke viewers to reconsider their own understandings of beauty and of normality.

————What is the most beautiful place you've visited?

In my head. Deep, secret places, where no one has ever been.

— INTERVIEW WITH TIFFANY LAMBERT

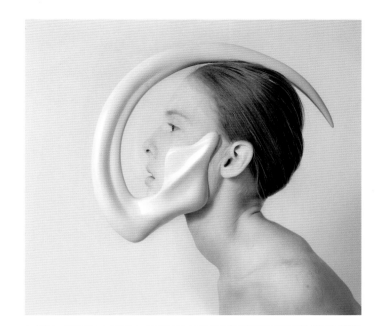

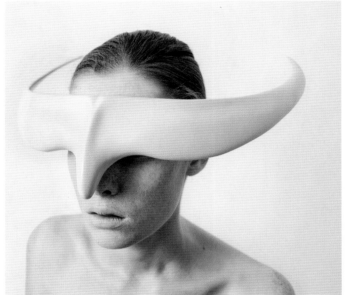

Wearable sculpture, from ANIMAL: The Other
Side of Evolution collection, 2012; Fiberglass,
polyurethane, rubber

TOP: 21 × 34 × 16 cm (8¼ × 13⅜ × 6⁵⁄₁₆ in.)

BOTTOM: 37 × 35 × 11 cm (14⁹⁄₁₆ × 13¾ × 4⁵⁄₁₆ in.)

OPPOSITE: 85 × 37 × 39 cm (33⁷⁄₁₆ × 14⁹⁄₁₆ × 15⅜ in.)

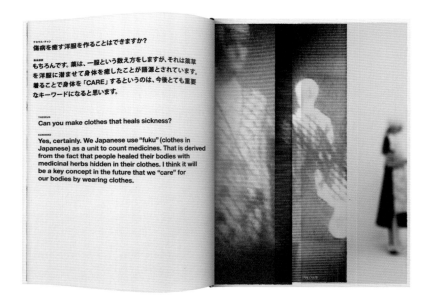

つづしゅん・チャン
傷病を癒す洋服を作ることはできますか？

もちろんです。薬は、一服という数え方をしますが、それは薬草を洋服に潜ませて身体を癒したことが語源とされています。着ることで身体を「CARE」するというのは、今後とても重要なキーワードになると思います。

Can you make clothes that heals sickness?

Yes, certainly. We Japanese use "fuku" (clothes in Japanese) as a unit to count medicines. That is derived from the fact that people healed their bodies with medicinal herbs hidden in their clothes. I think it will be a key concept in the future that we "care" for our bodies by wearing clothes.

Theseus Chan
—SINGAPOREAN, B. 1961—

Limitations are what give Theseus Chan the freedom to pursue his designs. The creative maverick works in an extremely organic fashion, often guided by only intuition and whatever resources are on hand. This seemingly irrational approach helped Chan consistently produce unconventional advertising and graphic design for clients ranging from high-fashion Comme des Garçons to streetwear-label Adidas. His pursuit of highly original works led Chan to leave mainstream advertising and establish his independent firm WORK in 1997. Rebelling against an industry lacking in imagination, Chan founded the magazine *WERK* in 2000, subsequently followed by *W__K W__K* in 2015, to further push the boundaries of graphic design production, and to extend his reach beyond Singapore. Collaborating with overseas creatives from Tokyo, New York, and London, each issue meshes the imperfect, the odd, and the handmade into beautiful, limited-edition "extreme printed matters" that have won him top design accolades globally and the cult status of an avant-garde magazine designer. — JUSTIN ZHUANG

————Tell us about how you approach design at WORK.
I work with very little—often with almost nothing, but this limitation gives me freedom. This forces me to find ideas and solutions by thinking rationally and irrationally.
————*WERK* magazine started as a personal project to experiment in design. How has the magazine evolved over the years?
It is more like a journey of self-discovery now. It is about connecting and disconnecting thoughts, experiences, and random ideas together. After *WERK No.20*, I did a rethink of my approach to designing the magazine. I came to the conclusion that the format has always been loose and searching, and the best way to design it is to not overthink. Hence, with *WERK No.21: MARTINE BEDIN* and *WERK No.22: DOVER STREET*

MARKET BEAUTIFUL CHAOS, I worked with very little time, materials, and resources. This allows me to be completely free to design it as and when ideas come along.
————What role does *WERK* play in your design practice, WORK?
With *WERK*, the approach is more personal and vague, but I do apply some of the dictums to commissioned projects that have more defined objectives.
————Every issue of *WERK* is a reinvention and a completely new design. What is a common thread through the entire collection?
It always starts off indistinct in the beginning, and as I work on them they evolve. One idea leads to another, and that is how things happened for *WERK*.
————*WERK* stands out from other magazines by consistently experimenting with printing and production techniques

in each issue. Can you tell us about your relationship with the craftsmanship of printing?
"Experimentation," "artisanal," and "crafts-manship" are neologisms for designers and marketers—I don't set out thinking in that fashion. I create my work according to how I envisioned them. I work with my printers to find ways to do more extreme printed matters.
————*WERK* meshes the clean and chaotic, often mixing highbrow fashion and art subjects with the lo-fi aesthetics of punk and graffiti. How do you make sense of this seeming chaos to arrive at fresh designs, such as in issues 21 and 22?
The odd, imperfect, used, distressed, broken, handmade, lo-fi aesthetics appeal to me, and sometimes the only way to get there is to unlearn what you have learned.

Back in 2012, I was introduced to Martine Bedin by Alison Harley. I was told by Alison that she will need some ideas to show Martine for her meeting. Instinctively, I rendered some spreads with those die-cut shapes, partly because I saw Martine's work with the Memphis-Milano group and partly because I wanted to create a book-object. The published version is almost ninety-five percent close to those first thoughts.

When Adrian Joffe agreed to collaborate on *WERK No.22* for Dover Street Market [DSM], there wasn't much time—less than six weeks, to be precise—to DSM's tenth-anniversary launch. We were only given a bunch of interior and exterior photographs to work with. Given the progressive thinking behind DSM, a retrospective approach was definitely not in order. Instead, I imagined what DSM would be like in the next ten years. From there, I reimagined the future by creating lo-fi visual collages with interiors and windows of DSM and images from NASA—a future where different elements clash and encounter each other in often ironic, energetic ways.
————What comes to mind when you hear the word "beauty"?
A person's inner beauty is what I look for and is far more important to me.
————What is the most beautiful time of day?
A time when I am at peace with myself and everyone around me.
————What is the most beautiful place you've visited?
I was traveling in an old, yellow bus across this river where the water is pristine and underneath it is a forest with trees and plants of every kind. The place is unknown, but I know I have been a few times in my dreams.
— INTERVIEW WITH JUSTIN ZHUANG

Theseus Chan, WORK, for Parco Publishing; Inside, *W__K W__K VOL. 1: ANREALAGE* Magazine, 2015; Printed by AlsOdoMinie; Hand-glued offset lithograph; Closed: 30.5 × 22 × 2.3 cm (12 × 8 11/16 × 15/16 in.)

Spread and cover, *WERK No. 21: Martine Bedin* magazine, 2014; Printed by AlsOdoMinie; Die-cut, hand-sprayed offset lithograph on paper; Closed: 30.5 × 22 × 2.5 cm (12 in. × 8¹¹⁄₁₆ in. × 1 in.)

Delfina Delettrez

—ITALIAN, B. 1987—

A fourth-generation member of the Fendi family, Delfina Delettrez creates designs that seek new ideas about jewelry and beauty for her generation. Delettrez's often-surrealist jewels reappropriate items that are deliberately odd, ugly, or taboo—sex, poisonous insects, bones, anatomy—as fantastical inspiration, set in luxury materials and finishes. A single earring with a pearl and ruby lips (2013) is a contemporary nod to Salvador Dalí's Ruby Lips With Teeth Like Pearls brooch (1949). In another piece (2013), a golden bee sits delicately between fingers, balanced on one end of an unclosed ring. Delettrez's more recent work centers on adornment that appears to float on the body. Phantom settings are used to mount pearls on rings and earrings (2014–15). And earrings are sold singly, suggesting the wearer adorn themselves with just one (or a mismatched pair), as though leaving the house sloppily clad and half-dressed, a subversion of conventional beauty ideals. — JUSTIN ZHUANG

————You have a love for surrealist works that is evident in your designs. What draws you to that movement, and how do you interpret it?

When you talk about the surreal, you speak the language of dreams. Everything is possible, anything can happen, anything can melt in absurd combinations that merge and almost liquify, like a cocktail of absurdities. I don't get inspiration from dreams—my inspirations are very lucid and manual. I play around with materials on my body, trying to melt the inorganic with the organic. I like when the boundaries between the flesh and the metal almost disappear to the eye. I like when jewelry almost resembles a magic trick, an illusion, magically suspended on the body.

There is also the more figurative surrealism, and this is where my creative process resembles the process of the subconscious —in dreams, where objects are constantly given new meanings. So if jewelry is usually used to adorn fingers, ears, wrists, and the body in general, in my creations I like to make the opposite happen. Body parts embellish jewelry shaped like hands, noses, fingers and eyes. It's a continuous exchange of cross-references between the body and the object. There is also a sense of freedom of not having to justify anything; nothing needs explanation. When I awake from dreams, I don't like to analyze or ask myself questions. I just let my senses get inebriated from the images and combinations that usually resemble a dance.

————How do you define your personal aesthetic?

Schizophrenic—it can be more pared down and minimal, or ultra organic, using real insects as gemstones. I have always had a passion for opposites, for unexpected combinations, for the destabilizing, for what disturbs you, but most of all, for what distracts and attracts. I never forget when I work that what repels is also what attracts the most. I like to mix different codes in one object, trying to make objects impossible to fit in just one category, making it difficult to give to the objects temporal provenance or [making them] unable to be explained with one adjective.

————Where do you find new sources for inspiration?

Having the possibility of adding or subtracting during the process gives you a great sense of freedom, but at the same time, it makes it so hard to say, "OK, the piece is ready," at its maximum potential.

I am totally open to everything. Everything has beauty; ugliness is very appealing to me. I appreciate it the same way I appreciate beauty. I never forget that in our subconscious opposites coincide. Everything has potential to be transformed. But, most of all, my inspirations are very personal. I don't hide that how I create comes from an egoistic attitude in that I create what I want to wear myself. I was never a jewelry person because I never felt jewelry represented me. I felt the need to craft my own pieces to reflect the needs of my generation—to make things that are different. I felt the preciousness of jewelry couldn't be based just on the material itself, but with the preciousness of a concept.

————Is it liberating to be a self-trained designer?

It is a never-ending learning process, and I find this exciting. It frees me to make a mistake. In Italian the word for mistake is errore, which also means to wonder, discover new horizons and new possibilities. I will never forget when one day I was left alone in my laboratory and couldn't resist experimenting with the machines. I placed three fine jewelry pieces in one of the machines to polish them, and later we discovered a perfect chaos. The three rings immediately fused together and melted, and that is when the Metamorphosis rings took life. This is what I call the gift of the mistake.

However, in order to make mistakes and take risks, you have to have a team of very skilled artisans who respect your vision, but also provide the best quality. The artisans keep the engineering and mathematical aspects of the jewelry in mind, like balancing the weight of the stones and making the pieces wearable and everlasting.

————You experiment with traditional jewelry-making techniques and materials, mixing them with contemporary references and materials. Is balance between these contrasts important?

My references are a mix of the past and future. There is a nostalgic side of me that is present in my work. Jewelry that carries meaning, memories, or that is functional attracts me. I want to create a new category: ultramodern classic. I like to resuscitate traditional jewelry codes, respecting them, but evolving them for our generation. For example my personal idea of an engagement ring is that it needs to become more elastic and open to new possibilities. This is why I introduced the idea of an engagement earring, an engagement bracelet, and an engagement nose diamond piercing—why not?!

————What does the use of irony allow you to achieve with your designs?

To have fingers crawling from your ears at first sight makes you lose the sense of orientation. It destabilizes you and then makes you laugh automatically. I like those two sensations condensed in one moment.

————What comes to mind when you hear the word "beauty"?

Beauty is not necessarily attractive, and ugliness is not always repulsive. I believe in both. Beauty, to me, is what is different, what has the power to make you vibrate positively or negatively. Whatever has the power of catching your attention or stimulates you. Our tastes are so vulnerable. They shift constantly, erasing our aesthetic certainties.

————What is the most beautiful time of day?

I love to wake up and feel that little sand at the end of my bed. I guess this is my favorite time of the day. It disorients me.

————What is the most beautiful place you've visited?

The "holiday room" I built with and for my daughter. It's an imaginative room, where we build the four seasons in rotation. In the winter, we build a summer holiday room, the floor covered with sand. Then we pull off our shoes and play.

— INTERVIEW WITH TIFFANY LAMBERT

Ring, from Fall Winter 2015 collection, 2015;
Diamonds, rubies, gold, silver

Single earring, from Infinity Spring Summer
2013 collection, 2012; Gold, enamel, silver

Ear cuff, from Gold Vein Fall Winter 2014
collection, 2014; Pearls, gold

Single earring, from Fall Winter 2015 collection,
2015; Pearl, diamonds, silver

Bee ring, from Infinity Spring Summer 2013
collection, 2012; Gold, enamel, silver

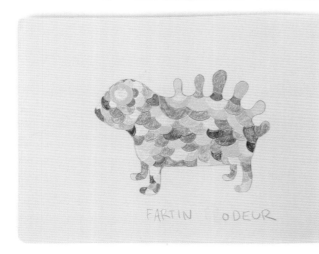

EYES-IK NEWTON

BILL-IAM ONYEABOR

FARTIN ODEUR

NONZALISEKO

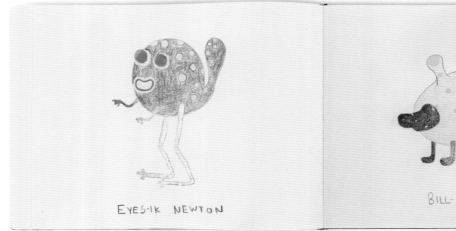

Sketches, 2015; early installation concept for
Beauty—Cooper Hewitt Design Triennial; Eyes-
Ik Newton and Bill-Iam Onyeabor; Fartin Odeur,
and Nonzaliseko

The Haas Brothers

—LOS ANGELES, CALIFORNIA, USA, FOUNDED 2010—

Twin brothers Nikolai (Niki) and Simon Haas (American, b. 1984) share a distinctive voice. Each imaginative, expressive piece they create—whether a chair, vase, table, tapestry, or otherwise—is characterized not only by a focus on texture and material innovation, but also by its sculptural, often anthropomorphic form. Their work provokes response. It is confrontational and humorous, discomforting and playful, exploring themes of nature, sexuality, psychedelia, and social equity. Underlying their aesthetic is an emphasis on material and technical experimentation, born out of an insatiable curiosity and years spent studying stone carving under their father, artist Berthold Haas. Brass, marble, ceramic, and fur are presented as fluid, supple, stalactite-like, and expressive forms. For their latest Afreaks collection (2015–ongoing), the Haas Brothers co-create fantastical beaded objects with women from South African townships, each imbued with the beader's personality to result in highly expressive forms. Simon developed beading algorithms based on natural phenomena, which the beaders are following to create hyperbolic-beaded vegetation for Cooper Hewitt's galleries. The collection represents a shift for the brothers into the realm of human equality. With the series, they present work defiant to categorization and share the stage with their collaborators, the Haas Sisters, to question the value of exclusive authorship. — ANDREA LIPPS

————How do you describe what you do?

NIKOLAI HAAS: I don't know what people are going to call us in two or three years. Certainly, we'll always be designers, but Simon's still a painter. I'm still a musician. We're both filmmakers. Now that we have this massive, ten-thousand-square-foot studio, we're constantly experimenting. And to have someone like your twin brother as a partner who supports you endlessly allows for this freedom of expression that we hold higher than anything else as artists.

SIMON HAAS: Yeah. One of the best parts of working with your twin is that even when we experience discomfort with each other's ideas, it's like a gigantic growth process. We're aware that that discomfort is probably shared by a lot of other people. By investigating our own reactions, we're able to understand other people's sensitivity, which is a very useful tool.

NH: That's what our whole career is about—freedom and liberty, and offering it to ourselves so we can explore what that really means and then try to find some way to make it more accessible to people around us. It's all about personal exploration and, at a larger scale, exploration of human emotion, in general.

————Tell me about your current way of working.

NH: Simon is always running this R&D department out of our studio. He came up with all of our material processes that are original, like our color-changing glaze, or our hex tiles, or our accretion process on our ceramics. All of those are Simon's invention. It obviously comes out of discussions that we share, but Simon really is at the forefront of pushing these ideas and being able to verbalize them in a way that allows for us to create the pillars of our belief system that we can apply to the work. Simon's this mad scientist who is creating a way of life for us inside of the studio. Then him creating these materials that are building blocks of an ecosystem that we've created inside of the studio.

SH: I always describe Niki as the "Picasso element," which is to say that there's a type of freedom of expression that is impossible to learn, that I think education can frequently remove from certain people. I think that there's a stigma attached to it when people call it "naive art." Niki has a facility and expressiveness with form that is impossible to replicate. If you were to separate us, I think you would find that my studies, though they're really interesting, they're meant to be tedious and unusable until Niki breathes life into everything that goes on. I would say that his work stands alone as sculpture, and mine stands alone more as science. Forcing them to marry is the same thing that we've been talking about with our reflecting on each other.

————Travel seems to be an important source of inspiration to you. How does this impact your work?

SH: It's important for us to be aware of our context, and to remove ourselves from our context in order to do so.

NH: If you're uncomfortable when you're making work, it creates a catalyst for better work. Traveling forces you to experience some level of humility because everybody around you knows their lives better than you do. They've got the place figured out. When you travel, you don't know where to get breakfast, where is a good running route, how to go about your day-to-day routine. It's nice for us to go somewhere because we get knocked back a peg. It helps us create empathy toward the rest of the world. It's all about keeping your mind more dexterous.

SH: Traveling prevents you from ever getting truly comfortable in your own situation. When you travel a lot, your home never feels quite the same when you get back. I think that's vital.

NH: We're very reactive because we always keep ourselves in this very uncomfortable situation. For instance, Simon and I were in this band, RRIICCEE, with Vincent Gallo. We had to go on stage and improvise entire sets with nothing planned ahead of time. We would do it almost naked on stage. It was like you had to be as vulnerable as you possibly could be in front of a bunch of people.

We're always trying to test new boundaries. We've been described as rogues and rebels, which is not what we're going for. We're just trying to explore ideas. A lot of that came from Vincent, and from this practice of being really vulnerable in front of people. It all comes back to creating empathy for other humans.

————What comes to mind when you hear the word "beauty"?

SH: I think that it's intangible. It's a recognition of something that is accompanied by a feeling of mystery. It's a mystery and recognition at the same time. It's a comfort, and it's a lack of understanding.

NH: My initial reaction is to connect it to lust, a beautiful woman or something, but it's deeper than that. It's like attraction to the unknown or the unachievable. "Beauty" is an elusive term, but it's visceral.

SH: It is like finding a pattern among chaos.

————What is the most beautiful time of day?

SH: For me, it is late night because I like to be alone.

NH: For me it has more to do with what I'm doing. Making a beautiful save as a goalie. (I play ice hockey.) Designing something that I think I've nailed. Having sex with my wife. Spending time with my godson and goddaughter.

————What is the most beautiful place you've visited?

NH: Iceland.

SH: South Africa.

NH: Simon hasn't been to Iceland yet. I think he might change his mind.

— INTERVIEW WITH ANDREA LIPPS

The Haas Brothers with the Haas Sisters;
Al-Gorilla, Eye-sik Newton, Neil Tongue, Bill
Nyeland, Isle Be Back, and Fungulliver, from
the Afreaks series, 2015; Glass beads, wire,
wood, mixed fiber stuffing, and cast bronze;
Courtesy of R & Company

Pepe Heykoop

—DUTCH, B. 1984—

The work of Dutch designer Pepe Heykoop straddles two worlds—the collectible pieces made in his Amsterdam studio, and the retail products made with women in an informal settlement in Mumbai, India, as part of the Tiny Miracles Foundation. Yet these two facets of his practice are not incompatible. Both reflect Heykoop's idealism and vision as a designer; both enable his exploration in the handmade. In fact, Heykoop's work in India led to the design of a lamp made from leather scraps, which became the genesis of his studio's Skin Collection (2011–ongoing). Recycling is at the heart of many of Heykoop's designs. The Skin Collection merges secondhand furniture with leather scraps discarded in the manufacturing process. The scraps—strewn aside because of deformations, scarring, or other imperfections in the leather—are glued into slipcover skins. The exaggerated, exposed seams create patterns suggestive of a cellular or mutant skin around the furniture forms. Recent pieces from the collection, such as the Mirror Chair (2013) and Tension Light (2014), demonstrate the evolving hybridized forms created within the series. The collection is evocative not only of skin and the body, but also of our relationship with objects found in our daily lives. — ANDREA LIPPS

————Tell me about your work.

In 2008, I graduated from Design Academy Eindhoven, and in 2010 my cousin, Laurien Meuter, started the Tiny Miracles Foundation in the slums of Mumbai to help some of the children in the red-light district go to school. The parents would take them out because the girls had to make money. So my cousin thought she should provide jobs for the mothers. And that's when she asked me, "Can you design some things which they can execute?"—which is how our collaboration started in 2010. At the moment, ninety women are working on a daily basis, and one hundred and fifty children are going to school, and everybody has doctor visits. It's a social project that really succeeds. It is something very different from the small-edition works that we are making in Amsterdam.

————How do you work?

I'm running the studio now for six years. I make one-off pieces because I want to convey a message. I am my only limitation. Like, does it fit the elevator to get out of the building? But it feels sometimes also a bit isolated, making pieces in, like, this kind of fairy-tale world.

The project in India, which I run together with my cousin, is completely different because we run the production from A to Z. I have to instruct them. I have to source the material in Mumbai. Then you have shipping and storage and the distributor, and then you have the contact with the shops. There are so many parties involved.

————How did the Skin Collection come about?

It started with the first project in India: a foldable lamp made of leather. It was the first time I worked with leather. I calculated approximately how many skins I needed, and we needed maybe one-third more skins than I thought. So I asked the guys who work with the skins, why do you need so many? And they showed me a bag full of offcuts. Suddenly I thought every jacket that's being made, every bag that's being made, every couch that's being upholstered would probably have the same amount of leftover. So I figured out that this is about twenty-five percent or thirty percent in normal production. And then I imagined how many leftovers there should be in warehouses.

I asked for this bag with all the offcuts, and back in the studio, I didn't know what to make out of it. Then I thought about the discarded furniture I pick up. I've always loved to cycle around in the city and to find nice chairs or lamps or whatever that people put out on the streets. You can glue them together and then paint it, but it will never look good. So I already did many projects by wrapping them with fabric, wrapping them with rope, whatever. But it always looked kind of homey.

And just at the moment that we started covering these objects in leather, then suddenly it felt like there was kind of a magic to them. We could change the most ugly object. There was no shape or material which we could not do. There was such freedom in that. And it is just with objects found on the street. Sometimes when a piece is displayed in a gallery window, you see people staring into the window. A year before, that same chair could have been standing in the street and everybody was just walking by.

————In your work, it's interesting that the beauty is related to the ethical deed.

And also in our India project, to me it's the same. It's just a very honest, open, transparent project that started by sending some girls to school. In this project, we don't want to just take. We want to do good for all the parties that participate in this project.

————What comes to mind when you hear the word "beauty"?

A recent project that I did was with a lot of small, wooden offcuts; there is a local saw mill that sells the wood offcuts to burn in the oven. I was actually a bit shocked these offcuts would just be burnt because there is like half a rain forest in there. It's beautiful: beautiful colors and smells and types of wood. So with, say, three thousand of these small sticks, I make a new chandelier. It has the same kind of magic like the Skin pieces. People open their mouth and grab their camera. And before, the same woods were sold to be burnt.

It's like this slogan, "From waste into wonder." That is what I say sometimes, turning waste into wonder. Because that's actually what this whole process is about, reusing the material. I would be foolish to say that I save the world by recycling a few pieces of leather, because I make just a handful of items, and we ship them around the world, and we drag them from show to show. That's not saving the world. But what might happen to these pieces is that they inspire other people to think about waste and how can we look at waste. I think that impact is much bigger than the actual piece.

————What is the most beautiful time of day?

I cannot answer that question because sometimes I don't even know what day it is. I don't even know if it's a Monday or a Friday. To me, it depends upon the weather. When I see a nice little sunshine breaking through the clouds, I enjoy that most.

————What is the most beautiful place you've visited?

Recently, the Himalayas. We were there for seven days with hardly anything. There was little to eat, and we were a bit lost, and it was really amazing. It was very beautiful because of the vast landscape. But it was also beautiful in the way that you have blisters on your feet and you walk and you walk and you walk, and you don't feel them anymore. You have money in your pocket, and you're really hungry, and you want to buy something, but the money is worth nothing because there is just nothing. We felt like prehistoric beings. You just walk and walk and walk, and around the corner still is another mountain. Endless.

— INTERVIEW WITH SUVI SALONIEMI

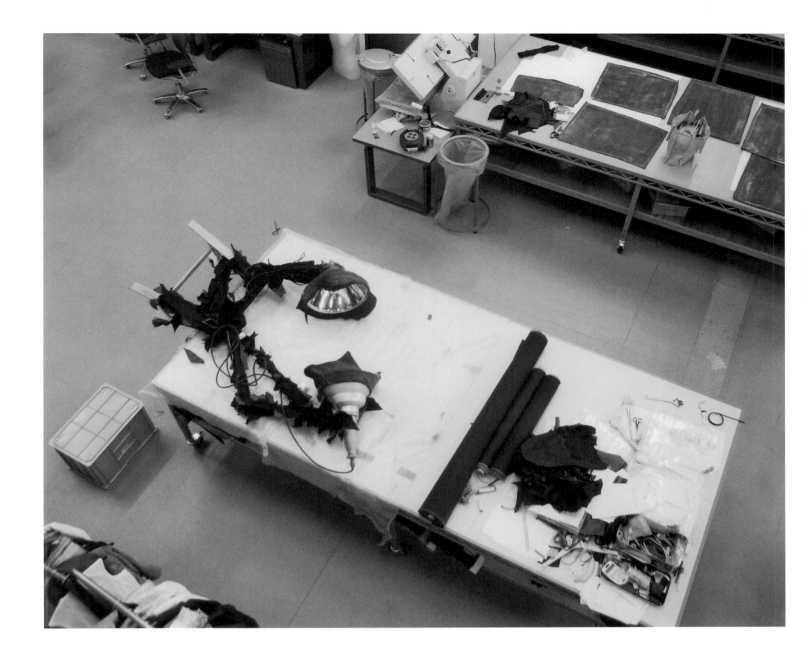

In Pepe Heykoop's studio in Amsterdam, his piece Skin vs G-Star Tension Light is being assembled from offcuts of denim.

Skin vs G-Star Tension Light, 2014; Jeans,
two lamps, melting pot; 200 × 130 × 50 cm
(6 ft. 6¾ in. × 51³⁄₁₆ in. × 19¹¹⁄₁₆ in.)

Mirror Chair, from Skin Collection, 2013;
Leather remnants, discarded objects;
80 × 60 × 45 cm (31½ × 23⅝ × 17¹¹⁄₁₆ in.)

Rad Hourani

—CANADIAN, ACTIVE IN FRANCE, B. JORDAN 1982—

Rad Hourani creates unisex, aseasonal clothes. His genderless silhouettes eschew trends in favor of timeless appeal, using sharp lines and a clean palette with minimal embellishment. Born in Jordan, Hourani grew up in Canada before moving to Paris. He launched his eponymous unisex line in 2007 and, in 2013, became the first invited member of the Chambre Syndicale de la Haute Couture to present a unisex haute couture collection. Hourani fashions unisex garments not to subvert gender roles, but to create an equalizing canvas that emphasizes the wearer more than his or her gender identity. Straight-legged pants and shorts, and architectural jackets, tunics, and tops can be worn by women or men, confronting normative ideas about fashion and beauty. In so doing, unisex clothing challenges conventional dress codes by liberating the wearer from them. Hourani gives further primacy to garment construction, driven by structure and precise geometry. He most often employs a limited color palette—black, navy, and gray—as in his Couture Collection #12 (2014) or Ready-to-Wear Collection #11 (2015). Alongside these neutral colors, Hourani's Couture Collection #14 (2015) veered into turquoise, red, and purple. He is a self-described visualist, pursuing fashion, photography, film, and art. — ANDREA LIPPS

———You are the first designer to present a unisex haute couture line. How did you arrive at designing a unisex collection?

Who decided that a man should dress in one way and a woman in another way? Or how different ages should dress? Who imposed these codes? All of my pieces are made to be unisex. Each piece can be worn by any gender or age. It doesn't make sense to me to limit things. It is about creating form that can be the present at all times without fitting in any past categories. I think it's about the yin and yang in all of us, the negative and positive, the masculine and feminine, the dark and light, the passive and active, the intuitive and logical, the cold and hot, the soft and hard. I want to be true to my vision and to the people who see themselves in it. It is very uncompromising.

———You refer to your clothing as timeless. Would it be accurate to also describe your clothing as universal, if the stated aim is to transcend gender, religion, age, place, and time? Why is this important?

Fashion is a trend machine; I have no interest in fashion. My interest is in the world and the people that live on this planet. My signature style is mainly based on symmetry and rectangular shapes. They help me achieve the unisex vision that I have been building for the past eight years. The geometry in my shapes is made of these two things, and I find that they make the human body look longer and more modern. I'm unconsciously attracted to architecture, and that's where all of it comes from. My unisex style has always remained

the same but with a certain evolution that expresses how I feel. My first collection in Paris in 2007 is still as timeless as my latest collection in 2015. I want to free my collection from all trends or seasons or references from the past. My designs will always be unisex, architectural, symmetrical, and graphic, and this is what keeps them timeless. Since my objective is to create garments that can be worn by anyone at any time, I subvert the biannual fashion calendar to some extent by fusing and blending seasonal stereotypes into an adaptable system based on aseasonal collections identified only by their sequential number. Therefore, I do not start every new season with a specific concept, but rather try to establish continuity from one to the next.

———Tell me about your process. Do you sketch? Where do you find ideas and inspiration?

I think a great deal about myself when designing. Of course, I didn't create a brand just for my own sake, but I believe that using what I would like to wear as a starting point to the design process is the most truthful and straightforward approach. It allows me to stay focused on my aesthetic and to assess my commitment to wearability, functionality, and comfort. Also, I have always been interested in creating something that looks minimal but is complex to make. For me, it is the most challenging process of work. I admire the craftsmanship of making something extremely luxurious without being showy. Attending to complexity and

simplicity at the same time is a very long process. It's all about *savoir faire*, working with only the best in every aspect: fabrics, tailoring, cut, fit, proportions.

———There must be challenges in creating and tailoring unisex garments. How do you design unisex clothes to accommodate the varying body types of both men and women?

Observation is essential for me. I took a full year to study and understand a male and a female body to create a canvas that can fit both. I've discovered this unisex canvas can make a body appear longer, slicker, new, and comfortable at the same time. I am not trying to dress a man like a woman or the opposite. I am creating a new way of dressing that makes people look modern without any limits.

———You seem to shy away from the term "fashion designer." Why? How would you describe what you do?

I find it very limiting to be set in one category. I don't consider myself a designer or a photographer or a filmmaker. I am all of those things in one. I want to express my vision through all mediums: design, art, film, photography, music. Call me a visualist.

———How do you define "beauty"?

Something that attracts your eyes with a great vibration in your body. It's personal.

———What is the most beautiful time of day?

Anytime when you are at peace with yourself, but I must say that a sunset is always beautiful to watch.

———What is the most beautiful place you've visited?

I would say the ocean in general. We know so much about the earth and above it, but we know so little about the inside of the ocean. Water is magical to me.

— INTERVIEW WITH ANDREA LIPPS

Ensembles, from Ready-to-Wear Collection #11,
2015; Double crepe jersey

Ensembles, from Couture Collection #12, 2014; Leather, silk crepe

OPPOSITE: Ensembles, from Couture Collection #14, 2015; Plastic nylon, silk crepe

Ensemble, from Fall / Winter 2013 Ready-to-Wear collection, 2013; Shredded trash bags

Gareth Pugh

—BRITISH, B. 1981—

Gareth Pugh's work resonates a dark, ebullient drama. Since his launch in London in 2005, the Central Saint Martins graduate has presented some of today's most avant-garde ready-to-wear collections. Replete with spectacle from the start—inflated clothing, Elizabethan ruffs, obscured models—Pugh's clothing is bold and uninhibited. In 2008, he received the Association Nationale pour le Développement des Arts de la Mode award, among the fashion industry's most prestigious prizes. Pugh's collections emphasize feminine strength while supplying a protective armor composed of structured silhouettes. His garments often contrast black and white, fantasy and severity, softness and aggression. An emotional intensity bubbles from these oppositional forces, suggesting a space that Pugh's longtime collaborator, Matthew Stone, calls "beyond; a space that relates to the sublime." For his Fall 2013 ready-to-wear collection, Pugh created a mountainous ball gown and matching cube hat made from trash bags, treating the material with every bit of care and attention as one would the most luxurious. His Fall 2015 ready-to-wear collection, inspired by national pride, presented warrior archetypes in leather breastplates and flared skirts. Pugh again demonstrated his irreverent material choices—a face-framing, funnel-neck bolero made of drinking straws mimicked the sheen of animal fur. It was black-on-black, confrontational and protective, and exquisitely executed. — ANDREA LIPPS

————There is a theatricality and performative aspect to your work. How did your early experiences—as a costume designer for London's National Youth Theatre at the age of fourteen, and early training as a dancer—influence you?
I think there is certainly a performative aspect to my work in the sense that I often begin with a character or a loose narrative in mind. For me, it has always been more about telling a story, rather than just pushing an aesthetic. I guess this also explains why when it comes to the show, I'm so fascinated by the idea of fully immersive presentation. A fashion show can be a compelling and emotional experience, and while you can't control what the audience takes away from it, you can try to ensure that the images penetrate. Over the past decade, we've utilized several perhaps unexpected elements in order to achieve this, and none more so than film and dance.

————Tell me about your process. What is the source of your ideas and inspiration?
It's difficult to pin down—it constantly changes, season on season—but I think that living and working in London is an important factor. There's always something of the city in my work. But, really, it can come from anywhere. We are all constantly exposed to so much visual information, so it's about trying to see past the white noise and focus on the things you carry with you. Whether it's something you've seen and remembered—a fabric, a material, an unexpected silhouette—or even just a feeling, I usually just try to go deep on that one thing, and naturally the ideas begin to unfold.

————You have presented precisely executed, unconventional materials for high fashion—balloons, PVC, bin bags, sackcloth, drinking straws—and have used conventional materials, unconventionally—fur, leather, chiffon. What drives your material choices?
It's easy to say that it's about using unconventional materials to make a point, or that it's about "make do and mend," but truthfully, it's just that some of the less traditional materials I've chosen to work with react in quite a specific way. Sometimes they just work, and so it doesn't matter if it's a luxury fabric or otherwise. If it works, it works, and I don't try to overthink it. It's a completely instinctive choice.

————How is emotion important in your work?
It's the single most important aspect. All you hope to achieve is that the work represents something emotionally honest and meaningful to you. Otherwise, it's totally pointless.

————There are often oppositional forces at play in your work. It is confrontational but protective; suggests chaos and control; incorporates black and white; presents a kind of utopic dystopia. Can you speak to this?
For me, it's about friction—like when two magnets oppose one another, and the energy and friction they create as they push away. The visual friction that can be created by combining two opposites is very interesting—it can sometimes create something quite unnerving. Opposites are in everything we do and everything we build. They are either black or white, positive or negative, good or

evil, masculine or feminine. I guess that's how we've learned to organize ourselves.

————What does beauty mean to you?
I think the way we appreciate beauty is entirely personal, and it's always in flux—it's constantly changing in relation to new experiences and exposure to new ideas. But that's what it means to be human. I think with regards to my work, it's something I'm constantly striving to create—to make an image that represents exactly what I thought or felt at the time—something truly perfect. And it's that search that keeps me going—perfection is something you never quite reach, or indeed never should reach. . . . It's that sense of dissatisfaction with what you've done that helps you to push forward and try again. . . . It's a constant and never-ending search.

————What is the most beautiful time of day?
I think perhaps very early in the morning. There's always such a sense of possibility.

————What is the most beautiful place you've visited?
I grew up near the sea, and as a teenager I used to spend a lot of time by the coast of my hometown, Sunderland, in the north of England. It's still a place that I think about constantly, and it's usually where I go when I need to get out of London. It can be very gray, and it's quite desolate in parts, but looking out to sea is an amazing experience. I love that sense of being on the edge of something; seeing all that nothingness in front of you is a truly humbling experience.

— INTERVIEW WITH ANDREA LIPPS

Ensembles, from Fall / Winter 2015 Ready-to-Wear collection, 2015

CLOCKWISE: Silk faille, neoprene, leather

Padded silk faille

Hand-cut plastic drinking straws, leather, patent leather, felted wool

Patent leather, plastic drinking straws, felted wool

OPPOSITE: Waxed leather, silk faille, buckram, steel curblink chain

Iris van Herpen with Jólan van der Wiel;
Magnetic shoes, black, from Magnetic Motion
collection, 2014; Resin, iron filings, base shoe;
30 × 22 × 26 cm (11¹³⁄₁₆ × 8¹¹⁄₁₆ × 10¼ in.)

Gravity stool, black and blue, from Gravity
series, 2013; Resin, iron filings; 46 × 34 ×
38 cm (18⅛ × 13⅜ × 14¹⁵⁄₁₆ in.)

Jólan van der Wiel

—DUTCH, B. 1984—

Dutch designer Jólan van der Wiel explores the impact natural forces have on form, wielding the conditions under which an object takes shape. While studying at the Gerrit Rietveld Academy, from which he graduated in 2011, van der Wiel developed and built the gravity machine for which he is most well known. The tool uses oppositional forces of gravity and magnetism to generate organic, armored forms made from a composite material of iron filings and plastic or ceramic. With the machine, van der Wiel creates tables and stools that sprout stalactites, fantastical architectural models, even dresses and shoes imbued with a primordial, prickly surface, made in collaboration with fashion designer Iris van Herpen. From his Amsterdam-based studio and workshop, van der Wiel continues to experiment with his gravity machine, pushing it to create ever-new challenging and elegant work. — ANDREA LIPPS

————Tell me about your background and entry into design.

I was born in the east of the Netherlands, a small village called Brummen. I went to Design Academy Eindhoven, where I ended up in Mobility, designing cars and bikes and that kind of stuff. But it was way too specific for me; I wanted to work more experimentally before I chose a direction. So I quit and started studying economics in Amsterdam. I'm always interested in the artistic part of things, but also I was interested in the business side. I thought it would be nice to combine this, but I could not find a way to— it was way too theoretical for me.

Then I went to Gerrit Rietveld Academy in Amsterdam, which is mostly an art academy; but they have a small department called designLAB, an environment for arts-related projects. With my graduation project, which was the gravity tool, I found a direction where I wanted to work and where I could start my own studio.

————How do you start the creative process? How much do you work with briefs, and how much do you self-initiate?

Ninety percent is self-initiated. And maybe ten percent is people will ask us for help. There is an organic process where we've done a project and out of that project comes a new idea, which we take into the next project. I also try to come up with small stories or a theme I want to work in. For example, our last project, we made a movie with a small team. We had about ten people working in the studio, directors and camera people, animation, studio makers. This ended up in the story *Journey of a Raindrop* [2014]. It's the idea that a water drop every day travels the whole world because it's evaporating and flying and falling down again. Actually it's meeting, every day, a lot of natural forces. I'm most interested in visualizing natural forces—magnetism or g-forces, or cold or warmth, or all the things that are invisible but have a very strong, shapable effect on material. They are all possible things to use for tools within our studio.

————How about the gravity tool? Where is the project now?

The idea was to come up with a prediction technique where a natural force is the designer of the object. We created a machine that has the same prediction methods all the time, but the objects, totally designed by this force, are always totally unique because magnetic forces are always changing.

I've worked now for three years with Iris van Herpen, who is a fashion designer. It's a totally different scale of working and is much more detailed, so that also gives us the possibility to create more sophisticated shapes.

We now are discussing with an architect how we can use magnetism as a tool for creating the shape of a building, not in the construction of a huge building, but more as a way of creating shapes, so all the time the design is made on the spot.

————What materials do you use with the tool?

Most of them are plastics, two components that we use in different flexibilities, so sometimes it's really hard or sometimes it's very flexible. It looks really dangerous, but it's soft to the touch.

We tried a lot of different materials. At that time, plastic was a good way because it doesn't shrink and it hardens very quickly and it's quite strong, but it's also very flexible. These shapes are very rough and sharp and pointy, so if it's too hard then it will break off or it will hurt somebody. So, that's why it was very important that it's a little bit flexible. Afterward, we worked also with cement and also with concrete and ceramics. There's still a lot to try out, but it's a very simple process. This tool creates within a few minutes this crazy work, different shapes all the time. It's always a unique piece, even in production.

————You said some companies come to you for help. What kind of companies?

Last year we worked with Dom Pérignon, the champagne company. They had these events where they launched a new bottle, and they asked us to develop an installation, creating organic shapes, and they thought about magnetism. So we developed a whole installation of a piece [The Power of Creation (2014)] with magnetic fluid over it, and this magnetic fluid was influenced by magnets moving in the neighborhood. It is nice to have those kinds of requests because it's a way of pushing us forward.

————What comes to mind when you hear the word, "beauty"?

I've always had the feeling that with beauty you should also have ugly next to it. Otherwise it becomes two beauties, so I always like to have beauty and ugly next to each other, so it's attraction and revulsion.

————What is the most beautiful time of day?

The time of the day would be one hour after I wake up. Then, you really have the feeling that everything can still happen, and you have all day in front of you.

————What is the most beautiful place you've visited?

In the Pienea in Spain, you have canyons. It's a very dry area and it's very hot, and there are small deep canyons you would never expect, and if you look in there, there's a sort of paradise where it's green and there's very nice birds and water and the atmosphere is really astonishing. It's so dry that you would not expect anything can live there, and you step into the cave and it's so fluid and colorful. That's the most beautiful place I know.

— INTERVIEW WITH SUVI SALONIEMI

Dragonstones, 2014; Magnetic ceramics, iron filings

OPPOSITE: Iris van Herpen with Jólan van der Wiel; Wilderness Embodied couture dress, 2013; Resin, iron filings

Noa Zilberman

—ISRAELI, B. 1977—

What many women spend thousands of dollars to hide, Noa Zilberman celebrates in an expression of delicate gold. Her Wrinkles jewelry collection traces the lines of an aging face. Crafted during her graduate studies at Israel's Bezalel Academy of Arts and Design, the pieces follow the grooves that settle naturally around the eyes, mouth, and brow—lines that Zilberman studied in her own face after the birth of her first son. The pieces seem to hover just above the wearer's face, an illusion that Zilberman says initially frightened her husband, who was not quite prepared to see the future take such a solid form. Currently working as an industrial designer, Zilberman continues to explore the materiality of products and personal ritual. — LAUREN SCIARAPPA

——What are your methods, your ways of working?

The Wrinkles project was all about the process. I had no vision of any type of finished product. I usually can visualize how things are going to look aesthetically and how they're going to be done conceptually, but when I started this jewelry project, I had absolutely no vision of where it was going. I like to play with materials, and many of the works come from there, from just playing with the material. In other works, I start with a concept, a vision, and I plan it and I go for it.

——How do you combine the fields of jewelry and industrial design?

In addition to jewelry, I design Judaica—Jewish religious artifacts, such as candlesticks and wine cups. Industrial design provides a broad way of thinking, focusing from outside to inside, from wide to narrow. That approach was also a part of my work when I was practicing as a silversmith.

I'm working now as the head of an industrial design team. What makes me a bit different from other industrial designers is that I always try to make my own models. I don't let production do it. I like to combine old-fashioned jewelry techniques, even techniques that nobody makes anymore. I combine them sometimes into new products. For example, filigree is not used a lot industrially, but we use it where I work.

——How did the Wrinkles series start?

It began as a class assignment during my second degree. It was about a year after my son was born. Everything feels different once you have babies. Not in a bad way, in a

good way. You're not who you were. You are something new. Wrinkles started out as a class assignment called "Repair." It started out by mapping. I was mapping my face with eye pencils. I was smiling to see what's left and then repeating it with eye pencil until I had made a map of me, of how I will be sometime in the future. Then I made a video with golden threads, and at the end I created the objects. The project was very personal for a long time, and then I made the jewelry objects so anyone can engage with it from the outside.

——What kind of feedback have you received?

Well, my husband was scared. He was the one that shot the video, and he was the one helping me. He said it scared him, the whole thing. He was glad when it was over. The feedback from my teachers was good. I actually didn't believe that a small school project would make it this far. The project was very sincere when I made it and was very honest.

——Do you consider yourself as mostly a designer of functional products to be used?

I've been in exhibitions, and I've done one-offs of all sorts, but I usually don't practice anything on myself. Before this, the work was never about me. I was never the subject. I did a pendant with maps of Jerusalem on them. I did cups that you transfer from one person to another. But I never did things that are about me in such a direct and personal way.

——Has this work changed somehow your practice?

I hope so. Wrinkles speaks about how I felt at the time, about researching myself and how I look, how I am going to look, what is

changing, what is me, what will be me. And now I'm a few years older and I have become a mother for the second time, and I'm not in that state anymore. So any kind of sequel to Wrinkles will be different, a bit more mature. And I really, really hope to do a sequel project.

——What comes to mind when you hear the word "beauty"?

Beauty changes so much from one culture to another, so you can't really describe it. When I made Wrinkles, I felt that I was making myself beautiful. It was beauty to me, but people that love me were very disturbed by it, so they didn't feel it was beauty.

——What is the most beautiful time of day?

The most beautiful time of the day is the beginning of the evening, when you look on one side of the sky and see a very, very dark blue, and then when you look on the other side, to the east, and you see that it's already pitch-black. That's my favorite hour of the day. My son likes to look out the window and pinpoint exactly the same hour. "Mommy, it's your favorite hour of the day now. Take a look outside the window."

——What is the most beautiful place you've visited?

There is a special place in the Israeli desert, called the Ramon Crater. I remember when I went there for the first time. I was a soldier, and I was on my way to my base, and I had to stay there. I woke up in the middle of the desert, and I saw it, and I felt it was the most beautiful place I'd ever seen.

— INTERVIEW WITH SUVI SALONIEMI

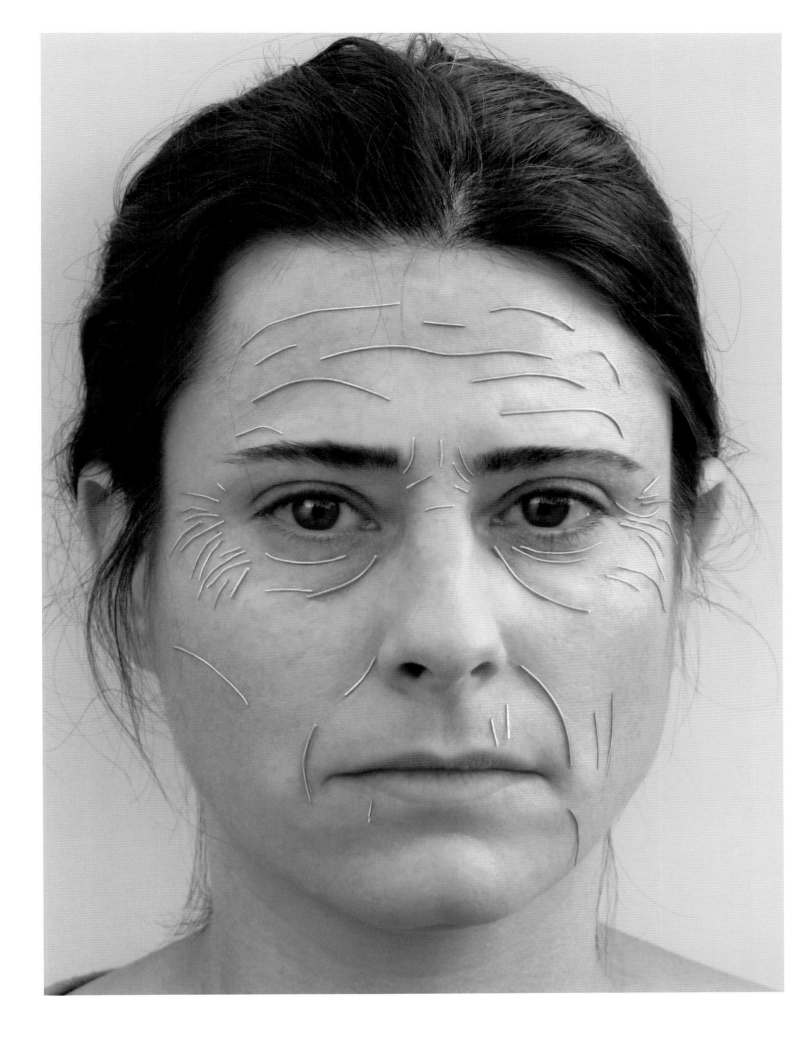

Wrinkles, from Wrinkle Jewelry collection, 2012; Gold-plated brass

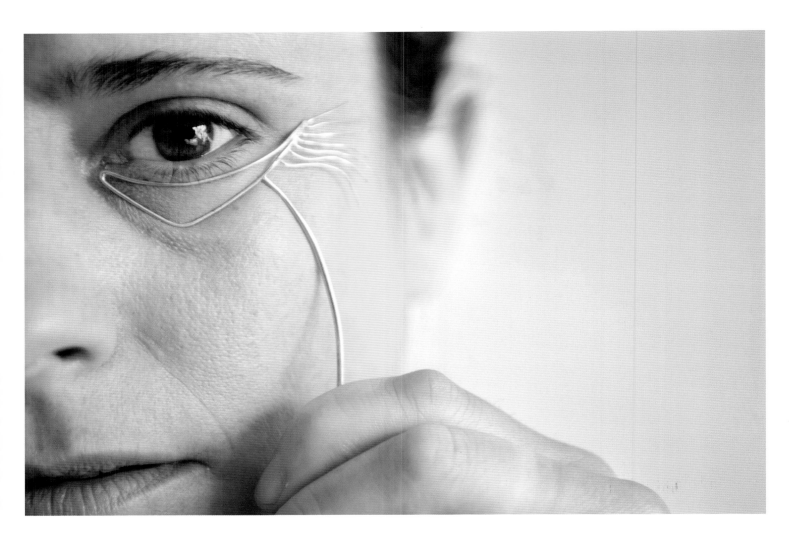

Undereye, from Wrinkle Jewelry collection, 2012; Gold-plated brass; 10.2 × 6.4 × 0.6 cm (4 × 2½ × ¼ in.)

OPPOSITE: Cleavage, from Wrinkle Jewelry collection, 2012; Gold-plated brass; 6.4 × 2.5 × 2.5 cm (2½ × 1 × 1 in.)

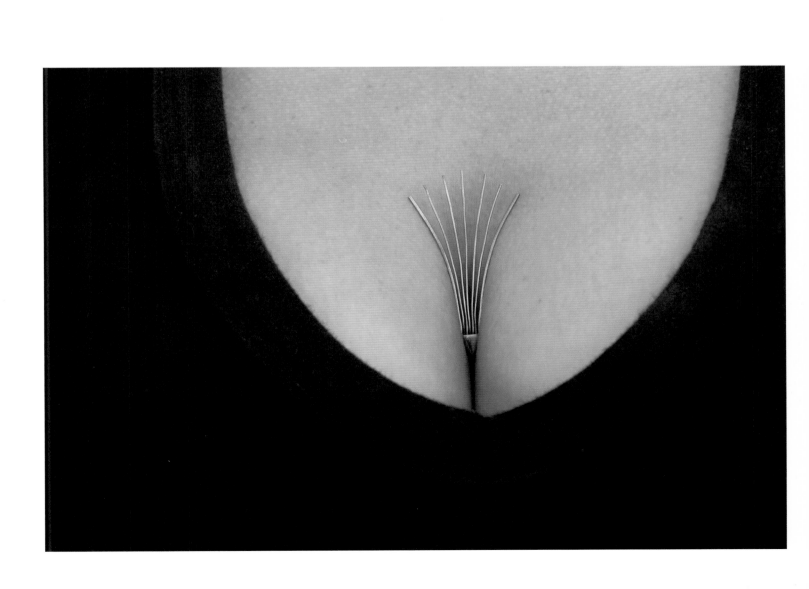

Elemental

Michael Anastassiades
Daniel Emma
Formafantasma
Emiliano Godoy
Industrial Facility
Daniel Rybakken
SO−IL
Trace Architecture
 Office (TAO)
Yeongkyu Yoo
Jean Yu

Some objects seek permanence, purity, and rest. Serene geometries and uncluttered forms draw energy and character from basic materials: wood, glass, stone, copper, a block of lava. Unassuming, almost anonymous objects invite intuitive interaction from users.

"I like to remove excess information from a product, so I keep on refining the design, taking away the excess layer after layer. With that process, you purify the idea, and this is when you end up with a pure essence of the product. It also manages to achieve a sort of timelessness."

———————————————————————— Michael Anastassiades

Michael Anastassiades

—CYPRIOT, ACTIVE IN UNITED KINGDOM, B. 1967—

Michael Anastassiades's work epitomizes pure form. He reduces a concept to its core, creating uncluttered, elegant, and timeless objects that remain imbued with a signature expressiveness. The Mobile Chandelier 9 (2015) is an exceedingly beautiful reduction in form, with curved and cantilevered arms that sway gently to subtly activate a space. The IC Lights (2014) for FLOS explore the balance and instability of a singular opaline-glass sphere. Statuary marble appears light and flexible in Miracle Chips (2013), a series of thin marble discs that successively curl in an abstract study of materiality. Fairest (2015) is a series of polished brass globes affixed to a wall almost like jewelry, intended to reflect the space around them. Anastassiades's work pairs simple form with luxury finishes and meticulous detailing, the precariousness of many pieces enabled by intricate engineering. Anastassiades studied civil engineering at London's Imperial College before obtaining a master's degree in industrial design from the Royal College of Art. He established his London-based studio in 1994 and, in 2007, launched Michael Anastassiades Ltd., overseeing all development, production, and distribution of his pieces. — ANDREA LIPPS

——Tell me what led you to where you are now.

I believe in evolution when it comes to the creative process. After graduating from the Royal College of Art, I set up my studio about a year later. It was quite a long process setting up a practice, not wanting to compromise. I felt like the expected career of industrial designers coming out of college was to start approaching manufacturers in order to produce their work and start cultivating relationships. I found that process draining because it relied very much on the internal politics of companies. And that's when I started to question this approach. It didn't feel right toward the creative process, and, for

me, that was the most important thing. I felt that my duty as an industrial designer was to get my work out for people to use and see.

I started with very experimental work. These projects were looking at a complex relationship that exists between the object and the user, which was much more immediate, more interactive. There was a psychological connection there. I also had a passion to design for industry, to design in larger quantities, and that's when I started questioning the values of aesthetics. I created products and eventually specialized in lighting.

Since 2007, I have had my own brand, for which I design and produce primarily light

fixtures under my own name. I'm very much involved in the whole cycle of design, from concept to product development to product manufacture to selling. And then only in the last few years, suddenly doors opened. Manufacturers and other brands have come to me and said, "We like what you do. We want you to do something for us." But I'm very selective.

——Where do your ideas come from? Where does it all start, the process?

Ideas, of course, come from anywhere. They are rooted in experiences, the environment, observations. Sometimes I'm more fascinated about what an object says to a user, examining the relationship that exists between the object and the user. That's very obvious in my early work, but I'm exploring that even now with the more everyday objects. On the surface, this is what they might look like, but there's quite a lot of layering involved.

——What is your aesthetic language?

I think the language is a very personal thing. I like simplicity when it comes to the aesthetic language. My work is often referred to as minimalist, but I prefer to use subtraction as a term to relate to. I like to remove excess information from a product, so I keep on refining the design, taking away the excess layer after layer. With that process, you purify the idea, and this is when you end up with a pure essence of the product. It also manages to achieve a sort of timelessness.

——What comes to mind when you hear the word "beauty"?

"Beauty" is such a relative term. I don't necessarily see beauty in terms of something that has a very high aesthetic value, traditionally. I think beauty exists when making an object that people can relate to. Design, at the end of the day, is about communication. You design something because you want to start a dialogue with somebody, with an audience that is there. So this idea of beauty is how successful you are in that process.

——What is the most beautiful time of day?

When I have time to think, when I have time to set my mind free from things to be creative. I wouldn't say it's a specific time, but it's more about having the luxury to be in a place free from certain commitments.

——What is the most beautiful place you've visited?

Home. But not my place in London where I live or where I sleep or where I'm based. Home is the place that I am able to feel comfortable. And that, for me, is really the most beautiful place.

— INTERVIEW WITH SUVI SALONIEMI

Michael Anastassiades for FLOS; String Lights with sphere fixture, 2014; Aluminum, polycarbonate; Light: 19 cm diam. (7½ in.), cord: 1200 cm (39 ft. 4⁷⁄₁₆ in.)

OPENING SPREAD: Mobile Chandelier 9, 2015; Black patinated brass, mouthblown opaline sphere; 145.5 × 110.3 cm (57⁹⁄₃₂ × 43²⁷⁄₆₄ in.)

Michael Anastassiades for Henraux Foundation;
Miracle Chips, 2013; Statutory white marble; Sizes
vary, up to 3 × 80 × 80 cm (1¾₆ × 31½ × 31½ in.)

Michael Anastassiades for FLOS; F1 floor lamp, from IC Light collection, 2014; Brassed steel, blown-glass opal diffuser; 135 × 27.5 × 20 cm diam. (53⅛ × 10¾₆ × 7⅞ in.)

Michael Anastassiades for FLOS; T table lamp, from IC Light collection, 2014; Brassed steel, blown-glass opal diffuser; 53 × 32.1 × 20 cm (20⅞ × 12⅝ × 7⅞ in.)

Daniel Emma

—ADELAIDE, AUSTRALIA, FOUNDED 2008—

The work of industrial design firm Daniel Emma introduces simple forms and colorful touches to everyday objects and environments. Partners Daniel To (Australian, b. 1984) and Emma Aiston (Australian, b. 1985) aim for designs that are enjoyable to use—or what they like to call "just nice"—as seen in Squeaky Clean (2015), a set of household cleaning tools elevated to beautiful objects that make chores a bit more pleasurable. Though the designs look minimal, often composed of basic geometric shapes, they are playful to experience. Their Cork Cone and Magnetic Tower pieces for Wrong for Hay (2014) are a block of cork or ash that unexpectedly attracts metal clips and stationery with a hidden magnet. The Australian duo first met while studying industrial design in Adelaide. After graduation, they moved to London, spending almost two years working for various designers. In 2008, they founded their practice and returned to Australia. — JUSTIN ZHUANG

———Tell us how you approach design. How do the two of you work together?

DANIEL TO: Our practice is about our collaboration of ideas. We only work on stuff that we both like. After coming up with the initial idea, we have separate roles. I'm better at a computer than Emma, but she is better at managing things.

EMMA AISTON: A Daniel Emma design is always equal parts Daniel as well as it is Emma. Daniel likes things quite minimal and I like things with lots of color. When it comes together, it's a mixture of colorful, minimal objects.

———I read on your website that you like to create designs that are "just nice." What do you mean by that?

DT: We're not making iPhones or things that would save the world. We're making everyday objects or environments that make you feel a little bit happier when you use them. You feel some value with our objects, rather than them being just another thing.

EA: We like the thought that our products can make people smile and give them a little bit of enjoyment. I guess that is "just nice."

———How does working in Adelaide, Australia, inform your designs?

DT: We were both born and raised here. My parents are from Hong Kong, and Emma's a multigenerational Australian. Our work is more inspired by modern Australian society, where there's a lot of immigrants and different cultures that you get to experience without having to travel. This authentic side of Australia is what inspires us. You couldn't say that our work is inspired by the landscape of Australia, like the red sand.

EA: We moved to London for two years after graduating. At the time, Adelaide didn't have much of a design scene. Coming home with some experience of what's happening in the world motivated us to pursue our practice.

Being in Adelaide allows us to take a step back and not be influenced by everything that's going on. In London, there was a lot of pressure to create unique design and be at the forefront of things. Whereas here, we're still part of that world because we exhibit our work overseas, but not being in the thick of it means we can take a more laid-back approach to working.

DT: A big influence for us is also growing up in Asia. I spent a lot of time in Hong Kong with my family. Emma has an uncle in Japan, too.

EA: The first design we ever came up with was inspired by Daniel's grandparents' apartment in Hong Kong. It is this stationery container that if you flip upside down is their apartment's light fitting. A lot of the colors that we use and how we combine them definitely comes from traveling in Asia.

———Can you talk about the Squeaky Clean set that we are featuring?

EA: Our design process quite often involves redesigning everyday products in some way. We look at objects that most people take for granted, and the challenge is to make them more enjoyable to use and nice to look at.

The Squeaky Clean set was for the Wallpaper* Handmade exhibition in Milan in 2014. We got asked to design a cleaning set by the curators of that show, and we thought about innovative ways of changing the aesthetic for a set of objects. For the [Cooper Hewitt] Triennial, we're doing a progression from the original set. We're not trying to turn them into a Dyson vacuum cleaner, but we like creating small, useful objects that have some nice design qualities.

DT: We're not trying to revolutionize the objects. Sometimes the change is as simple as a material or a color. The object is always very recognizable but with a slight difference.

———Your works play a lot with elemental shapes. Is that how you see the world as well?

EA: Yes and no. We like things to be simple. From my perspective, I'm not particularly good at drawing, so I quite often am breaking things down into those basic shapes and forms to be able to create what I'm thinking.

DT: When we first did a range of desk accessories, we set up some criteria and wanted to have two forms intersecting. Those two forms had to aid the function of the object.

EA: It's very easy just to chuck a triangle on something and make it part of the aesthetic, but for us, we're always incorporating the different forms into the function of the object. The shape of our things is always a result of the function.

———Could you describe what beauty means to you?

DT: It is very similar to the way we described "just nice." An ugly thing can be beautiful, as long as it brings some sort of happiness or enjoyment to what you're doing. Even when you have a bad car, there are all these quirks about it that only you know from driving such a shitty car. It creates a memory for you, and that is the nice thing. It's like music. As much as sometimes I hate pop music, I might associate it with a really nice memory. Therefore, I think it's a nice song.

EA: Beauty in design is very subjective. People can be quite superficial in deeming something beautiful or not. I always try to look for the beauty in ugly stuff.

———What is the most beautiful time of day?

DT: Probably morning. The air is nicer earlier in the morning.

EA: First thing in the morning. We get up very early. I get up at five o'clock every day. Knowing that you're awake before lots of people is a really nice feeling. There's a sense of achievement when you've been up already for four hours when some people are just rolling out of bed, and knowing that you've had a good chunk of the day to be able to do things. We're both very much morning people.

———What is the most beautiful place you've visited?

EA: The beach is five minutes from our house, and it's a beautiful beach. Going there on a nice, wintry day, when there's hardly anyone there. Even in summertime, it's not very busy, but going there when you're the only person on the beach and it's a bit windy, but it's still beautiful; it's nice.

DA: There's a road in Victoria—the state next to us—called the Great Ocean Road. From a nature point of view, it's a really beautiful and amazing place. To us, it's weird, because Australia, in general, is quite dry, but it's so rain foresty.

— INTERVIEW WITH JUSTIN ZHUANG

Daniel Emma for Wrong for Hay; Cork Cone pin holder and Magnetic Tower clip holder, 2013; Natural cork, natural ash; 13 × 9 cm (5⅛ × 3 9/16 in.) and 10 × 6.5 cm (3 15/16 × 2 9/16 in.)

Squeaky Clean set, 2015; Acrylic, nickel, polished aluminum, natural fibers, foam, soap; Dustpan and broom: 11 × 15 × 13 cm (4⁵⁄₁₆ × 5⅞ × 5⅛ in.), cleaning powder: 16 × 4 cm diam. (6⁵⁄₁₆ × 1⁹⁄₁₆ in.), scrubber: 7 × 6 cm diam. (2¾ × 2⅜ in.), sponge: 10 × 6 × 3.5 cm (3¹⁵⁄₁₆ × 2⅜ × 1⅜ in.), soap: 7 × 6 × 2.5 cm (2¾ × 2⅜ × 1 in.)

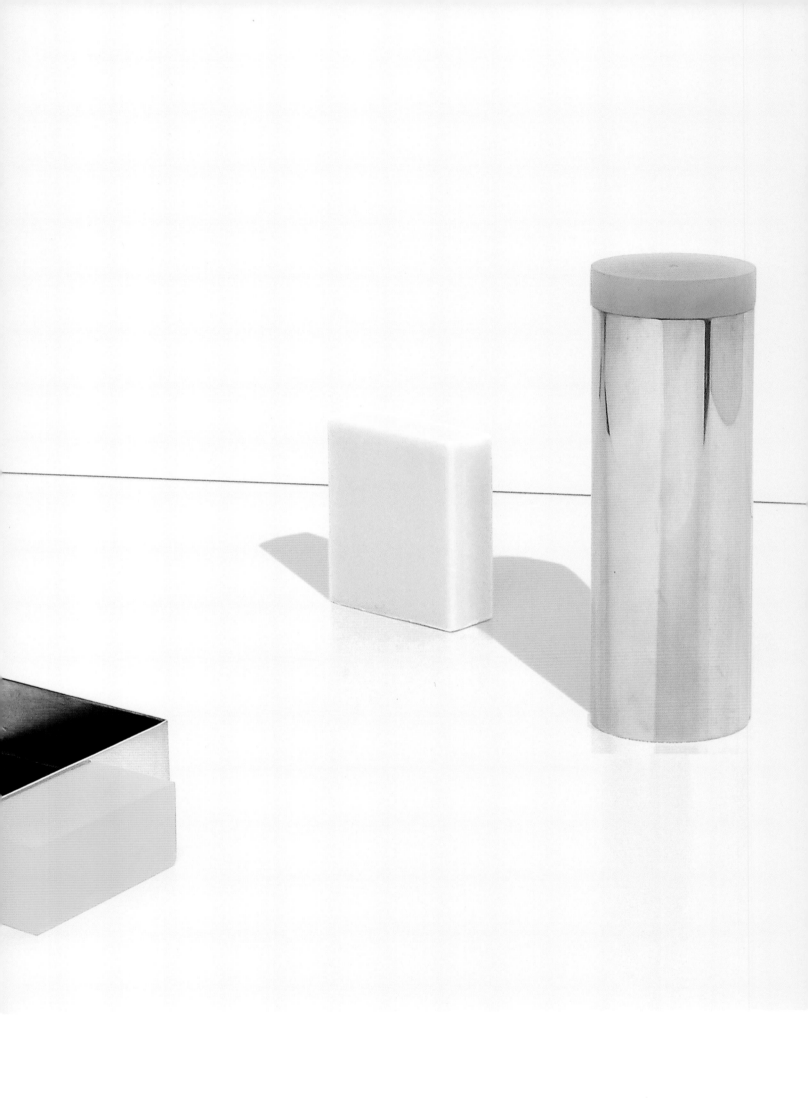

Formafantasma

—AMSTERDAM, NETHERLANDS, FOUNDED 2009—

For Andrea Trimarchi (Italian, b. 1983) and Simone Farresin (Italian, b. 1980), the duo behind Formafantasma, beauty is essentiality, which can be seen in their work. The pair met while studying communication design in Italy, and both obtained their master's degrees from the Design Academy Eindhoven in 2009. Rooted in research, Trimarchi and Farresin distill a concept to its essence, rigorously considering its origin, production, and contemporary narrative. Their analysis results in elegant, evocative objects. Among their most successful projects are those centered on materials studies, such as plastic, leather, charcoal, or glass. In the case of De Natura Fossilium (2014), the studio investigated lava within the subtext of Sicilian culture around Mount Etna, an active volcano that erupted in November 2013. Extreme experimentation rendered lava a viable material for design, both as a liquid blown like glass and as fibers woven for textiles. Basalt, a volcanic stone common to the region, was foundational, used to create tables, seats, and bowls. In wrestling with the landscape, Formafantasma derives expressive and specific forms, respectful of the link between objects and cultural heritage. — ANDREA LIPPS

——Tell me about your practice—the importance of materials, craftsmanship, your anthropological approach, and interest in cultural heritage narrative.

SIMONE FARRESIN: I will start with the element of craft in our work. We often collaborate with craft-based companies, which is important for us because craft is a way of exploring ideas within our own studio. It allows a possibility for experimentation with a very hands-on approach as opposed to industry, which is much more about delivering a very precise idea that is going to be repeated thanks to industrial production. Craft gives you this chance to keep on experimenting and testing ideas very quickly, and that's how we developed the project De Natura Fossilium in the studio. Material investigation is also important to us because I think humans have a very physical relationship with materials. We have the feeling that if we manipulate design on that level, it can be much more radical than just on the formal level. Also, I think there is a very specific ability that material has of communicating with the user.

We are very much interested in design that not only looks at or envisions the future, but also how it relates to the past. Design is often a discipline interested in what is happening next. This is important, of course, because it leads to innovation. But it doesn't mean that innovation and the new shouldn't be linked to what happened before. I think this attitude can lead to much more consciousness in the field.

——Why is this connection to history so close to you?
It is like removing all those connotations about something that we have constructed over time to get back to its essence. If you think back to the conception of a specific technology or material, we can't neglect that our current perception has been constructed over time. So looking back is a way to go to the core of things for us.

——Kind of like peeling back or unfolding layers.
Yes, an unveiling. It's a search for clarity.

——How do you start working on a new series?
The most important part is the beginning, the dialogue between me and Andrea, both verbally and visually. We start to visualize our ideas by collecting existing images as a way to create a common ground between the two of us. Then we write, sometimes, a bit, to define the idea behind the work. Then there is, of course, the research if it is about a new material, or the historical research, and then there is the model making, or the material sampling. The last part is the finalizing with drawings and the final model.

I simplify the process, of course.

——Tell me more about the De Natura Fossilium project.
The project started many years ago. We have been very fascinated that southern regions of Italy are very much not industrialized. They are seen as a place for tourists. We were interested in working with the local producers and local materials. We were drawn to Mount Etna specifically, connecting it to production because the volcano is still active. It is like nature that is excavating itself, providing materials for producing things. And then we started wondering what we could do with this material. This was the most experimental part, working with the lava.

Working with some samples of lava we collected at the volcano, we realized we had quite a quick cooling time. At the beginning, we were thinking we would have resulted with sort of liquid stone, but the lava contains high levels of silica, the main ingredient in glass, and with this quick cooling down, the material turns into a sort of glass. This was a difficult investigation because glass is nowadays a very industrialized product. There are only a few companies that are refining glass. So what we did is almost redoing glass from scratch.

The reason we have the obsidian mirror in the collection is linked to the glass pieces—obsidian is a kind of naturally occurring glass. In our process with the glass pieces, we were basically trying to repeat what is already done in nature with obsidian. The glass pieces are our own engineering of nature. And in each of these glass pieces—and in the mirror—there is always a piece of raw material or rock in it, tying it back to the raw material.

——What comes to mind when you hear the word "beauty"? How is it related with your practice?
We never start out thinking about beauty. We seek to construct a narrative. But if the element of beauty arises, perhaps it is a very intuitive presence. For instance, with De Natura Fossilium, we had never used such geometric forms as the ones we used in the work. The form language can vary intuitively based on the work. We later realized we chose those forms because the whole work was about controlling nature, was all about shaping it, forcing it to become a material, to become a form, to become an object. So the language we used was a very dramatic and controlled form, almost brutalist. There was this certain tension in the work, again that idea as if you are peeling off layers and getting to the core of something. So when we work with a material, we try to understand the language of that material, its essence. And by searching for that, beauty arises.

——What is the most beautiful time of day?
We both agree it is breakfast. We very much love cooking and spending time at a table because it's a moment that you share with others.

——What is the most beautiful place you've visited?
We recently spent some time in a traditional *ryokan* in Japan, which is a traditional Japanese house, which was absolutely wonderful, and we loved to wake up in the morning. And then there were the paper windows, and light was coming through, and then the shadows of plants were on the windows. We thought that was one of the most beautiful ways of waking up ever.

— INTERVIEW WITH SUVI SALONIEMI

Mount Etna is an active volcano in Sicily
that erupted in 2013. The landscape is littered
with lava rock.

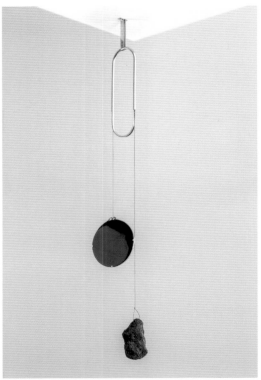

De Natura Fossilium collection, 2014; Courtesy of Gallery Libby Sellers

CLOCKWISE: Alicudi vase; Mouth-blown lava, lava rock, Murano glass, textile; 35 × 35 × 25 cm (13¾ × 13¾ × 9¹³⁄₁₆ in.)

Iddu mirror; Obsidian mirror, lava rock, brass; 150 × 40 cm (59¹⁄₁₆ × 15¾ in.)

Lipari bowl (detail); Occhio di pernice basalt, lava rocks, brass, textile; 35 × 35 cm (13¾ × 13¾ in.)

1991 stool and 1614 stool; Basalt, brass, textile; Both: 60 × 30 × 30 cm (23⅝ × 11¹³⁄₁₆ × 11¹³⁄₁₆ in.)

OPPOSITE: Athena textile; Basalt fiber, cotton; 90 × 120 cm (6 ft. 2¹³⁄₁₆ in. × 47¼ in.)

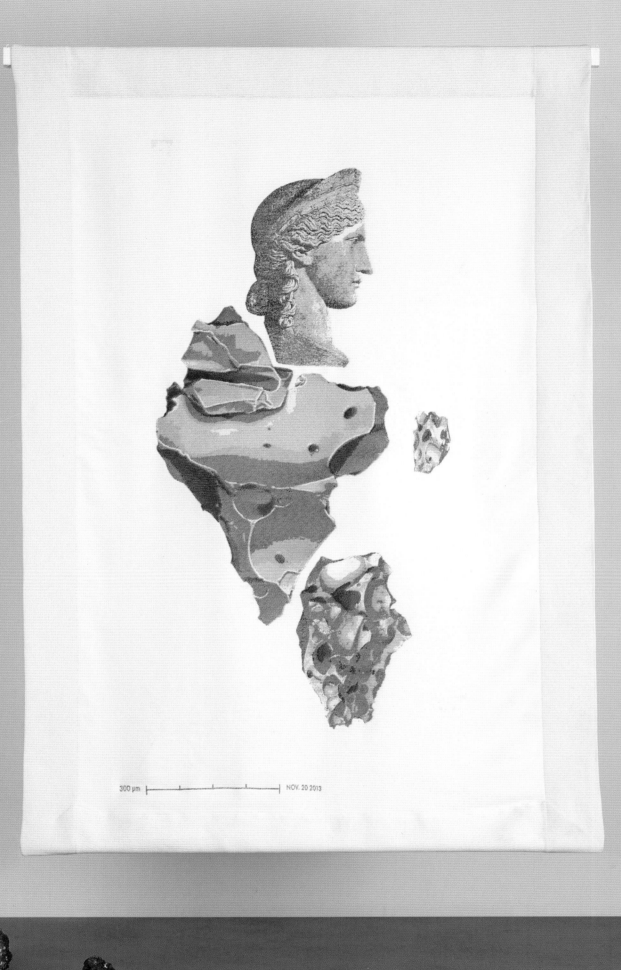

300 μm |⸻|⸻|⸻|⸻| NOV. 20 2013

Emiliano Godoy

—MEXICAN, B. 1974—

Emiliano Godoy employs ethical constraints and an analytical design process to stimulate creativity and invention. His reverence for people and the environment is illuminated in every detail of his products and furniture pieces. Godoy was born in Mexico City after his parents and siblings emigrated from Argentina in the 1970s, fleeing that country's dictatorship. He studied industrial design at Ibero-American University in Mexico City and completed his master's degree at Pratt Institute in New York City in 2004. Committed to a socially and environmentally sustainable practice, Godoy's office in Mexico City designs products for a range of local manufacturers, including Nouvel Studio, Arta Ceramica, and Pirwi (a company Godoy helped found). HIs office also works with international companies such as Ecoist, Masisa, and Krv Kurva. By seeking out sustainable materials and developing processes that rely on skilled labor and local materials, Godoy creates visually rich, surprising outcomes that are informed and enhanced by solid values. — ELLEN LUPTON

————What were the major turning points in your career?

I started studying industrial design here in Mexico City in 1992, which was the year of the Earth Summit [United Nations Conference on Environment and Development] in Rio de Janeiro. I ended my studies in 1997, the year when the Kyoto Protocol was signed. I completed my master's in 2002, the year of the [Earth Summit] in South Africa. Throughout my career, I've been seeing how the academy and industry haven't really tackled the environmental issues discussed in other spheres of industry and commerce from a design point of view. From the start, I wanted to use viable industrial processes and make products that were not just one-off, artistic pieces. I opened my own design office even before I graduated, and from that moment on, I've always worked in offices or workshops or companies that I started.

————Tell me about your methods and how you work.

I start by analyzing which spheres of life are affected by a design project—the environment, the economy, society, culture, symbolism, politics, functionality, and technology. For example, in the environment, a project should strive to be environmentally regenerative. In society, the project should strive for equality. And in politics, a project should be active. If the project involves suppliers or raw materials that come from a country that has some political issue that I oppose, I shouldn't use it in the project.

————Explain how this relates to your glass Pablo bowls.

I designed the bowls for Nouvel Studio in Mexico City. They do glass-blown pieces, and they're part of a larger glass manufacturing company. When you make any glass piece, the biggest impact in terms of energy use is melting the glass. For melting the glass, the company uses the cleanest available fuel source in Mexico, which is natural gas, and they keep the process as clean as possible. How could I reduce the energy use even further? When I did a life cycle assessment of the glass manufacturing process, I realized that mold manufacturing consumes a lot of energy. Most molds are made out of steel, so I looked for other materials that could withstand high temperatures while needing less energy to manufacture. I ended up using molds made out of volcanic stone from Mexico City, so there was no transportation related to that. I needed to make sure that the people working in the stone quarries were working in good conditions and that those suppliers were meeting a high social standard.

————What comes to mind when you hear the word "beauty"?

For me, beauty usually boils down to proportions. In a few projects, I started to notice that everything was correct except for a couple of measurements. Keeping proportions in harmony with each other creates beauty. On the other side of the question, there is symbolism and meaning. For example, let's say you're doing an embassy for a country, and you make the building out of reinforced steel with no windows and a single door guarded by two military guys. Maybe the proportions are beautiful. Maybe the quality's perfect, and maybe the building in itself is beautiful if you saw it as an object, but the meaning is wrong. The meaning of that embassy is about fear and not about diplomacy.

————What is the most beautiful time of day?

I have a two-year-old son, and he rises up like the sun, and it's amazing. He's the definition of what an American would call a morning person. He wakes up, and he's ready to play and to smile and be happy, so morning is the most beautiful time of the day for me.

————What is the most beautiful place you've visited?

The Rothko Chapel in Houston is basically an octagon with paintings inside and a place to sit. It's a nondenominational chapel. You maybe won't say that it's beautiful, but the feeling that I got from it has stayed with me for quite a long time. It's very dark. It's not necessarily a sophisticated or sensual space, but the feeling you get inside of it is amazing.

— INTERVIEW WITH SUVI SALONIEMI

Production of a Pizzelle vase using a tool that resembles a waffle maker, 2014.

Emiliano Godoy; Manufactured by Nouvel Studio; Pedro and Pablo bowls, 2012; Blown glass; Pedro bowl: 10.2 × 36 cm (4 × 14⅛ in.), Pablo bowl: 8 × 27.5 cm diam. (3⅛ × 10⅞ in.)

Emiliano Godoy; Manufactured by Nouvel
Studio; Vases, from Pizzelle series, 2014;
Blown glass; Sizes vary, up to 42 × 22 × 8 cm
(16 ⁹⁄₁₆ × 8 ¹³⁄₁₆ × 3 ⅛ in.)

Industrial Facility

—LONDON, ENGLAND, UNITED KINGDOM, FOUNDED 2002—

Sam Hecht (British, b. 1969) and Kim Colin (American, b. 1961), cofounders of Industrial Facility, lend a clarified vision to the industrial design field. Having studied industrial design and architecture, respectively, the pair critically engages the cultural, spatial, and performative context of each object, optimizing form to function. The result is simple, intuitive objects that last. Formwork (2014–ongoing) for Herman Miller is a collection of modular desk accessories that began with an anthropological study of what people keep on their work surfaces. The forms were designed around not just pens, scissors, and paper clips, but also hard drives, power cords, and eating utensils. Cantilevers keep small objects visible and accessible. Containers stack to maximize a small footprint and become topographical when paired. The Semplice light (2013–ongoing) for Oluce dematerializes the archetypical table lamp by eliminating the lamp base and stem in favor of an inverted glass cone. — ANDREA LIPPS

———Tell me about the origins of Industrial Facility.

KIM COLIN: Sam and I met coincidentally, and we started a conversation from our different disciplines. My discipline is architecture, and his is industrial design. We were both interested in the other's discipline. Sam was always aware that industrial design is a young subject and is not as rooted in thinking and writing as the tradition of architecture, which we speculated was because architecture is conjectural. In other words, a lot of projects don't get built, but they still influence culture because they're written about; they enter into the discourse and are digested over long periods of time.

Yet because the timeline of industrial design is so productive—especially in mass production—and an enormous contributor to popular culture, it remains odd that there is so little critical writing about it. Sure, there are some practitioners who have written about it, but, generally, the discipline isn't considered thoughtful. It is a commercial discipline. It serves industry and isn't described in terms of cultural contribution. We, of course, have a different point of view. When we receive a brief, we look outside it to understand the bigger context rather than just responding with things. That's what architecture brings to the perspective—when you create architecture, you design not only the building on the site, but in the city, considering the landscape, the community. In other words, you're always looking outside of the thing.

———How do you arrive at form, and what value does it have for your practice?

KC: What value does form itself have? Well, if we didn't have form, we wouldn't have the thing. [Laughs] We're not formalists, if that makes any sense. We're not obsessed with the form. We're not obsessed with a certain radius, a certain color, anything like that. I think the function grows ahead of the project, and what we see are the elements that are important about the project.

For instance, sometimes the client will come with a brief. They see the world in a certain way, and their research has driven them to that point or justified that point. And then they come to us, and we have a different point of view. We're outsiders to that information. We learn that information, but we also have our own experience in many other fields. And I think our eyes to the world are much broader in a way.

———Tell me about the importance of function in your practice.

KC: We spent our first several years trying to take functions out of products, removing as many things that seemed extraneous to the actual use and enjoyment of the products. Often, R&D departments try to squeeze in a new function thinking it is what persuades us as consumers, that the object does more than the competition's. But that's a bit of a trap. Once you get past the point of purchase and you take it into your home and live with it, you don't care about the twenty functions that you're never going to use. It's not an asset; it's a waste that you went that far. So, why shouldn't we be using things that are easy to use, a pleasure to use, not a burden to use, that don't demand a lot of our attention.

———What comes to mind when you hear the word "beauty"?

KC/SAM HECHT: It is difficult to locate just where beauty resides in the product: is it in its making, its use, its form, the personal memory it may signify, or its cultural relevance? Or is beauty found in the equilibrium of all of these things?

We are supporters of the idea that things that are man-made should remain incomplete to demonstrate the impermanence of all objects. This is interesting but very difficult to apply technically to mass-produced goods, when industrial design relies upon consistency and repetition by its own nature. But there remains some value in awareness that beauty remains open in at least its thought rather than necessarily in aesthetic execution. In some ways, to stop design before the temptation to idealize its presence—that is when beauty resides in the object. This requires enormous courage on not only the designer's part, but particularly the company's.

For us, beauty remains a difficult and abstract concept, not necessarily an ideal or related to truth or perfection, but nevertheless an untouchable quality, bigger than any object. Beauty is therefore, by nature, immaterial. We can locate it when we find a product that is almost impossibly between time and space: it functions very well within our concrete, material world and is also somehow transcendent in the relationship it forms to its context. This context adds something that the object alone can never completely hold; the relationship between the thing and its space is everything.

———What is the most beautiful time of day?

KC: Sunrise or sunset. Both equally because the light is so incredible at those times of day, and you see the change happening quickly.

———What is the most beautiful place you've visited?

SH: It's probably the desert. I try to visit the desert at least once a year. This is an immense luxury, but where some people buy expensive clothes, I prefer a trip to the desert. This year I visited the desert of Anza Borrego [California], and it was extremely beautiful.

— INTERVIEW WITH JUSTIN ZHUANG

Industrial Facility, for Oluce; Semplice lamp, 2013; Blown glass and metal; 44 × 31 cm (17 5/16 × 12 3/16 in.)

OVERLEAF: Industrial Facility, for Herman Miller; Formwork series, 2014; ABS plastic with non-slip silicone base; Sizes vary, up to 5.7 × 24.8 × 30.5 cm (2¼ × 9¾ × 12 in.)

Daniel Rybakken for Luceplan; Ascent lamps, 2013; Extruded aluminum in anodized black; 64 × 10 cm diam. (25³⁄₁₆ × 3¹⁵⁄₁₆ in.)

Daniel Rybakken
—NORWEGIAN, B. 1984—

Daniel Rybakken seeks connections between man-made and natural beauty. Raised in Oslo, Norway, Rybakken studied industrial design at the Oslo School of Architecture and Design, and completed his master of fine arts at the University of Gothenburg School of Design and Crafts in Sweden. Rybakken's career began with his Daylight series (2008–2010), which simulates the experience of natural sunlight by projecting bright shapes onto walls or bringing light into a room sideways as though from behind a curtain. The series offers an alternative to standard over-head incandescent lighting solutions. His Counterbalance (2012) and Ascent (2013) pieces for lighting design company Luceplan are crafted around intuitive gestures; their simplicity belies the fixtures' internal complexity of design and engineering. Employing dynamics and movement, Ascent allows the user to control the intensity of light with a simple up-and-down motion. Although he gained his initial success as a lighting designer, Rybakken is also exploring furniture design and public art. He is currently based in Gothenburg and Oslo. — LAUREN SCIARAPPA + ELLEN LUPTON

————Tell me about your practice.

I spend time sitting and thinking, and then my first model is very similar to my end result. When I start sketching an idea, I start imagining how it would be photographed and communicated. It's like I'm sketching a photo of the piece. I did a piece in Paris that was hung on the wall of a building, with two sheets leaning against the facade. I drew that as a photo.

————You have had great success with lighting. Where is your work heading now?

My whole career began with my Daylight pieces. By starting with lamps that criticized existing lamps, I got assignments from companies like Luceplan to design more traditional lamps. Now, people want me to

design lamps quite similar to what I do with Luceplan. They can't imagine me doing anything else. I'm doing my first chair, a stackable chair for a Danish company. This project was self-initiated, because nobody asked me to design furniture, so I took that step on my own.

————What is the place of conceptual ideas and philosophy in your work?

Ideally, I would like to do conceptual pieces that are put into production. Even now, after I've won so many awards with lighting, my Daylight pieces have not been put into production, because they are called art or conceptual design. A lot of designers are afraid of calling what they do "art." Yet there's

more money in art. It's more commercial, in a way. The pieces that I've done that were classified as art installations—like the Daylight Entrance (2008–2010)—have been more professional, with better terms and more money for me as a creator. If I did the same piece as a designer, they would probably say, "It will look nice in your portfolio. You could do it for free."

————Would you like to do more large-scale public art projects?

Absolutely. I think I can manage to do that and create objects for serial production at the same time. They can inspire each other in both directions. Some people classify art as objects without function. If it has function, then it's craft or design. Of course art has a function. And design has a function, too, but that doesn't necessarily mean, "Oh, this is something ergonomic," or "I can hang my jacket on it." Design can be connected to the senses and emotions, the way a lot of art is.

————What comes to mind when you hear the word "beauty"?

I use the word "aesthetics" instead. Maybe "beauty" feels superficial, as if it's only about the outer shape. Beauty can be something honest as well. It doesn't need to be Botox or a silicone outer layer. It can be about the natural beauty that lies in materials, and honesty around how things are made. Design is communication. It's a language that can be spoken in different ways. Raymond Loewy designed a pencil sharpener that was aero-dynamic, and that was criticized, because why does a pencil sharpener need to be like that? It's not flying. It's standing still on the table. But then you add styling, and styling is regarded as a bad word within design. We need to separate beauty from styling.

————What is the most beautiful time of day?

I feel the most creative in the morning. You have your whole day in front of you, and you can shape it any way you like. If you get up really early, there's a special atmosphere. People are waking up, going to work. A city comes to life.

————What is the most beautiful place you've visited?

What I find beautiful are areas with a lot of sky. A town is always filled with skyline, with different buildings all around you. When you get out into open areas, you see a lot of sky. My girlfriend has a cabin in Lysekil, on the west coast of Sweden. There is one area where we can walk out along the coastline and see almost one hundread and eighty degrees of sky and water, so you feel that you're inside an enormous dome. That is a different kind of beauty than the man-made beauty of amazing buildings in Paris or New York.

— INTERVIEW WITH SUVI SALONIEMI

Raising or lowering the lamp head adjusts its brightness.

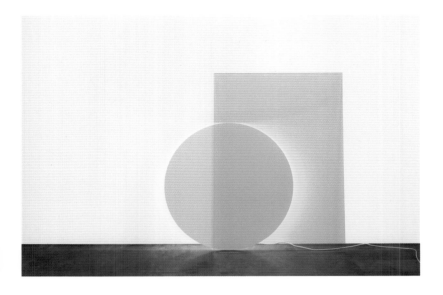

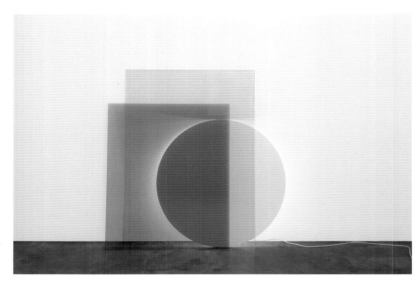

Daniel Rybakken and Andreas Engesvik for e15;
LT04 COLOUR floor light, 2014; Solid-colored
pink laminated glass, signal white powder-
coated steel; Sizes vary, up to 105 × 75 × 1.3 cm
(41^{15}⁄₁₆ × 29½ × ½ in.)

SO-IL

—BROOKLYN, NEW YORK, USA, FOUNDED 2008—

At the core of every SO-IL project is an attempt to invigorate the rich experience of space. Founded by Florian Idenburg (Dutch, b. 1975) and Jing Liu (Chinese, b. 1980), who were later joined by partner Ilias Papageorgiou (Greek, b. 1980), SO-IL works at a range of scales—building, interior, and installation—designing architecture that heightens awareness of place and its surroundings through a considered use of material and immaterial elements. This pared-down yet direct approach is evidenced in simple, clarified designs that host dynamic experiences. For the Greek Pavilion at the Venice Biennale (2014), SO-IL proposed covering a rocky valley on an Aegean island with a veil that refracts light, mitigates heat, and transforms wind into a soundscape. It is a singular gesture to create space enabling a kaleidoscopic sensory experience of landscape. SO-IL's design for Amant—a private arts gallery (expected 2017) to be built in Brooklyn, New York— presents large, fluid concrete shells draped over gallery spaces. In the firm's hands, the concrete forms are rendered an expressive suppleness and carry light delicately into the interior. — JUSTIN ZHUANG

————I've read that Florian was a drummer and Jing wanted to be a writer. How do those impulses translate into your design practice?

FLORIAN IDENBURG: There are obvious and well-explored relationships between music and architecture—composition, structure, layering. I have never thought much about the parallels in my case, but since you ask, I can see a few aspects carrying through. One to highlight could be that the musical experiments I engaged in with a group of friends was about finding a certain hybridity between the digital and the analog. We mostly performed live, merging electronic music (samplers, drum computers) with instruments played by humans, blurring their oppositions.

JING LIU: There are even more obvious relation-ships between literature and architecture. However, over the years since I have chosen the path of architecture, it has revealed to me the unique properties it possesses. Architecture is unmistakably visual, physical, visceral, and more democratic to a certain extent. I have come to realize the incredible power embedded in these aspects.

————Your projects vary in scale and form. What unifies them?

SO-IL: At the core of every project lies an idea that through the employment of material or immaterial elements we create a heightened awareness of one's relationship with a place and/or with others. Architectural form is the medium in this process, a device that dis-sects, reconstructs, and eventually amplifies the physical and sensorial qualities of our surroundings. This augmented experience creates a distance between user and space and, we believe, triggers a more critical reading of the world around us.

————Talk me through your design process. What role does each of you play?

SO-IL: As a generalization, one can say that Florian is the uninhibited, restless producer of both very bad and very good ideas. Jing is more critical and reflective, but at the same time makes bolder and enduring moves. Since 2013, SO-IL has a third partner, Ilias Papageorgiou, who is adept at seeing through ideas and poignant in establishing conceptual and aesthetic integrity. Through a continuous dialogue, ideas gain precision.

————You've talked about the importance of experience, materiality, and light in your designs. Could you elaborate on this?

SO-IL: In a bland way, one can say that all an architect does is put "stuff into the world." Undeniably, there is a lot of stuff already here, and lots of it lacks any sense of purpose beyond a short-term, economical one. We believe the world is wondrous and humans have the ability to enjoy space as much as one can enjoy food or music. We believe the "junkspace" around us has inhibited our ability to fully experience the richness of our environment. With our projects, we are trying to reinvigorate this spatial sensibility that is latent in all of us.

————There is an elemental simplicity in your designs—the muted palette and visible structures. Can you talk about this aspect of your work?

SO-IL: We try to get to the core of an over-arching idea by reducing all elements that are just distractions and superfluous. We use the elements we have to work with to strengthen that single idea, rather than adding (to) a cacophony of well-intended sub-solutions. Often this approach leads to seemingly simple forms and structures; however, the physical sensorial experience is dynamic, layered, and complex.

————What is the role of beauty in your work?

SO-IL: Beauty, as present in the discussions in our studio, has an ungraspable quality. Beauty lingers in the peculiar territory between the familiar and the sublime, the comfortable and the fearful. On this scale, we often linger around the darker side of it, tiptoeing to glimpse the barely discernable figure in the darkness. Beauty is a form of intelligence, a way to perceive, understand, and imagine the world around. And so it is a vehicle to augment the relationship with the world around us.

————What comes to mind when you hear the word "beauty"?

SO-IL: Beauty is the attribute that weakens our protective layers so we can acknowledge our humanity and fragility. Beauty is for the courageous ones.

————What is the most beautiful time of day?

FI: Very early morning.

JL: The most beautiful moments of the day can come to you at any given time. It's the air; it's the noise; it's the color; it's the inner voices.

ILIAS PAPAGEORGIOU: I like the evenings. It's a time of reflection, the in-between state of the day that is ending and the one that is about to start.

————What is the most beautiful place you've visited?

SO-IL: The natural world has left many lasting impressions, but as architects, we'd like to call out a built place—the Salk Institute [La Jolla, California], by Kahn. It frames the natural with stuff, does very much what we aspire to, creating a heightened awareness of our physical being on this unique planet.

— INTERVIEW WITH JUSTIN ZHUANG

SO-IL with project team Ted Baab, Seunghyun Kang, Andre Herrero, and Kevin Lamyuktseung; Context rendering, Veiled, Aegean Sea, Greece, concept design, 2014

SO-IL with project team Ted Baab, Seunghyun Kang, Andre Herrero, and Kevin Lamyuktseung; Model, Veiled, Aegean Sea, Greece, concept design, 2014; Plaster, metal; 12.7 × 48.3 × 109.2 cm (5 × 19 × 43 in.)

SO-IL with project team Kevin Lamyuktseung, Ted Daab, Kerim Miskavi, Max Hart Nibbrig, Lucie Rebeyrol, and Pietro Pagliaro; Renderings of sculpture gallery and interior view toward terrace, Amant private arts gallery, New York, USA, expected 2017

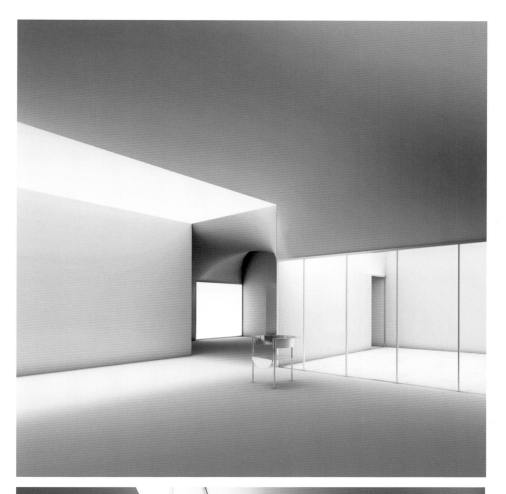

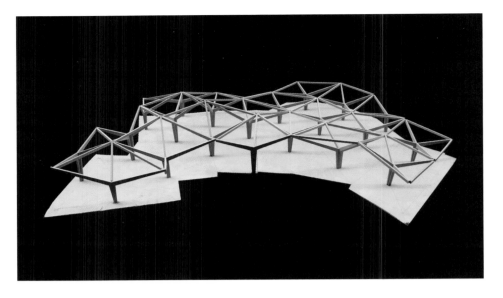

Trace Architecture Office (TAO)

—BEIJING, CHINA, FOUNDED 2009—

Contrary to contemporary architecture that tends to be globalized in production and obsessed with spectacular form, TAO's work responds to the specific conditions of a site. For the firm's founder, Hua Li (Chinese, b. 1972), architecture should be inseparable from its environment. Li studied at Tsinghua University in Beijing before moving to the United States to pursue his master's at Yale. After practicing in New York, Li returned to China to run Universal Architecture Studio, working on mega-projects such as large sports facilities and mixed-used complexes. In 2009, he started TAO, a practice to return to smaller works. His brand of architecture—creating a structure deeply rooted in its context—is evidenced by Tree Clubhouse (completed 2015) in Grand Canal Forest Park, Beijing. The structure is inspired by the forest. Cantilevered beams are suggestive of branches; the supports are evocative of trunks. The building is primarily constructed with natural materials, including wood and rammed earth from the surroundings. This is the beauty of Li's works, which are sensitive to the landscape and light of the environment—a trace of architecture indeed. — JUSTIN ZHUANG

————Tell us about TAO's approach to architecture.

I start from thinking about the nature of human activities in architecture and the nature of place. This becomes the beginning point that I call "origin." From this origin, my feeling about the atmosphere of a place starts to evolve, vaguely giving me hints, clues, and then memories and imaginations, through hand sketches, gradually turn into forms. It's always a mutual action between feeling and thinking. The site, program, climate, technique, all these conditions that I call "gravity," will be confronted during the design process. It is gravity that makes my design specific and concrete.

————Can you talk us through Tree Clubhouse? Why turn to a tree as the key element of your design?

The site is in a park full of trees by the Grand Canal River on the east side of Beijing. The client didn't give a clearly defined program,

which meant the space must be flexible for different functions (restaurant, bars, event space, gallery, office, etc.). When a program doesn't give much to me, I look at the site to capture the sense of place. The river and the trees were the strongest character of the site, so I thought to create a place where people can sit under the tree and enjoy the view of the river—just like what everyone does in a park, even without architecture. This became the beginning point. We developed a structural unit looking like a tree, organized it in a grid, and we got the form! When you start with something simple, you can capture the most desired and powerful thing. Later on, the structure, material, landscape, mechanical system, drainage, all these elements are conceived and developed following the original intention.

————I read that you've learned "to live a simple life." How does this impact your practice and view of architecture?

Somebody once said, "Complexity is a seduction." I think to embrace simplicity is an attitude. It creates more chances to get closer to the nature of things, rather than being entertained by all kinds of illusions.

————You've also said that form for TAO is not about abstraction or representation but about "meaning recorded in the process of making things." Could you elaborate on this?

I believe architecture is not just an autonomous form created by an architect, but is also an organism evolving all the time through its own history. So if you only look at form as "form," you are an artist. But as an architect, one needs to look at more. To understand the making and evolutionary process of a building will make the form more profound and meaningful.

————You prefer working in locations that are untouched by globalization. What are the challenges in practicing architecture in such contexts?

I call these "strong sites." Their unique character and specific conditions stimulate and inspire me. The challenge is how to work with local builders and find the appropriate technique to build. I always try to maximize the usage of local resources. I believe a building is like a plant: it must grow well in the right soil. Of course, in a globalized age, you can build anything, just like you can relocate plants into any context. But it's not sustainable. There is extra cost to achieve that and maintain it. By doing so, you consume lots of energy and produce lots of waste. It's part of the economy, but it's not part of the ecology.

————What comes to mind when you hear the word "beauty"?

Harmony, silence—beauty exists beyond words.

————What is the most beautiful time of day?

It depends on my mood. A slice of sunlight in early morning, the quietness of late afternoon, the stone path lit by the midnight moonlight—these moments can all be beautiful to me.

————What is the most beautiful place you've visited?

There are two small towns: Mechernich in Germany and Gubbio in Italy. I visited them both by coincidence, and I was fascinated by their mysterious and labyrinthine spaces. The anonymity of place exiles me into an unknown world, and that, to me, is very beautiful.

— INTERVIEW WITH JUSTIN ZHUANG

Structural model of Tree Clubhouse, 2013

OPPOSITE: Architect Hua Li surveys the construction of Tree Clubhouse, Grand Canal Forest Park, Beijing.

OVERLEAF: Tree Clubhouse exterior, 2015

Yeongkyu Yoo

—KOREAN, ACTIVE IN USA AND SOUTH KOREA, B. 1971—

Yeongkyu Yoo designs pure, clarified objects. He omits superfluous decoration to intuitively emphasize an object's function, resulting in elegant forms suggestive of the work of Kenya Hara. After having worked for companies including Nike, iriver, and Samsung, Yoo established cloudandco in 2010 as a design firm to deliver his simple, pared-down aesthetic to a commercial market. The Bottle Humidifier (2012) for 11+ is a considered design, intended to seamlessly integrate into an environment—whether on or off—with its clean, minimal form and white matte finish. The humidifier's USB power cable, typically a secondary design element, becomes the object's only decorative expression, in orange. The World Clock (2014) can display the time in twenty-four different cities by simply rolling the clock. The clock hands adjust accordingly. Type 01, an aluminum speaker currently in development, will feature a minimal form with leather carrying strap. Yoo also provides creative direction for industrial design as part of the Microsoft New Devices team. In this role, Yoo helps oversee the headset, packaging, and accessory design of Microsoft's HoloLens (expected soon), illustrating his expertise in clarifying complex technology with simple, user-centered design. — ANDREA LIPPS

————What were the early inspirations that led you to design?

I was born on Jeju Island, South Korea. As a little boy, I grew up playing on the beach all day, enjoying the beauty of the ocean and nature. I appreciated the beauty of everything so much and loved drawing, and it took me to studying design at the university. I soon realized that design can make people happy and create better lives. The process of designing made me happy, and I still enjoy it. My life and my work are inseparable in a good way, and I feel lucky.

————What is the ideology behind your practice?

I believe that good design is timeless. Design is the result of a long process of deep consideration. This includes not only an aesthetic view that satisfies people, but also social responsibility since we face more environmental problems from the outpouring of new products every day. I do not add decorative elements that are not necessary to an object's primary function. An object has to be simple and pure to convey a message. I try to keep my design as pure as possible, eliminating unnecessary elements and thinking about how to successfully deliver the beauty of simplicity to a commercial market.

————Tell me about your process and working methods.

A general design process when working with a corporation is a long consultation from research, concept development, rendering to manufacturing. Going through this process makes the design concept very different from the original thinking, which can be frustrating. While this is one part of my work, I maintain more creative freedom with my self-initiated design work. I initiate a project and design that is ready to be manufactured as first intended, and then I look for a suitable client to propose. These kinds of projects keep me motivated as a designer.

————Your work is closely related to technology and engineering. What is the relationship of your design work to these fields?

Sometimes people think good design and new technology belong in very different worlds, but for me this is where new opportunities lie. Design can be pure and minimal in the technology world. When designing something like an invention, I think about how to visualize the form of complicated technology, introducing it to users in a friendly way so that they can enjoy it and use it intuitively without feeling overwhelmed by the technology.

————What was the inspiration for many of your products?

Most of my designs for everyday products, such as the Bottle Humidifier, start from observations about objects I'd like in my everyday life. My ideation doesn't require a specific time or place, so I keep my pen and idea book for rough sketches nearby all the time.

The idea of the Bottle Humidifier sprung from the realization that there wasn't any humidifier with a minimal and simple form that would fit my life. This motivated me to design the humidifier and to look for a partner for its manufacture. I believe there is market opportunity for people who love timeless design.

————What comes to mind when you hear the word "beauty"?

Beauty is pleasure and the motivation to design things.

————What is the most beautiful time of day?

When I am focused on sketches listening to music.

————What is the most beautiful place you've visited?

Yongnuni Oreum on Jeju Island, which is a volcanic cone in my hometown. This is a beautiful small hill, and its smooth line from flatland to the hill naturally meets the sky, which gives another charm.

— INTERVIEW WITH SUVI SALONIEMI

Sketches for Bottle Humidifier, 2012, by Yeongkyu Yoo and cloudandco, 2012

Yeongkyu Yoo and cloudandco; Manufactured
by 11+; Bottle Humidifier, 2012; ABS Plastic,
polycarbonate; 20 × 8.7 cm (7⅞ × 3⁷⁄₁₆ in.)

Yeongkyu Yoo and cloudandco; Manufactured
by 11+; World Clock, 2014; ABS Plastic,
polycarbonate; 5.9 × 8.5 cm (2⁵⁄₁₆ × 3⅜ in.)

Yeongkyu Yoo and cloudandco; Manufactured
by 11+; World Clock, 2014; ABS Plastic,
polycarbonate; 5.9 × 8.5 cm (2⁵⁄₁₆ × 3⅜ in.)

Jean Yu

—KOREAN, ACTIVE IN USA, B. 1970—

Jean Yu's work—critically acclaimed for over a decade—operates outside the temporal rhythms of fashion. Born in South Korea, Yu moved to New York from Los Angeles to study at the Fashion Institute of Technology in 1990. She became best known for her soft yet architectural underclothes, which magically embrace femininity while eschewing traditional female tropes of lace and padding. She is meticulous in her craft and committed to every cut, as evidenced in the Overflow bodice (2015) created for the Design Triennial. The garment reveals its construction: the bodice is configured from a single piece of silk that meets the lower piece at the waist. The sculptural form exposes a rolled edge, key darts, and only the slightest bit of lightweight, white boning. Achieving a sophisticated simplicity through strategic layering of transparent fabrics and dramatic cutting techniques, Yu emphasizes that one should feel nothing when wearing her work. — ANDREA LIPPS + SARAH SCATURRO

———Tell me about your background. What led you to fashion design?

I believe it was the language barrier that led me to the visual medium. We migrated to the States from Korea just after I turned seven. My parents found a house in the suburbs of Southern California almost immediately. It was an enormous adjustment. I found that there was no place for my Korean words, and I learned to rely on my eyes to understand the new world. Fine art and fashion were natural draws and provided the opportunity to offset the language handicap. Whereas my interaction with fine art was confined to classrooms, fashion had an immediate and continuous application. Every day, we dress. From this daily routine, I learned to see clothing as a communication tool. Dress gave insight into social order and cultural context.

———Tell me about your shop 37=1.

Building the shop turned out to be a great learning experience. In working with my architects, David Khouri and Roberto Guzman, I discovered a subculture of shared values. Architecture seeks full integration of idea and construction throughout the design process. What thrills me is technical prowess in execution. The "how" is everything. My commitment to quality control encompassed not only manufacturing in NYC, but also installing it in-house. I also decided to put retail, wholesale, and public relations under a single roof to develop a cohesive brand message and experience.

The shop was a jewel box tucked away from the thoroughfare in SoHo. The ceiling and wall surfaces were clad in high-gloss, white acrylic panels that were smooth to the touch. Whenever possible, the glass doors located at the front and back of the lengthwise walls were open to allow cross ventilation. The delicate pieces hanging from an invisible wire became a free-floating choreography of retail merchandise. The physical layout led the client toward the dressing room in direct proximity to a hidden rack, where dress and lingerie pieces were offered ready-to-wear and made-to-measure.

———Tell me about the lingerie you design. How did it begin?

Lingerie was born of a compulsion for all things to be beautiful inside and out. It was a standard and an approach that became a category. In ready-to-wear, the industry demands newness as the jumping-off point. Fashion design is about planned obsolescence in aesthetics; whereas, architecture and industrial design are about aesthetic durability. My clients are of the former, but my personal values belong to the latter. This made for a conflict and an opportunity.

———Talk about your aesthetic approach.

I'm innately drawn to dynamic tension in all media. Perhaps it's working through the polarity within: negotiating the space between establishment and antiestablishment, East versus West. The design signature developed from slow and quiet study. Looking at it again and again. What's there, what's not there. It is an intimate process and result.

———What comes to mind when you hear the word "beauty"?

When I see something beautiful, it's arresting. It hurts. Yet beauty can be a moving target. How it is defined is specific to time and place. Then, there is universal beauty, the kind that awakens us from ourselves. It has a transporting quality. I feel light and buoyant and can move past the "container" to feel connected to all else. Beauty is like a design scheme to pave the way to where you want to go but didn't know existed.

———What is the most beautiful time of day?

I don't really have a beautiful part of the day. I like the changing light.

———What is the most beautiful place you've visited?

It's more like a time and place. We were sixteen, or so. Lauren, my buddy, and I made for a road trip to the Four Corners: Arizona, Colorado, Utah, New Mexico. Along the way, we were nudged to Taos, New Mexico. There, we were invited to take a bath in the natural hot spring at the foot of the Rio Grande. "Sure" was an involuntary reflex to all things hot springs. Taos is quite high in elevation, so it was a bit of a trek to make it down to the gorge. We started after sundown, and it was pitch-black, with only the moonlight to guide us down along the narrow dirt path. Steep. Narrow. No guard rails, no flashlight, nothing. Also, it was January and really cold. My hair formed icicles. Somehow we made our way to the small pool with hot steam stirring just above it. It was a most welcome sight. To improve the circulation, hot and cold rotation was recommended, the latter being the roaring river that runs through several states before hitting Mexico. "Sure." With that, we slipped into the liquid black of ice and safely returned to the hot bath with all limbs intact. And as if it were a special reward for surviving that, we were treated to a spectacular display of chiaroscuro. Visible up one side of the gorge was a thick blanket of snow glowing with the reflection of the full moon, and on the other side, an indefinable shape of black vortex. It was more than beautiful. It was epic.

— INTERVIEW WITH SUVI SALONIEMI

Designed by Jean Yu; Photographed by
Robin Broadbent; Overflow bodice, 2015;
Silk gazar netting

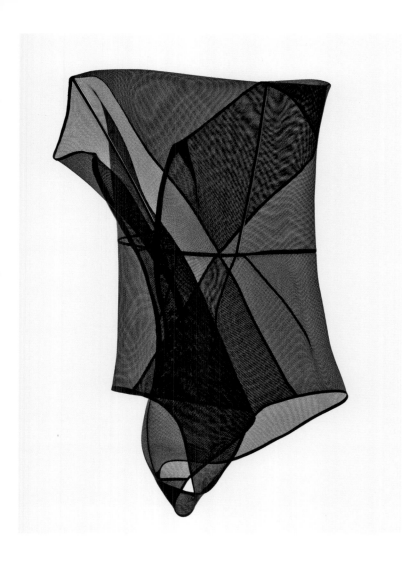
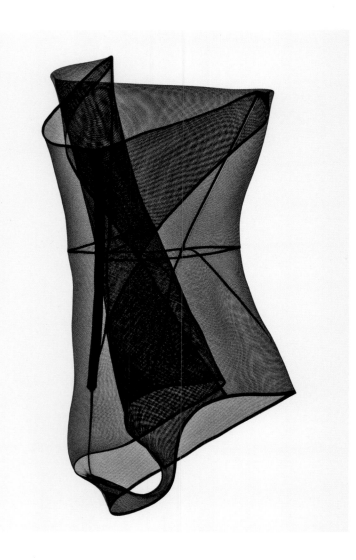

Designed by Jean Yu; Photographed by
Robin Broadbent; Overflow bodice, 2015;
Silk gazar netting

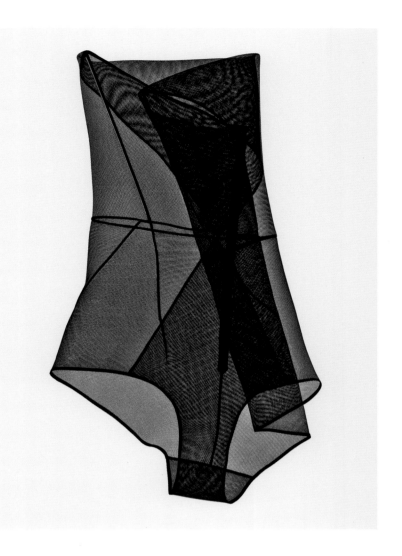

Emergent

Neri Oxman
Daniel Brown
Alexandra Daisy
 Ginsberg
Aaron Koblin
Jenny E. Sabin
Kyuha Shim
Simogo
Olivier van Herpt
Ken Wong

These contemporary designers employ digital systems to generate unexpected forms. Emulating nature and embracing code and mathematics, they create rules and processes that determine the final outcome of a project, working with data flows and user interactions to create responsive forms.

"We are inspired by all things in nature—the growth of trees, the formation of the glass sponge, swarm intelligence, the birth of planets. We seek the logic of formation rather than the description of form itself, particularly forms of logic that are often concealed, such as force fields guiding the distribution of calcium in trabecular bone. We then translate these phenomena to the product or building scale."

——————————————————— Neri Oxman

Neri Oxman

—ISRAELI-AMERICAN, ACTIVE IN USA, B. 1976—

Neri Oxman designs for, by, and with nature. Oxman and her team seek to do away with the "world of parts" approach to manufacturing, where products and buildings are made from discrete parts with distinct functions. In Oxman's approach, coined Material Ecology, computation, fabrication, environment, and the materials themselves are inseparable. Oxman earned a PhD in design computation at the Massachusetts Institute of Technology after studying architecture at the Architectural Association in London and the Technion—Israel Institute of Technology; she also studied medicine at the Hebrew University of Jerusalem. Oxman founded the MIT Media Lab's Mediated Matter group, which operates at the intersection of computational design, robotic fabrication, materials engineering, and synthetic biology. The group applies this knowledge to design, from the micro scale to the building scale. Wanderers An Astrobiological Collection, created in 2014 with Stratasys, is a series of 3D-printed, wearable, synthetic organ systems that could help humans survive the harsh conditions found on distant planets. The team recently unveiled GLASS, a new method for creating glass structures with 3D-printing technology. — ELLEN LUPTON

———Tell me about your current way of working.

All our projects seek to enable variation of material properties and behavior as part of the fabrication process. Our studio is a predictive practice, a laboratory in which the future of design is being actively and empirically created. We don't regard ourselves as problem solvers, but as solution seekers to problems that may not yet exist.

———Tell me about the ideas behind Wanderers, your spectacular exploration of wearable technology.

Wanderers is about traveling beyond the planet Earth, to hostile landscapes and deadly environments with crushing gravity, gaseous ammonia, prolonged darkness, and temperatures that would boil glass or freeze carbon dioxide. *Wanderers* externalizes and augments the digestive system [gastrointestinal tract (Mushtari)], the integumentary system [hair (Zuhal)], the skeletal system [bone (Otaared)], and the nervous system [brain (Al-Qamar)]. 3D-printed wearable capillaries are created for the interplanetary pilgrims of the future, designed to be infused with synthetically engineered microorganisms. Each design is a "codex" of the animate and inanimate, with an origin and a destination: the origin being engineered organisms, which multiply to create the wearable within a 3D-printed "wearable organ," and the destination being a unique planet in the solar system. The origin and the destination engage multiple scales, from the atomic to the cosmic.

One of the Wanderers, Mushtari, was further developed to become the first demonstration of a multi-material, 3D-printed, photosynthetic wearable. It has been redesigned to house synthetic microorganisms that fluoresce bright colors in darkness,

produce sugar, and manufacture biofilms. The wearable can change color, create food, and produce biological tissues, such as insulation for the body. Mushtari was designed to host two bacteria—a photosynthetic cyanobacterium and E. coli—housed and controlled in a network of millimetric fluid channels. The design is inspired by the geometry and material properties of the intestinal tract. Channels housing a photosynthetic bacterium use stiff, clear material to expose the bacteria to external light. The length of the entire system is greater than 59 meters [193.57 feet], and each channel ranges in diameter from 1 to 2.5 mm. Using a process known as "bitmap printing," this project is the first of its kind to achieve volumetric translucency gradients in extremely high resolution (a few microns) as well as hollow channels. Like living tissue, the design object has locally varying properties, such as color, rigidity, and opacity. Ultimately, the incorporation of synthetic biology in product and architectural design will enable the transition from designs that are inspired by nature to designs made with and by nature, to, possibly, designing nature herself.

———What's the inspiration behind GLASS?

With GLASS (2015), our goal was to embed life within architectural structures and thus to reimagine Kisho Kurokawa and Kenzo Tange's vision of a metabolist architecture—a true material ecology where building skins can exchange liquids and gasses with the environment. Ancient yet modern, enclosing yet invisible, glass was first created in Mesopotamia and Egypt 4,500 years ago. As a material, glass can be molded, formed, blown, plated, or sintered. From the discovery of the core-forming process for bead making in ancient Egypt, through the invention of

the metal blowpipe during Roman times, to the modern industrial Pilkington process for making large-scale flat glass, each new breakthrough in technology resulted from prolonged experimentation and ingenuity, and gave rise to new uses and possibilities. Our GLASS project unveils a first-of-its-kind, optically transparent glass–printing process called "G3DP." In this additive manufacturing platform, the upper chamber acts as a kiln cartridge, while the lower chamber serves to anneal the structures. The molten material gets funneled through an alumina-zircon-silica nozzle. The project synthesizes modern technologies with age-old tools and methods to produce novel structures with numerous potential applications.

———What comes to mind when you hear the word "beauty"?

Beauty must not be heard, but rather listened to. If you seek beauty, it will cease to exist; it dissolves the moment it solidifies. I prefer to talk of the sea, or describe the crown of a weeping willow. Not to talk of "beauty." Beauty cannot be hunted, only discovered. If you seek it, it will never find you.

Beauty and function unite in nature and in vernacular architecture. Human spongy bone or the craft of thatching are formations characterized by simple rules linking material to geometry, geometry to structure, structure to function, and function to the environment. And in both of these examples, beauty and purpose are indistinguishable. Similarly, architectural expression has always been tied to technique. This is true for adobe brick construction in the Persian Citadel of Arg-é Bam and for the steel-frame constructions of modern architecture. Digital fabrication is at the heart of a new age where technique and expression unite. The moment we generate a choice between beauty and utility is the moment we compromise our calling as designers.

———What is the most beautiful time of day?

Evertime.

———What is the most beautiful place you've visited?

Neverland.

— INTERVIEW WITH ELLEN LUPTON

Wanderers was set as a collaboration between Oxman's Mediated Matter group at the MIT Media Lab and Stratasys and the Laboratory of Professor Pamela Silver at the Department of Systems Biology, Harvard Medical School. Researchers include Christoph Bader, Dominik Kolb, Will Patrick, Sunanda Sharma, and Steph Hays. The Glass 3D Printing Project was created as a cross-disciplinary collaboration between the Mediated Matter group at the MIT Media Lab, The MIT Department of Mechanical Engineering and the MIT Department of Materials Science and Engineering's Glass Laboratory. Researchers include John Klein, Michael Stern, Markus Kayser, Chikara Inamura, Giorgia Franchin, Shreya Dave, Peter Houk and Prof. Neri Oxman. We wish to acknowledge Corning Incorporated, Skutt Kilns, and Joule Unlimited for their support.

OPENING SPREAD: Neri Oxman and MIT Media Lab Mediated Matter group; Rendered by Deskriptiv: Christoph Bader and Dominik Kolb; Produced by Stratasys; Rendering, overall view of Zuhal, from Wanderers collection, 2014

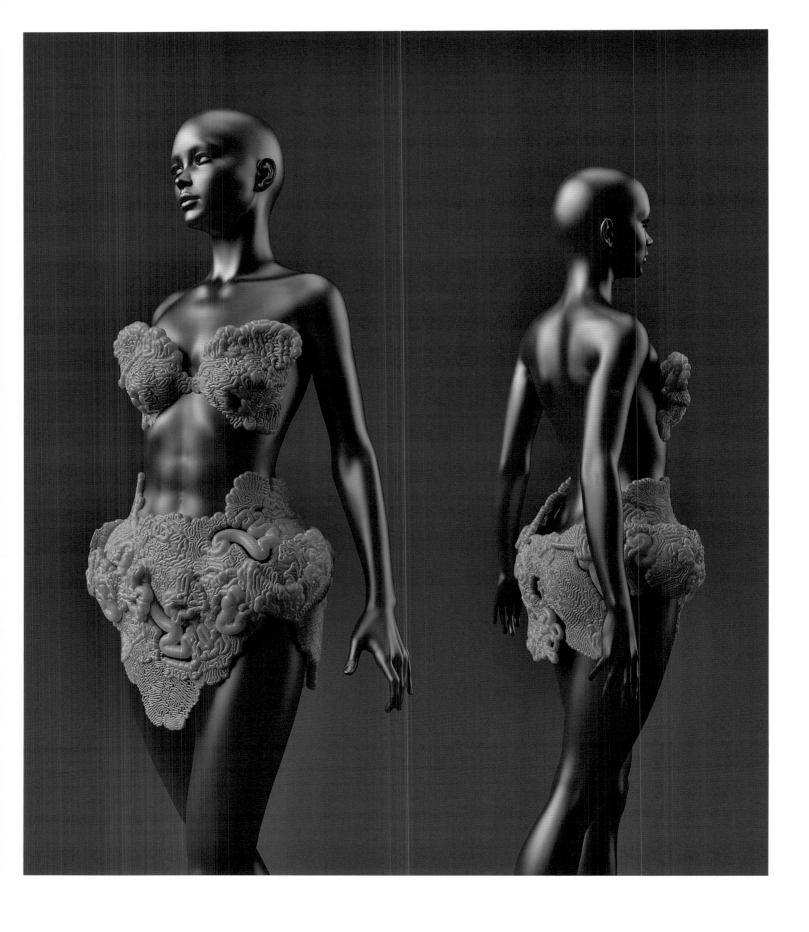

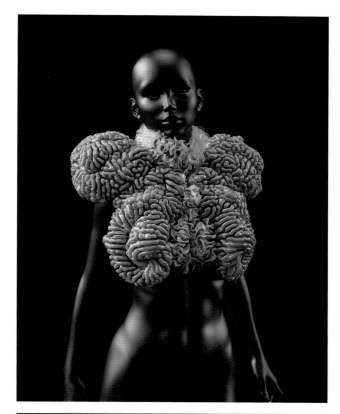

Neri Oxman and Mediated Matter in collaboration with Stratasys and Deskriptiv; Rendered by Deskriptiv: Christoph Bader and Dominik Kolb; Produced by Stratasys

Rendering, front view of Al-Qamar, from Wanderers collection, 2014

Rendering, back view of Otaared, from Wanderers collection, 2014

OPPOSITE: Rendering, overall view of Mushtari, from Wanderers collection, 2014

Daniel Brown

—BRITISH, B. 1977—

Daniel Brown, considered to be among the top media designers of his generation, always knew his field would be computer graphics. He was practically to the manor born—his father, artist Paul Brown, founded one of Europe's first computer graphics companies—but it was his innovative work with Roy Stringer and the digital marketing and consultancy group Amaze, and his own personal website Noodlebox (1997), that propelled his career in the 1990s. Best known for his inventive and playful interactive animations, he went on to initiate the visually stunning and lush *On Growth and Form* series (2000–ongoing), which uses mathematical formulas to generate and "grow" flowers in never-repeating patterns. He continues to contribute to the series with new generations of flowers, demonstrating the ever-increasing capacities of the technology based on algorithms. Using the computer-graphic game technology of his youth, he strives to evoke emotion and aesthetic appreciation in the immersive experiences he creates. He creates work for the SHOWstudio website and posts his own experimental pieces on play-create.com. — PENNY WOLFSON

————Can you tell me how you got started?
My introduction to the design industry was not typical. Although my father founded one of the first computer graphics companies in the late 1970s, by the time I was five my mother and father had divorced, and I was living in Liverpool. At the time, the typical Apple Macintosh computer cost around £10,000 (US$15,500) and was not accessible to the average person. My break came when a friend of my mother, Roy Stringer, who owned a small multimedia company, invited me to come in on weekends and use his company's equipment. Roy saw that I had talent and ambition, and started offering me work on the weekends and summer holidays. Later I would go on to work for Roy while he was at Liverpool John Moores University Learning Methods Unit. This department was later spun into an offshoot company, Amaze, and I worked for them when I left school. Around that time, the late 1990s, I produced an experimental website called Noodlebox using a cutting-edge piece of Adobe software. It went on to receive many accolades and established both my and Amaze's reputation in the fledgling web design industry.

Back then, the multimedia industry was very much dependent on designers who could do a little bit of everything—coding, designing, video, 3D—but by the early 2000s, I was starting to realize that I was not the best photographer or graphic designer or illustrator. I decided to focus on computer programming and instead collaborate with creatives who were the experts in their own respective fields. In 2001, I left Amaze to join photographer Nick Knight's experimental web project, SHOWstudio, which gave me access to collaborate with artists, designers, and celebrities such as Björk, Naomi Campbell, and Nick himself. Coming off the work I had produced for Amaze and SHOWstudio, the London Design Museum awarded me their Designer of the Year prize in 2004. Later that year, I chose to set up my own niche company, providing specialist creative technology services to my clients.

————It is interesting that you describe yourself foremost as a coder.
From an early age, I was always most interested in art and computers. My mother is a math lecturer and piano player, and my father is a painter and computer programmer. With both disciplines around me as a constant influence, I realized early on that computers could be a fantastic tool for creativity, well before the days of Photoshop.

In my teens, I was struggling to think of a career that matched both passions, but then by pure luck, the digital media industry came along. The nature of the job required both creative and programming skills. From there, I went on to be interested in what is formally known as "computational aesthetics," or "generative design"—in creating computer programs that can produce new art forms.

————How do you work? What's the process—the source—of your ideas? Your philosophy?
In the nineties I worked as a typical multimedia designer, doing a bit of graphic design, a bit of animation, a bit of video editing. Very much a bit of everything, and I always kept the sketchbook with me to jot down ideas. However, in 2003, I sustained a spinal injury while on holiday in Barcelona. I spent a year in hospital and lost most of the function in my hands. I'm lucky that with suitable adaptations I can still use a computer and type. From that day on, I unwittingly became a specialist "generative designer." All images that I create are now made by the computer code that I write, rather than "by hand"!

————Tell me about the work On Growth and Form.
I started the *On Growth and Form* series in the late nineties. The original piece was merely intended as a technical exercise to demonstrate what is known as "fractal behavior." However, the London Design Museum saw it and asked if they could display it as part of their *Web Wizards* exhibition. It ended up being one of the most popular pieces of work in the show, and I realized that digital flowers were a way that members of the public could appreciate computer processes aesthetically. So over the past fifteen years, I have created new generations of flowers to demonstrate the ever-more-powerful abilities of technology.

The name On Growth and Form comes from the title of a book by D'Arcy Wentworth Thompson. In it, he uses mathematics to model how particular plants and animals could come to have the shape they do. My flowers use essentially the same process but in reverse. I start with mathematical formulas and try to visualize them in a beautiful way. In 2013 the D'Arcy Thompson Zoology Museum in Dundee approached me and commissioned this work in honor of the book.

————What comes to mind when you hear the word "beauty"?
I have a very traditional, romanticized sense of aesthetics, inspired by flowers, painting, theater, even fashion. I'm interested in how computers can compute that sort of imagery.

————What is the most beautiful time of day?
Dusk, somewhere hot, such as Barcelona....

————What is the most beautiful place you've visited?
There are far too many places for me to mention, so I'll go for the patriotic option and say where I was born, near the corner of Huskisson Street and Percy Street in Liverpool, facing the Anglican cathedral.

— INTERVIEW WITH SUVI SALONIEMI

OPPOSITE: Daniel Brown, for D'Arcy Thompson Zoology Museum; Stills from Darwin flower animation, from On Growth and Form series, 2013; Real-time 3D (OpenGL / DirectX) flowers engine

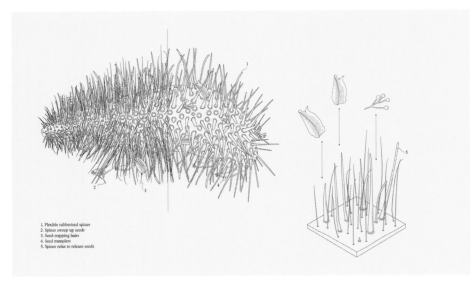

1. Flexible rubberised spines
2. Spines sweep up seeds
3. Seed-trapping hairs
4. Seed transfers
5. Spines relax to release seeds

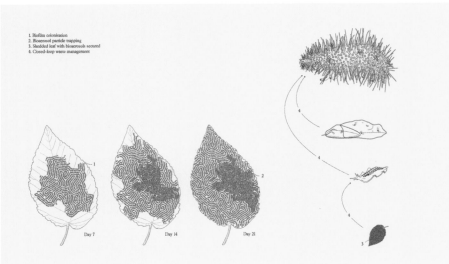

1. Biofilm colonisation
2. Bioaerosol particle trapping
3. Shedded leaf with bioaerosols secured
4. Closed-loop waste management

Day 7   Day 14   Day 21

Alexandra Daisy Ginsberg

—BRITISH, B. 1982—

Ask Alexandra Daisy Ginsberg what led her to enter the Royal College of Art's inaugural Design Interactions program after studying architecture at Cambridge and design at Harvard, and she explains: "It was never a planned diversion." The same could be said of her engagement with science, in which Ginsberg has no formal training. Yet her work belies such modesty. It is incisive and provocative—bold, elegant, and empathetic. Ginsberg is forging tighter connections between design and science, exploring design approaches that visualize aesthetic and ethical futures enabled by biotechnology. Designing for the Sixth Extinction (2013–ongoing), for instance, investigates the impact synthetic biology could have on biodiversity and conservation. It imagines newly designed organisms intended to sustain and revive endangered ecosystems—a slug that neutralizes highly acidic soil, a porcupine-like device to collect and disperse seeds, a self-replicating biofilm that attaches to leaves and traps airborne pollutants. In her constructions, Ginsberg engages the tradition of a landscape painter. She presents patent diagrams for the fictional organisms, suggestive of intellectual property, engaging a narrative design approach to yield new knowledge about ethical issues. — ANDREA LIPPS

────What is your starting point for a new project?

Generally, I get a bee in my bonnet [*laughs*]. It's often stimulated by something I've heard in a conference or something that seems surprising or a piece of research that I've read. It then is a process of stitching together different ideas. For instance, with Designing for the Sixth Extinction, I was increasingly seeing mention of the "sixth extinction," and simultaneously, other kinds of synthetic-biology-related ideas around ecology emerging, a constellation that seemed very strange to me. The discourse about conservation and synthetic biology is situated within this techno-utopian attitude of synthetic biologists: the promise of saving nature. It was really about how to work all those bits together into a narrative to seek new insights.

────What do you think design has to offer to science?

I think there's more freedom to be normative, to suggest how things could be, because the space is less prescriptive. There's room for provocation. My experience with synthetic biology is that there is an increasing sense from the field that the public is scared of synthetic biology and the technology will be rejected. While I'm researching my PhD I'm not getting directly involved in what in the UK is called "public engagement," to avoid being hired by science to help soften the message. I think some designers are happy to do that and that's fine, but for me, because I'm interested in the ethics of the science, it makes it much more complicated. That's why I'm not perhaps a conventional designer. I have a more political and normative agenda. I'm interested in the ethics of it. So it makes a traditional design relationship problematic.

────You're not engaging design as solution. It's more like design as medium.

Yeah, it is this idea of design as a question-asking tool and making it more critically engaged. But it leaves me in a tricky position as a practicing designer, because if the design is removed from the commercial context, what's left? That's the next step of working in critical perspectives on design: working out how it evolves or develops.

────Is it possible to leverage design fictions, or design for creating narratives, to effect greater change?

I'm not sure. In the very techno-utopian fields—I include TED and *Wired* in that area—there isn't much room for critique. You can't really dissent. If you dissent, you don't get included. So how do we allow space for critique and for critique to be seen as a useful tool for innovation? That's the positive spin on it. Why is it useful to dissent? I think it is really useful. It's part of the democratic process. I think a lot of criticism that comes

Autonomous Seed Disperser Patent, from Designing for the Sixth Extinction, 2013

Bioaerosol Microtrapping Biofilm Patent, from Designing for the Sixth Extinction, 2013

toward critical design and speculative design is that it's not measurable in its impact. That's part of the discussion that's going on at the moment.

Are ideas like this what led you to pursue your PhD?

In a way. The techno-utopianism—the blind faith in design and technology—is what I'm focusing on: how design is not just co-opted but part of that myth building. It's called "The Dream of Better." I'm looking at the myth of progress, why we think the future is going to be better, how we think that design helps make the future better. Because I would argue that design makes things worse as well as better, yet we have this implicit understanding that designing something improves it. The act of planning and designing is a process of amelioration.

What is a better future? What role does design play in constructing this idea of "better"? And the applied practice-based part is how might we use design to imagine alternative visions of better? How do we use design to imagine a better future that might *actually* be better? I'm increasingly hopeless about that possibility, which is an interesting existential hurdle. Can we use design to help us understand what "better" might be?

So where do you go from there?

Good question. It's really complicated. My value in synthetic biology as it matures is being pushed toward public engagement, and I don't really want that. In a way, I'm left to wonder whether design like this can't be in the service of science. Maybe it needs to be in the service of society, and help elicit those values and communicate them back to science.

At the same time, so much of what I'm interested in is how design gets its own voice and its own value system back. Because it's always been in service, and the origins of industrial design are very much about making stuff to sell. Can design be anything else? If it stays too much in the service of science, nothing really changes. It's just selling stuff.

Ideas.

I think design can work really well in helping design tools to actually communicate and teach science. I think that's a really great idea. But the kind of work I'm doing is slightly nuanced and maybe still quite ill defined. There remain problems with the projects and manifestos that use design for debate. Saying that the perspective of design is for debate is complicated, because you're skewing the debate. People may believe that it's real. Using the language of design convinces people that the future's already here. So there's all this stuff, basically, that's really unclear and needs to be teased out. Because if you make a dystopian future or show the negative possibilities of a new technology, then you're not going to get funded by science. But I still think that those kinds of projects have a lot of value, because they can help us shape the direction that we want our future to go in.

It ultimately is a very ambiguous, messy space.

Yes—which is why it's interesting.

How do aesthetics and science— specifically synthetic biology—interact in your practice?

Synthetic biology doesn't have an aesthetic at present because it's mostly invisible. But I think the experience of it can be aesthetic. Aesthetics is definitely an area of interest for me: imagining and exploring a potential aesthetic of synthetic biology. To me, it's a way to imagine what the values of a future and of a technology could be, but also the potential of a material that doesn't yet exist.

What comes to mind when you hear the word "beauty"?

I'm quite obsessed at the moment with naturalness and aestheticized nature, which is definitely something in Designing for the Sixth Extinction. For me, beauty is a goal system for how we judge and enjoy and have an emotional response to something. Beauty can be incredibly ugly. I think something could be seen as beautiful in provoking an emotional response that produces pleasure. I think about beauty a lot when it comes to design. You feel slightly guilty enjoying beauty, because it's understood as somehow shallow, but I don't think it is. I think it's something deeply emotional.

What is the most beautiful time of day?

It depends which climate [*laughs*]. If I'm somewhere hot, it's definitely the early morning, just as the sun comes up.

What is the most beautiful place you've visited?

South Africa. (Where my family comes from!) It's the scale of the landscape that's awe–inspiring. It's not like anywhere else. It's the same as the Grand Canyon, where you just feel very, very small. I've been reading Simon Schama's *Landscape and Memory*, which is so evocative of the awe-inspiring power and terror of nature, so I'd say the mountains of the Cape.

— INTERVIEW WITH ANDREA LIPPS

Alexandra Daisy Ginsberg

Rewilding with Synthetic Biology, from
Designing for the Sixth Extinction, 2013

Aaron Koblin

—AMERICAN, B. 1982 —

The work of digital media designer Aaron Koblin could best be described as data reimagined. If that doesn't sound exciting or beautiful, just look at *Light Echoes* (2013–ongoing), with Ben Tricklebank, a series of long-exposure photos that capture light from a laser projected onto a landscape, akin to temporary graffiti on the rural terrain; or the interactive video *Just a Reflektor* (2013), created with Vincent Morisset and which lets viewers control the video's effects, turning them into the "reflector." Humans' relationship to technology has been a subject of reflection for hundreds of years, but in Koblin's hands, this sometimes elusive dynamic skips along the interface of technology and art, resulting in work that can be fragile, monumental, comic, intimate, and elegant. Koblin has collaborated with people in the music, video game, and advertising worlds, and has won accolades as diverse as an Emmy, a Clio, a Grammy, a National Design Award, and a National Science Foundation prize. Koblin recently cofounded Vrse, a virtual reality company, with director Chris Milk. — PENNY WOLFSON

————Tell me about your current way of working.

I love to be doing tons of different things at the same time and try to figure out how one can inform the other. The thing that unifies most of the projects is an intense curiosity, often stemming from the technology or the application of that technology to our lives and how it's affecting humanity. I've been really interested in systems thinking: how can we either visualize existing systems, which usually means starting with a data set and visualizing that, or visualize new systems from new data sets, which tell us something interesting about ourselves or give us insights into society?

————How do you see your work evolving as these technologies change and advance?

A lot of the things that I work on are a direct response to the changes that we're seeing in technology, and in our relationship with technology. In a project like Flight Patterns (first launched in 2005)—which utilizes airplane traffic information and which I've revisited a few times—the data set is actually getting more and more refined. The paths of the airplanes themselves are actually changing, as the GPS units get more accurate and the airplanes get more automated. A lot of the character of the data set itself is changing. I think that's happening with a lot of technology. The data we're getting has better granularity, more time sampling, more accuracy. That really changes the picture.

————Where does your inspiration come from?

I have a running list of things that strike me as curious and interesting and worth spending some time with. I constantly reprioritize that list, try to figure out which thing I'm most interested in spending time on. The hard part is actually eliminating items and deciding, "OK, I'm going to work on this, and not that." And then trying to also understand why I'm making those decisions as I am.

————How did you find yourself at this intersection between art and technology? Was it something you were always drawn to, or did you come with a specific idea of what you were going to do?

I've always been interested in making things. I've also been really interested in technology, and I had access to a computer at a really young age. I got into computer games, but I ended up ripping the computer games apart and building new games, more than playing the games that were made.

————Which games?

The first game I got into was *Lemmings*. . . . Just this idea that you had these little creatures that you were taking control over and manipulating to do these tasks for you. From there, I went on to simulation games. *Civilization* was probably my all-time favorite game. At the same time, I liked very story-driven games, like *King's Quest* and those kinds of more fantasy/adventure games.

The combination of those ideas led to my interest for doing interactive music videos and other more narrative-driven technology experiments. I was less into arcade games, fighting games, and things like that, and more into simulation, strategy games, and action/adventure character games.

————There's obviously some interpretation, on your part, of data that you incorporate in your projects. Could you speak a little bit more to that aspect of your work?

It's this great opportunity to extract the essence and amplify the story that you're interested in, and make a pretty subjective interpretation of this data source into something that becomes or conveys knowledge.

For me, it's usually exactly that: distilling, trying to understand what are the parameters or attributes that make a relevant, interesting story, and then blowing those up and turning them into something.

————One of the things that strikes me about your work is your ability to see beauty in everything, even in things that may be invisible to us. What comes to mind when you hear the word "beauty"?

It's a very elusive thing. For a while, I used to think that beauty was synonymous with complexity, but I think it's obviously a lot more nuanced than that. A lot of things that I think are beautiful are really complex, not necessarily visually but complex in what they mean. To a certain extent, beauty is the combination. I don't want to say that beauty is novelty over complexity. Though those things can often be beautiful, beauty can also be tranquillity and simplicity. I'm really interested in that idea of visualizing the invisible—making tangible the intangible—because it recognizes that thing that we're all aware of and puts it in the spotlight, allowing us to focus on it and really appreciate the essence.

————What is the most beautiful time of day?

Sunrise has to be the most beautiful time of day. It's so rarely seen, but filled with the optimistic potential of new beginnings. The colors of sunrise are so intense and build so quickly, yet gradually. I can't help but think about the science of light rays being refracted in the atmosphere as the angle of light gradually increases, but at the same time it's magical, and analog, and mysterious.

————What is the most beautiful place you've visited?

I'm pretty interested in what's happening with virtual reality right now. I've been somewhat skeptical because of what we've been able to achieve, technically. We're really at a tipping point where it's about to turn into something very interesting and able to really make us question what we mean when we say "space."

Our ability to interface with our own senses will allow us to simulate and create spaces that have a scale and have a sense of presence, and therefore, have intrinsically embodied existence, which is pretty exciting and also quite scary, to make it work.

We're going to be relinquishing a lot of power, and we're going to be creating a lot of vulnerability by strapping ourselves into these devices. With that can come really interesting experiments and interfaces and experiences. It's quite possible some of my favorite spaces in a year or two might not exist in a way that could be experienced right now. . . .

— INTERVIEW WITH TIFFANY LAMBERT

Director Vincent Morriset testing the video effects with his phone for Arcade Fire's *Just a Reflektor*, 2013.

Aaron Koblin and Vincent Morisset for Arcade Fire; Stills, *Just a Reflektor*, 2013; WebGL, Three.js, WebSockets, WebAudio, getUser-Media(), Device Orientation, Google App Engine, Google Compute Engine, Google Cloud Storage; Video, 7:33 minutes

Aaron Koblin and Ben Tricklebank; Stills,
Light Echoes, 2013; Video, 1:38 minutes

Jenny E. Sabin

—AMERICAN, B. 1974—

Jenny E. Sabin proposes new ways of thinking about architecture. Her work fuses architecture with biological and material sciences, mathematics, and digital technology to generate new building forms. Sabin explores diverse material trajectories not typically associated with building, ranging from textiles and ceramics to dichroic film, to interrogate the aesthetic interface among form, material, fabrication, and human behavior. PolyThread (2016) is a temporary, inhabitable pavilion proposed for the Cooper Hewitt galleries, continuing Sabin's research into knitted textile structures. Its parametric form reflects advances in high-performance composite fabrics that will absorb, collect, and deliver light in response to the gallery's conditions and presence of visitors. PolyBricks (2014–15) are mortarless, 3D-printed ceramic bricks whose forms are inspired by bone composites and dovetail joints. Sabin's structural research investigates ceramics as a viable building component in contemporary generative architecture, manufactured with almost no waste. Sabin has degrees in ceramics and interdisciplinary visual arts, and earned a master's in architecture from the University of Pennsylvania. She is principal of Jenny Sabin Studio, an experimental architecture studio, and director of Sabin Design Lab, a research and design unit. Sabin is the recipient of numerous awards and honors, and serves as assistant professor of Architecture in Design and Emerging Technologies at Cornell University. — ANDREA LIPPS

——What are the sources of your ideas and inspirations?

The primary inspirations have been biology, mathematics, and materials science. I'm interested in how craft-based techniques and media such as textiles and ceramics provide a material realm that can accept these dynamic processes, textiles being an incredible way to explore analogically the notion of the extracellular matrix, a dynamic meshwork or web that one can work within.

The idea behind matrix biology is that half the secret to life resides outside of the human cell or the cell itself. You have code, or DNA, which influences form and function. But then you have the extracellular matrix, which is the environment that the cells interact within. For me, over the years, this has presented a series of really potent ecological models to consider, looking at what, in biological terms, is known as reciprocity, this kind of dynamic feedback between environment and how

events within that environment act upon and influence code. It's a dynamic choreography between environment and form. They're not separate; they're inextricably linked.

A longtime collaborator, cell and molecular biologist Dr. Peter Lloyd Jones has been a huge influence and inspiration. Another collaborator is Dr. Shu Yang, who's a materials scientist. One of the things that we've been looking at is the topic of structural color. She looks at the wings of butterflies, for example. With the butterfly wing, the color that we see with the naked eye is not pigment based. It's entirely about reflection and refraction of light and manipulation of pattern and geometry. At a nano-micro scale, if you look at one of these wings, you just see white and variegated patterns. We've taken some of those principles not just as inspiration, but also as a way of starting to transfer those ideas and technologies into architecture.

——Can you talk about your process?

I never know what the final form is going to be when I start, which is in contrast to how most architects work and think. I'm interested in designing more like nature does, where you start with a set of very simple parameters or variables. Through iteration and multiple generations, it's possible to develop much more complex results. That's given rise to a really productive way of thinking and working where the final form is never post-rationalized. It's finished when you've gone through all of those phases, what I like to call "productive contamination", where material, fabrication, and contextual constraints are incorporated along the way and throughout the design process.

——How do you see your aesthetic evolving as both science and technologies change and advance over time?

My design methodology is very process heavy. I tend to look at part-to-whole relationships and the development of complexity—not just formal complexity, but spatial complexity. Through these new technological leads in making and fabricating—alongside our ability to script, hack, and design our own digital tools—the architect is now in a position of facilitating the making and constructing process. We now think three-dimensionally, parametrically, dynamically. I'm interested in how that's impacting our built environment; how we can meaningfully deal with that in our design processes from a cultural, economic, even political standpoint; and how, ultimately, that's giving rise to a shift away from the thrust of Cartesian orders of column, beam, arch. I would describe it on a meta level, as a much more feminine space that's horizontal, about meshworks, about topology, about connectivity, about nonstandard forms and structures that are much more variegated.

Produced by Sabin Design Lab, Cornell University: Jenny E. Sabin, Martin Miller, Nicholas Cassab-Gheta, David Rosenwasser, and Jingyang Liu Leo; PolyBrick series, 2014; Ceramic, maltodextrin, alcohol; 15.2 × 15.2 × 7.6 cm (6 × 6 × 3 in.)

We're not there yet, in terms of how this will impact architecture in the built environment.

I'm interested in what I like to call "the topic of personalized architecture". How do we start to tune and adapt our material environments? Not just literal moving architecture, like interaction design, but something that's much more sympathetic and empathetic, integrating the human body into the design process.

—Tell me about your current research and projects.

In the studio, I'm doing front-entry stoop elements, public street furniture, and facade accent paneling for a thirty-one-unit, mixed-use housing development project in North Philadelphia. It's pretty exciting, because it's the first permanent architectural project that we've done. The project is called *PolyVine*. It's a highly ornamented set of interventions that are inspired by the local history of the site, which was a vineyard.

In my lab, I have a new collaborative research project funded by the National Science Foundation, where we're looking at geometric and material principles across multiple length scales related to the topic of kirigami. Kirigami is slightly different from origami in that it's folding, but with the addition of the strategic placement of cuts and holes. The project is in collaboration with a theoretical physicist, a bio and environmental engineer, and a materials

scientist. We're interested in scaling up these folding principles and, on the architectural end, looking at how that can give rise to prototypes and material assemblies that fold and adapt to environmental cues that might be highly functional, or also about how we as humans interact with them. We just finished a prototype called ColorFolds (2014) that we had installed at Cornell University for the past four months.

In another trajectory, we are continuing to explore and experiment with knitted textile structures initially developed as a pavilion titled myThread (2012) commissioned by Nike, Inc. Here, we are working with high-tech responsive yarns and are in turn embedding this technology into much larger adaptive knitted textile architectures. One of the two contributions for [*Beauty*] will be a new knitted structure that people can inhabit.

The PolyBrick project, which is under the broader topic of digital ceramics, is also ongoing. We're directly 3D printing variegated ceramic bricks, starting with the idea that the brick as a module hasn't been questioned for centuries. Why not start to look at more novel, nonstandard natural forms?

—What comes to mind when you hear the word "beauty"?

For me, beauty is biological. It's material. It's about the human body. When something reaches a certain spatial resonance in its morphology. It depends on how you approach

the term, whether you're coming from issues of aesthetics or theory, but I like to approach it analogically in terms of thinking about a result that is the product of deep inquiry, where geometry, pattern, materiality, and biological principles stemming from the human body are inextricably linked as a way of thinking. I've found that engaging this as a process develops radically beautiful forms that are difficult to entirely understand. I'm interested in where the natural and the synthetic meet and the spatial and material beauty that emerges from this intersection.

—What is the most beautiful time of day?

I live part-time in Ithaca, because I teach at Cornell. I have a place on the west side of Lake Cayuga, right on the lake. For me, the most beautiful time of the day is early morning. The bird life on the lake is incredible, and the light is stunning, so there's that level of natural beauty. It's also the only time of the day where it's completely quiet and I get a lot of work done and I'm not bombarded with the craziness of the day and managing everything else.

—What is the most beautiful place you've visited?

I love cities, too. I would go a little crazy if I only lived in Ithaca. I like to have a duality, one foot in an urban environment, the other in a more natural environment.

— INTERVIEW WITH TIFFANY LAMBERT

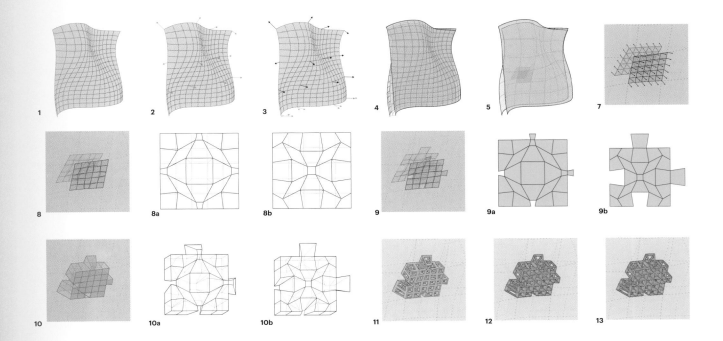

Illustration of algorithm to determine shape and placement of bricks to build a structure, PolyBrick series, 2014, by Jenny E. Sabin, Martin Miller, and Nicholas Cassab-Gheta.

OVERLEAF: Produced by Jenny Sabin Studio: Jenny E. Sabin, James Blair, Simin Wang, Martin Miller, Meagan Whetstone, Brian Heller, and Nicola McElroy; engineering by Daniel Bosia, AKT Engineers; fabricated by Shima Seiki, Dazian Fabrics, and Smucker Laser; installed by Leslie Cacciapaglia, Aaron Gensler, Mi Young Kang, Rachel Kaplan, Jae Won Kim, Zhongtian Lin, Liangjie Wu, Youngjin Yi, Zhenni Zhu, for Nike, Inc.; myThread Pavilion, New York City, USA, 2012

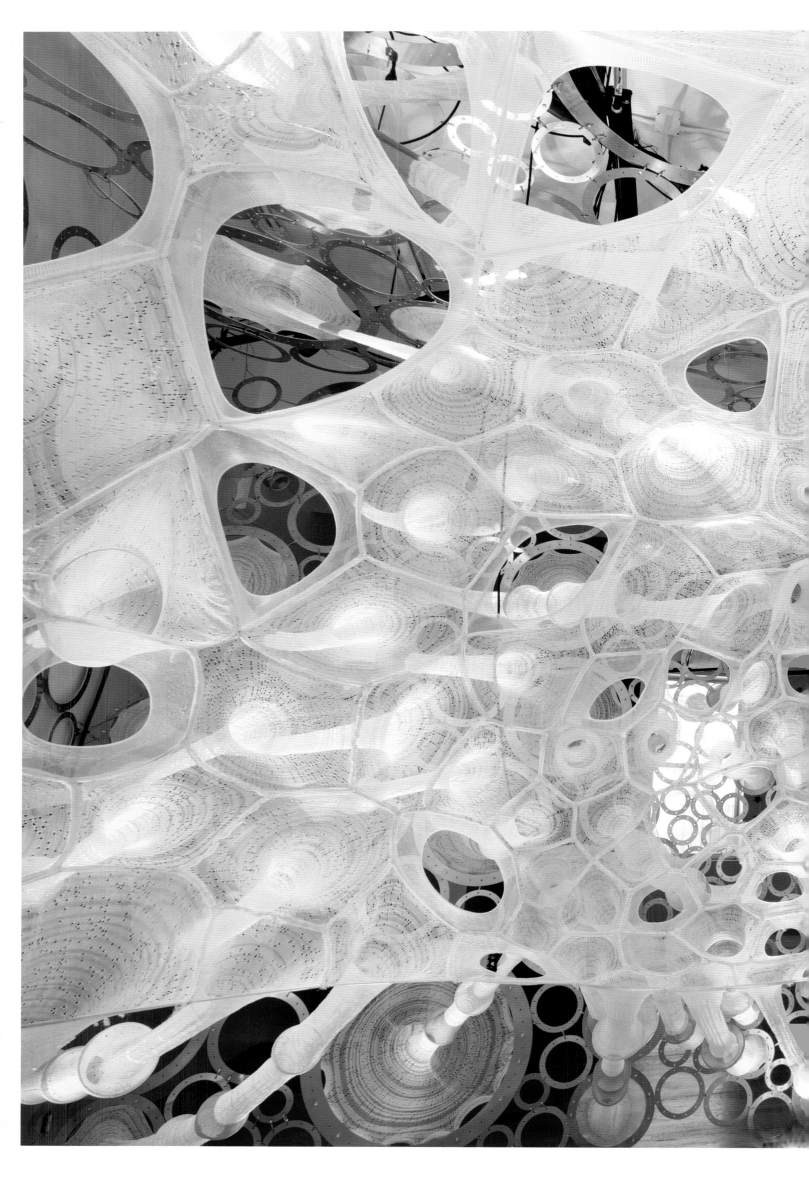

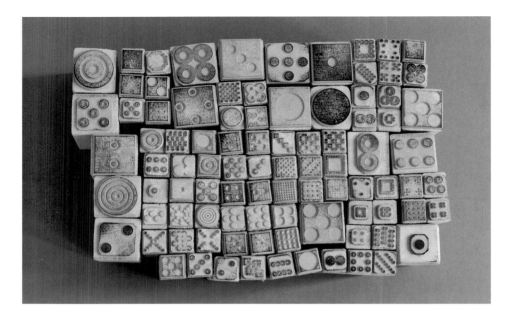

Kyuha Shim

—KOREAN, ACTIVE IN USA, B. 1982—

Kyuha Shim creates his own rules and tools for generating graphic forms, ranging from code-driven letterforms to complex data visualizations. The Korean-born designer and researcher has studied and worked in the United States, the United Kingdom, the Netherlands, and Korea. Seeing through Circles (2013) explores raster systems for screen-based typography by translating pixels into a physical, analog process. By analyzing how letterforms are displayed digitally in pixels of different shades of gray, Shim designed sixty rubber stamps whose visual densities roughly match the brightness of sixty corresponding pixels. He implemented this system in a series of hand-stamped prints. Grid Brush: The Art of Selection (2014) produces richly colored letterforms in 2.5 dimensions from a warped scaffold of parallel lines; by varying the number of lines, the weight of the stroke, and the choice of colors, Shim generated a luscious candy shop of unexpected outcomes. — TIFFANY LAMBERT

————Describe the differences between computational design and graphic design.
It is hard to differentiate the two disciplines because graphic design now encompasses many new media and computational features. Designing computations can be a part of graphic design. The important part is the context. My practice is situated within a computational environment, but the computational systems I design, in turn, generate typography and images, either on-screen or in printed matter.

————Many people working in the realm of computational design and data visualization create work derived from the language of data, and there is an interpretive aspect to that. Much of your work, however, seems rooted in the opposite—to start with the graphic or visual element and then apply code. Could you talk about your approach?
I usually start from a diagram and think about the possible parameters that I can drill out of the content or context. In this way, I'm more interested in the relations between program parameters and visuals. In order to realize my content in the digital platform with computational parameters, I have to translate the content into code. This takes three stages. The first is characterization, which is the foundation of my understanding; this is when I conceptualize and specify the problem. The next is integration. This is comparable to a mix- or mashup of possible ideas within the situation. The final stage is generation. Here, we see new configurations, variations, visual cohesions, and consistency of the outputs.

————Is there room for "randomness" in your work?
Chance operations play a critical role in my work, as they brings an infinite flow into the sequence of graphics. Random methods in computation actually generate pseudo randomness; the conditions are slightly different from pure chance in the real world, such as flipping a coin or throwing dice.

————Does your inspiration come from the field of graphic design, or do you look to other disciplines?
Parametric design was widely used in architecture during the past decade, but rarely in graphic design. With parametric modeling, designers can concentrate on building a system that generates various cases instead of dealing with single details in design. Designers can therefore achieve a myriad of iterations by modifying the value of parameters. They can also add new input parameters or conditions into the algorithm to extend the variations. In my research, I bring parametric methods to graphic design production for printed matter.

————You work with the intangible—code, data—as well as the tangible—the outcome or end "thing" that you've designed. Would you say a primary concern is the narrative of making visible what is not?
My practice is situated in art, design, and technology, with particular interest in the language of systematic and playful patterns in design and computation. Data becomes the primary medium in creating a complete, narrative system informed and driven by integrated processes of visualization, fabrication, and installation.

————We live in a time where people have greater access to the tools of design, whether digital-imaging tools or tools of manufacture like 3D printing. What is your take?
This may not directly answer your question, but my recent exhibition, You Shape Tools Shape You [RCA, 2015], represents how I see code/rationale/logic as designers' tools. The interaction with our tools is a continuous and reciprocal activity [of shaping and being shaped], and the procedural sequence is considerably faster—so much so that it is perceived to be simultaneous. The use of tools involves logical thinking processes much more than the assembly of physical compartments. The show reevaluates what tools have become in relation to design practices, moving away from the traditional model in which a tool is simply an instrument used to carry out a function.

————What comes to mind when you hear the word "beauty"?
For me, beauty emerges from a mixture of parameters. This mixture is not a single variable form but a group within a hierarchical object. The results of my systems are determined by relationships between parameters. Likewise, moving images can be achieved by morphing these values. The conditions and parameters are more important than the individual aesthetic choices that I make in my work.

————Where is the most beautiful place you've visited? What is the most beautiful time of day?
The John Madejski Garden, in the heart of the Victoria and Albert Museum, is a five-minute walk from the RCA. It is especially beautiful at night, when both the building and the lighting are reflected in the water.

— INTERVIEW WITH TIFFANY LAMBERT

Rubber stamps for the production of Seeing through Circles, 2013.

Seeing through Circles, 2013; Hand-stamped print; 42 × 29.7 cm (16⅝ × 11¹¹⁄₁₆ in.)

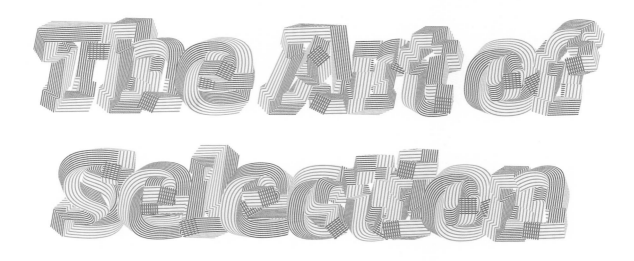

Iterations, from Grid Brush: The Art of
Selection, 2014

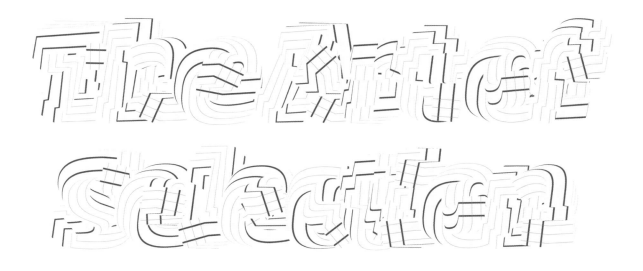

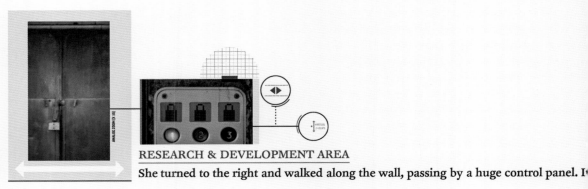

ANALOG. ZOOM [X 35]

STRATEGY & MARKETING AREA

RESEARCH & DEVELOPMENT AREA

She continued her exploration deeper in

She turned to the right and walked along the wall, passing by a huge control panel. I

split in half, a couple of the others had one or several limbs missing. Anna headed straight to what she figured would be the exit – a large steel door with no handles. *A keypad ...figures.*

Simogo

—MALMÖ, SWEDEN, FOUNDED 2010—

Small and mobile best describe Simogo and its games. In just five years, Simon Flesser (Swedish, b. 1982) and Magnus "Gordon" Gardebäck (Swedish, b. 1976) have set the mobile gaming industry abuzz with a string of hits that challenge traditional gaming conventions. The duo broke out together from a games company to make a bigger impact by staying small. With Flesser designing visuals and audio and Gardebäck working on code, Simogo creates immersive environments that offer multisensory gameplay. *Device 6* (2013) is a work of interactive fiction. It uses typography as part of the interface—lines of type stretch out and change direction (forcing one to do the same with the device), leading the player around a mysterious mansion. Illustrations in the text offer views into the rooms and their contents, revealing clues to help the heroine, Anna, through the adventure that lies ahead. Part novella and part puzzle, the game combines sound, text, and graphics to create a unique experience that takes the idea of e-publishing in a new direction. *The Sailor's Dream* (2014) is a cinematic experience of gameplay, directed not by the linearity of levels or challenges, but by a whimsical, aestheticized world of short stories, music, and toys. — JUSTIN ZHUANG

——————Can you tell us your backgrounds?
SIMON FLESSER: "Simogo" is a contraction of our two names, Simon and Gordon. We met at a game studio in Malmö, where we both worked for three years or so. I previously worked on the effects and animation for movies and commercials, while Gordon programmed security systems. I don't really have an education, except for spending a year and a half learning 3D graphics and an internship at a video effects company.

——————What is Simogo's approach to games?
We do the work that we are excited about, and a big thing for us is to try and make things that have not been made before—at least in games.

——————How do you divide your work in the studio?
Gordon does mainly the programming in our projects, while I work on the art and sound. It differs from project to project, but we design the things together, including the philosophy behind the mechanics of the game. My interest is more in the theme, vibe, and audiovisuals of the story; whereas, Gordon is more about the functional design of a project. In our more recent projects, we've also collaborated with friends and other freelancers.

——————Can you tell us more about your work process and source of ideas, such as in your detective game Device 6?
Device 6 took about six months to make. We don't really have a method, and we're actually not really good at planning, either. For *Device 6*,

the idea came from our previous game *Year Walk* [2013], which is based on this folklore and Scandinavian horror tradition called Årsgång. That game had a companion app with facts about Scandinavian folklore, which gave the game a larger narrative. When we finished that project, we both wanted to do a game almost strictly based on text, because we were excited about the prospects of how much you can communicate with so little. But we also knew we didn't want to make something that was one hunred percent text-based, because just reading it would not take advantage of being on a digital platform.

We talked about maps quite a lot at this time, because when we start a project, or—at least for me—I usually draw a map of the places in the game, even if they don't have a map in the game. It helps me to create spaces for the places in the game and see how everything is connected in the work. I just sketch it on a paper with circles and little roads. *Device 6* was based on this thought of describing a place not only with text but sort of geographically. We didn't really have a detective story before we had the form.

Around the same time, Jonas Tarestad, who helped write the story for *Device 6*, and I were getting into spy fiction, and we were particularly inspired by Patrick McGoohan's show *The Prisoner* from 1967. *Device 6* has a lot of things in common with it, from the game's social commentary to its title, which references the "Number 6" character McGoohan plays.

——————What did *Device 6* lead to next?
The Sailor's Dream is the culmination of the things we learned from *Year Walk* and *Device 6*. One part is creating text-based projects, and the other is creating around narratives rather than challenges, as found in traditional games. *The Sailor's Dream* doesn't have any puzzles or challenges at all. It's a totally free, open narrative where you can dive into the things that you want and at your own pace. Basically, you are at sea and can enter different islands containing items with stories to tell. So you'll read the separate text stories and have to piece together a larger narrative. What we wanted to explore more with this game was the advantages of a digital platform and using mixed media. *The Sailor's Dream* not only uses text to tell some of its story, but there are also songs that depict the stories of the characters, who are all connected by the ocean in some way.

——————Is beauty an important element in your work? What does it mean to you?
It's a really tough question. I'm inclined to think visually, because I do visual things, so I want to say that it's when I see something beautiful. But it's also not something that I can really explain because it's intangible. When you really can't explain why something is beautiful, then maybe that is beauty? It's hard to say there is a formula for beauty. It's when you see it, you feel it, or you just know it—so I would say it's a very personal thing.

Beauty can come from many things. At least for me, it's important that my work is something that is visually pleasing, and the experience of it also feels good in your hands. It all has to work like cogs in clockwork—everything has to sing together. That is what creates beauty.

——————What is the most beautiful time of day?
Early morning, when everything is quiet, especially if I can wake up before everyone else and just have the world to myself. That is a beautiful time of the day.

——————What is the most beautiful place you've visited?
It's, I think, all about the context. A place is only place. It's about who is inhabiting the place, at what time, and what is happening in the place. So, I'd say that only situations can be beautiful—and I, thankfully, have too many to list them.

— INTERVIEW WITH SUVI SALONIEMI

OPPOSITE AND OVERLEAF: Stills from Chapter 2, *Device 6* game, 2013

She continued her exploration deeper into the room, to the left. It was becoming hard to move. There was junk cluttered around in big piles everywhere and racks filled with all sorts of technical equipment formed small corridors along the wall.

She turned to the right and walked along the wall, passing by a huge control panel. It was lit, as though active, but it was unclear what it...

In the corner stood a large table.

Every seat was occupied by small bears, except the chair at the head of the table. Anna didn't recognise all of them, but she could identify Lord Nelson, Napoleon and General Custer. There was a big map of Europe laid out on the table and bear models were placed at London, Paris and Berlin.

There weren't there before, were they?

she tripped over a lever on the floor and heard something activate behind her. She turned her gaze, and noticed three shooting range targets hanging from a wire by the brick wall.

PRODUCT EVALUATION AREA

All around her were panels, buttons, screens and cables that together formed the skeleton of an outdated - yet unarguably advanced - operation. An earthen floor and weeds by the corners contrasted the high tech surroundings. This was truly a shell, nothing more than floor brick walls stuck in the ground. She stepped by an enormous magnifying glass device. Around it stood a couple of mannequins that all had melted in different ways. One had its torso split in half, a couple of the others had some or several limbs missing. Anna headed straight to what she figured would be the exit - a large steel door with no handles. — *A biped... figure.*

Well, I guess I'm all set should I need any giant ants around here, then.

it climbed the wall the against hanged put sounds unpleasant several

A terribly unstable looking ladder was the only way down. It made

Whoever made this ladder should be hanged.

Dear Lord, what is this place?

If anything this looked more like a research facility, or a missile silo. There was a lot of technical equipment on the floor before and in the centre of it all stood a cylindrical container housing three rockets.

This castle looked nothing like the inside of its twin. Although similar on the outside, this one was made up of a single large room. A shaft of a castle.

She led the last of the bears behind her, and entered the twin castle. It was pitch black. Anna took a couple of steps in the darkness. Big spotlights on the walls lit up and music started to play. She was standing on a small steel platform.

LAUNCH FACILITY

d that it was best not to press any buttons.

Only an idiot would start to push buttons randomly in a place like this.

A notice board on the wall left Anna somewhat perplexed. There were numerous papers pinned to the board, many of them marked "Operation Goldilocks", "Project Sun" and "Top Secret". *It seems like a bright idea to leave it here, then.* The room was the home of a thousand projects. Few of them finished, all completely mad. Toys seemed to have been turned into weapons and weapons into toys. Thankfully, none of these products had ever graced the market ... as far as Anna could tell.

DEVICE 2
Audio Visual Output Chip
(Secondary Simulation Device).

· Sight and hearing simulation transmission to DEVICE 4.

Developer Notes:
· Audio output 100% literal.
· Visual output 75% literal, 25% figurative.

She noticed a shape that looked decidedly human, covered by a white sheet. Anna pulled it quickly and jumped back - just in case. A doll with blonde hair stared at her. There were cords going to the back of its head. It smiled happily at Anna.

Hiding from the bears are you, Goldilocks?

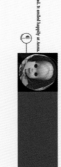

Hoping to find some answers behind it, Anna increased her pace towar

Too it released

'call/answer'. It seemed that the bear wasn't alone. It had the company of two other stuffed companions.

She gave it a closer look and noticed a speaker embedded in its stomach, protruding from the fur. Below the speaker was a little red button marked

A bear was standing on its hind legs and staring straight into Anna's eyes. On closer inspection it appeared to be rather immobile. And, in fact, quite dead and stuffed. Anna calmed down, and giggled at the absurdity of it all.

She felt the presence of someone - or something. As she turned towards the bridge railing she almost fell over in shock.

an option. The bridge appeared to stand thirty feet tall.

Olivier van Herpt

—DUTCH, B. 1989—

At the intersection of the digital and analog, as well as design and tools, sit the works of Olivier van Herpt. An industrial design graduate of the Design Academy Eindhoven, he is interested in the interplay between digital tools and their physical output, and is constantly tinkering with methods and means of production to yield new and interesting designs. Challenged by the limits of 3D-printing technology, van Herpt successfully designed a 3D printer that can not only produce larger forms, but also work with ceramics instead of just plastics. He has used this to print various pottery collections that blur the line between what is made by the human hand and the machine—a beautiful showcase of the craft of digital manufacturing. For van Herpt, design is not a closed practice, and he wants to create machines and tools that empower others to create as well. He hopes that as the technology becomes accessible to many, the beauty of 3D-printed objects will blossom. — JUSTIN ZHUANG

————How were you introduced to 3D printing?

A few years ago, I started thinking about how I could make machines that let others make. I experimented with my first 3D printer to see what these machines were capable of, and, although 3D printing was fun, the machines were limited, and you could not make human-size objects. So I set off designing and building a 3D printer of my own that was capable of making large, functional things. 3D printing is a complex interplay between material, shape, function, software, electronics, engineering, material science, design, and creation. The challenge of making machines is balancing out these things.

3D printing lets one manufacture many different forms, textures, and colors that otherwise would not be possible. By developing a 3D-printing process for a more noble and beautiful material—ceramics rather than plastics—I was able to make better, more functional things. I also found ceramics to be interesting since there are so many forms of it and you can vary, change, and mix many types of clay. At one point, I was unable to build things larger than 40 cm [15 ¾ inches] because they would collapse due to the wet clay used. After much iteration, I was able to overcome this challenge and build larger things using a new extruder and hard clays. This kind of a pure interaction with the material would not have been possible with plastics.

————So you built your own 3D printer to produce your ceramic wares. What is the role of tool building in your design process?

I believe that you need to extend and improve technologies. I want to be at [the] knife's edge of technology, pushing the envelope. This is because I believe that improving the methods and means of production will yield new, interesting, functional objects. Due to this, I spent two years developing a 3D-printing ceramics technology, continually improving

the extruder and making new versions of it. After iterating many times, I'm now able to make objects that measure 40 by 80 cm [15¾ by 31½ inches].

The form of the 3D printer and extruder are completely dictated by function. There is no final shape for either device, and they are constantly improved as I learn and explore making better things. I do take aesthetics into account, but the key driver is the functionality. There is no fat on the machine, nothing unnecessary. The vases exist to demonstrate the technology. Hopefully, they are interesting, and new objects will emerge from them. For the vases, function follows form because their shapes are dictated by the capabilities of the machine. They are made specifically to illustrate the possibilities. The reason I make machines is so that interesting objects can be made not only by me, but by others as well. I want to collaborate with others and let other people make and design. To me, the final output of the work is the increase in some small way of the sum total of things that can be made. It's not about me making a thing; it's about making a machine that lets many people make things that were not able to be made previously.

————One common element of your 3D-printed projects is the attempt to bring the hand into the machine. What are your thoughts on the dichotomy between technology and craft?

I see no dichotomy between technology and craft. If you work with digital manufacturing —3D printing, software, or machines—you always collaborate with the tool. Sure, it enables the making of internal structures, textures, and shapes that could not be made by traditional means. But still, this process is open to direct human intervention. It is a dance between you and the machine. In technology, there are mistakes and imperfections, too. As designers, a lot of us feel at arm's length when using digital tools

to make. We often feel like we have to force a human fingerprint on a design, make visible the human touch. In a way, we are increasing the abstraction level and putting a chain of tools between the object and us. But in the final analysis, a paintbrush or pencil is also technology that we use to make. Likewise, I think that while taking into account that we are becoming more distant to the object, the process of creation may be different, but it does not somehow change the nature of authorship or expression.

————What are your thoughts on the aesthetics of 3D-printing design right now?

With the adoption of more materials and processes, the collective beauty of 3D-printed objects increases each and every day. With so many people having access to so many of their own "factories," it is a march of tens of thousands toward more beautiful things. Many can now make what they want, and this may lead to many things deemed ugly. I'm hopeful that we will end up making many things that are found to be beautiful—either by only one person or by many.

————What comes to mind when you hear the word "beauty"?

I do not understand beauty. I know beauty when I see it. I try every day to make beautiful things. I want to make them, but as soon as I have, my mind wanders to a more beautiful thought of a more beautiful object. In so doing, I don't find the things I make beautiful. I hope one day to make a beautiful thing. But, as to what beauty means or who would find it beautiful, I do not know the answer to your question. Beauty is a fleeting dream of an object, thought, or moment. An intangible impossible, an elusive, effervescent, ultimate expression of a goal beyond the furthest reaches of our imagination and ability. We strive to create and experience it whilst not understanding how to do so or what it is.

————What is the most beautiful time of day?

The night. It is quiet, calm, and peaceful. I work best at night. I can focus more on the projects I'm working on when the world is dark. Buildings are different then; lights dot the landscape; and the world changes. Shapes, shadows, and light are all more sculptural while being draped in peace.

————What is the most beautiful place you've visited?

I find it difficult to separate place from experience. If you've had a bad experience or, likewise, are exploring a place while in love or whilst celebrating success, it will disproportionally alter your feelings toward this place. I have found many places beautiful but find it impossible to determine which place is beautiful itself.

— INTERVIEW WITH JUSTIN ZHUANG

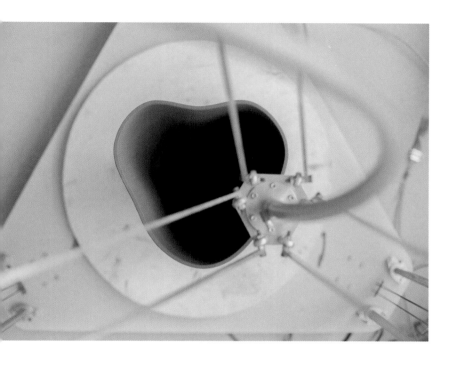

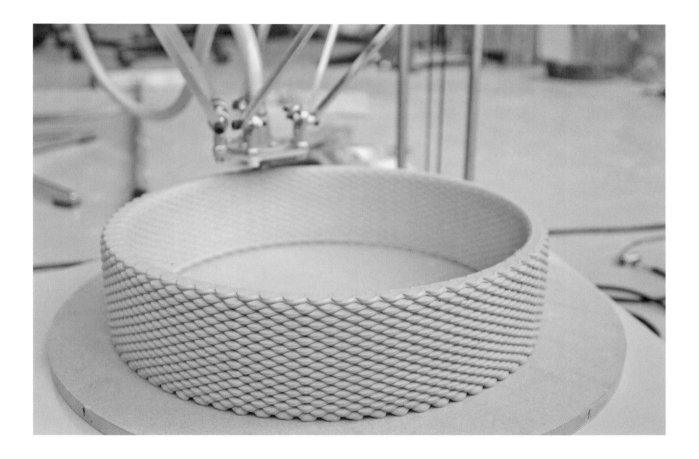

Van Herpt's 3D printer can print objects up to 80 cm (31½ in.) high and 43 cm (16¹⁵⁄₁₆ in.) wide, 2014.

The ceramic 3D printer builds objects layer by layer, 2014.

Printing a ceramic form for the 3D Woven collection, 2014.

OVERLEAF: Experiments and works from the designer's studio, 2014.

Ken Wong

—AUSTRALIAN, B. 1982—

The desire to create compelling user experiences is what inspires the interface design company ustwo to push the boundaries of digital products, including video games, dissolving the medium's conventions of violent competition and mindless challenges. Ken Wong, lead designer of ustwo's genre-bending game *Monument Valley* (2014), uses aesthetic intrigue to engage a wider community. Unlike traditional games, *Monument Valley* is built around how users interact with touch-screen devices, and it centers on the experience of architectural beauty and complexity. *Monument Valley* enables users to interact with isometric buildings inspired by temples, monasteries, and churches from around the world. For Wong, video games are an emerging creative form that combines art, engineering, and design. As with film, games allow him to create worlds for users to discover and explore. — JUSTIN ZHUANG

————Describe your practice and working methods.

The old way of making video games is centered around the fantasies of teenage boys. We got good at making games about jumping and shooting and running, and games that resemble sports competitions. But games can be more like art, more like movies or films or theater or architecture. We can advance the making of video games by taking a step back and looking at who is actually playing these games, and how are they playing. Games are played by everybody—by children, by women, by all sorts of people. They're playing in groups; they're playing on the Internet; they're playing on their smartphones or tablets.

At ustwo, we decided to make a new mobile game with no restrictions. Our boss said to us, "Don't worry about trying to make a profit. Just make it amazing, and we have faith that it will benefit the company." We took a look at the way people interact with touch-screen computer devices, and we shaped *Monument Valley* around that. A lot of games are supposed to be challenging—there's an aspect of difficulty to them. We realized quickly that *Monument Valley* is not meant to be a difficult game. Many people enjoyed our early test versions of *Monument Valley* because they like seeing beautiful things unfold through their interactions.

ustwo is not a game company. ustwo is a visual design agency, so we approach things in a more design-oriented fashion. We weren't burdened by preconceptions of what a game is. In fact, a lot of people don't think of *Monument Valley* as a game. They're more comfortable calling it a piece of interactive art, of visual art, or a beautiful app.

Our approach involves a lot of user testing. Throughout the whole project, we invited our colleagues and friends and other people visiting the studio to try out *Monument Valley*. By observing them, we could see whether they were having fun, or whether they were frustrated, or whether they got stuck. That's the way that you create a good user experience. Games are not just isolated products that we put out to the universe. What we're actually designing is the user experience.

————Tell me about the visuality of *Monument Valley*.

My background is in illustration and in concept design for video games. When I joined the company, I had the opportunity to suggest some ideas for our next game. I did that by making illustrations of some ideas. One of the ideas that I pitched was an isometric floating building, inspired by M. C. Escher. This picture drew a lot of interest and enthusiasm from my teammates and from the rest of the company. That's how the project got started. That image set the direction for the game. It was going to be visually oriented, with strong colors and a minimalist design. It would communicate ideas visually—with hardly any text. I'm passionate about architecture, so I was looking at temples and monasteries and churches from Spain and North Africa and India, and looking at all these amazing shapes and textures and colors. We don't see enough of that in video games. In *Monument Valley*, architecture is the main character.

Video games are an emerging art form. Many of the visual artists who have been involved have worked more like craftsmen, where they're making things to spec. Artists are now realizing that they have more to offer. Art can be the main point of the game. If a video game is a visual feast, beautiful to look at, that can be more important than having interesting or fun game-play mechanics. There is also a design component. A poem can be beautiful, or a song can be beautiful, even though they're not visual. Game design can result in a feeling of beauty, whether that's through the story, or through the mechanics. Two things that video games do very well are mathematics and geometry, which we know are beautiful. A snowflake is beautiful, and patterns are beautiful. M. C. Escher explored patterns and repetition and geometric paradoxes, and he fused that with his skills as an illustrator. We did something similar with *Monument Valley*. We're exploring the beauty of geometry and mathematics, using the medium of video games.

————What comes into your mind when you hear the word "beauty"?

My job as an artist is to provide stimulating material for other people. I take what I find beautiful and interesting and poetic and moving about the world or in my imagination, and I put that in a form that other people can interact with, whether that's a game, or it's a print, or it's pictures on my website. Then it's up to people to respond and make up their own minds about what the meaning is, or whether it is beautiful. At the end of the day, if people say that it's beautiful, then who am I to argue with them?

————What is the most beautiful time of day?

I do my best work between about midnight and four a.m., which is when, unfortunately, everybody else is asleep and when I should be sleeping, too, if I need to be working the next day. But somehow, in the dead of night, that's when my creativity works best, and I get great ideas.

————What is the most beautiful place you've visited?

Hayao Miyazaki, who made the films *Spirited Away* (2001) and *My Neighbor Totoro* (1988), has a film company called Studio Ghibli. The studio has a museum in the suburbs of Tokyo. It's not like Disneyland, where you pay money, and you line up, and there are rides, and there's junk food. The Ghibli Museum is very small, and it only lets in a certain number of people every hour. It is the most spiritual place that I've ever been to, because it isn't a shrine to a religion, to gods; it's a shrine to childhood. Everything about the museum is about how magical and amazing it is to be a child, as expressed through the movies that Studio Ghibli makes. It's just a very serene, beautiful place.

— INTERVIEW WITH SUVI SALONIEMI

Ken Wong for ustwo studio; Digital illustrations,
(clockwise) Labyrinth, Moon, Interlude, Descent;
Monument Valley game, 2014

Ken Wong for ustwo studio; Digital illustration,
Spire, *Monument Valley* game, 2014

Ken Wong for ustwo studio; Digital illustration,
Lost Falls, *Monument Valley* game, 2014

Extravagant

Here lies the domain of glamour, seduction, and excess. Rich materials and shimmering, sometimes deceptive surfaces create an aura of luxury and erotic possibility. Extravagance feeds desire, rather than following function.

"I'd like to create a pair of snails; a larger one and a smaller one. Suddenly, one of the craftsmen said, 'You won't believe it—I have had at home a pair of shells for a long time. One looks like the mother and the other one like its daughter as they are the same color and shape.'"

———————————————————————— Stefan Hemmerle

Hemmerle

—MUNICH, GERMANY, FOUNDED 1893—

A Hemmerle jewel is unmistakable. The fourth-generation, high-end jewelry firm, established in 1893, is known for its striking designs. In 1895, Hemmerle was appointed purveyor to the Royal Bavarian Court and has since built a reputation for high-quality, technically sophisticated traditional jewelry. The house underwent a major transformation in 1995, when Stefan Hemmerle took control of the firm with his wife, Sylveli. Under their direction, Hemmerle developed what is today its signature bold aesthetic. In 2006, they were joined by their son, Christian, and his wife, Yasmin. Hemmerle pairs high-quality stones with a distinctive mix of metals and materials—a diamond-and-iron ring; or earrings with aquamarines, jasper, and concrete. Nature is an endless source of inspiration, seen in Hemmerle's snail brooches, eucalyptus brooch, or honeybee earrings. The family searches for special stones, sometimes waiting years until finding a mate, such as with the cameos or pink tourmaline-and-sapphire earrings. The design of each piece is often inspired by a central stone or material, and is a collaborative process for the family and their workshop. Each piece is shaped through iterative sketches and then handcrafted in Hemmerle's atelier, taking up to five hundred hours to complete. — ANDREA LIPPS

———Tell me about your process. What is the starting point for each jewel?

CHRISTIAN HEMMERLE: The way we work is very creative and sometimes very spontaneous. We start with the gemstone and create the jewel around it because we want to respect the beauty nature has created. We don't try to force whatever stone it may be into a shape or form. Therefore, each and every piece is individual, different, unique, and exciting all over again.

STEFAN HEMMERLE: We are guided by the beauty of the gemstones we find. We are extremely happy when we are able to combine stones that complement each other. Then we can start to think about what to create out of them. We do not wish to repeat our pieces and are always thinking innovatively.

———What is the source of your ideas and inspiration?

CH: Stefan taught me that inspiration can lie in every thing: each element, shape, form, or even thought. Reinterpreting them and pushing the boundaries can result in something new.

SH: We look all over to find these inspirations, in literature or in travel. For example, in the Hagia Sophia in Istanbul, I saw this carpet with a fantastic design on the floor. In the cathedral, I studied the dome. I took out my pencil and put it down on paper. This later inspired me to create a pair of earrings. The same can happen when you are around nature. I have found inspiration in pine trees; it is amazing how pinecones have such regularity in their construction. Nature gives us the best guidelines.

CH: Then you can interpret that inspiration.

———One sees this in your use of materials. You pair unconventional materials with more conventional gemstones. You bring in many elements from nature, such as the shells in your snail brooches, or acorns, or wood. What drives your material choices?

CH: We don't use unconventional materials just because they are different. It truly goes back to the fact that we want to give each and every gemstone the perfect home. Sometimes to find that, to bring out all the different hues of a gemstone, classical materials are not enough for us. That's why we started using unusual materials, and each and every one has an intriguing point. It gives a new aspect and a new beauty to our pieces.

SH: Exactly. For example, we discovered one very small Lingam stone. Lingams are olive shaped and come in different colors and patterns like brown and gray, often with lines. They are not considered precious stones, but it's the beauty of each stone that you see. Using their natural beauty, we created a pair of earrings. Combining them with diamonds and mounting them in copper resulted in a highly unusual, yet exquisite pair of earrings.

———How would you describe the Hemmerle aesthetic?

SH: We are very focused on proportions. It is in the proportions that you can feel the aesthetic. If you look at the proportions of our pieces, most of them are balanced, like in nature. This is the Hemmerle shape, the Hemmerle aesthetic.

———Your jewels are highly wearable, a bit of a rarity in the field of high jewelry.

CH: Stefan has always had the belief that there's nothing more boring than jewels in the safe.

Inspired by that, we want to create something that, for the connoisseur, is visible as a jewel, and for somebody else, it might not be. We always say that we want the client to wear the jewel, and never let the jewel wear the client. The collector should feel comfortable with the piece; it should feel like a second skin.

SH: It should be part of them and their daily life.

———Tell me about the snail brooches. They are spectacular!

SH: I was walking with our dog in the neighborhood. I'm always trying to look at little things, and I discovered this snail, which I picked up from a tree. I wanted to see how it reacted. Of course, it immediately retreated into its shell. That stood in my mind. I went to the workshop and said, "I'd like to create a pair of snails; a larger one and a smaller one." Suddenly, one of the craftsmen said, "You won't believe it— I have had at home a pair of shells for a long time. One looks like the mother and the other one like its daughter as they are the same color and shape." The next day, he brought them in, and they were perfect. We made the model, and that's what they became.

CH: We try out a lot of things in our workshop. In the case of the snails, we started by making models, as we occasionally do. To a certain extent, you can envisage a final design with a model, and this gives us the opportunity to adjust elements of it to ensure that the proportions and balance are correct. It's wonderful to have a workshop where we work together to push the boundaries of design.

———What comes to mind when you hear the word "beauty"?

CH: It is that which lights up your heart. Beauty makes you happy and puts your mind in a good place.

———What is the most beautiful time of day?

SH: The most beautiful time is when I wake up or when the sun is going down. Both are times when there are different lights that can create different moods.

CH: I prefer mornings, especially when Florian [our son] gets up. The sun comes up and the light comes in, and it's a beautiful moment in the day.

———What is the most beautiful place you've visited?

CH: Luxor in Egypt. It is a place with a rich heritage, with amazing aesthetics that have remained untouched in a very fast-changing world.

SH: It is difficult for me to choose because I've been fortunate to have seen so much of the world. I would probably have to say Egypt or the Tuscan countryside in Italy.

— INTERVIEW WITH ANDREA LIPPS

OPENING SPREAD: Earrings, 2013; Copper, white gold, sapphires, spinels, rubellite, tourmaline; Each, approx.: 6.7 × 2.9 × 1.3 cm (2⅝ × 1⅛ × ½ in.)

OPPOSITE, LEFT: Small snail Brooch, 2014; White gold, diamonds, snail shell; Approx.: 6 × 3.2 × 3 cm (2⅜ × 1¼ × 1³⁄₁₆ in.)

OPPOSITE, RIGHT: Large snail Brooch, 2014; White gold, diamonds, snail shell; Approx.: 8.8 × 4.4 × 3.8 cm (3⁷⁄₁₆ × 1¾ × 1½ in.)

Eucalyptus brooch, 2013; Brass, bronze, white gold, diamonds; Approx. 5 × 1.1 cm (1¹⁵⁄₁₆ × ⁷⁄₁₆ in.)

Honeybee Earrings, 2014; Bronze, iron, pink gold, red gold, amber; Each, approx.: 2.9 × 2.6 × 2.6 cm (1⅛ × 1 × 1 in.)

OPPOSITE: Earrings, 2014; White gold, cameos, diamonds; Each, approx.: 6.2 × 3.3 × 1.3 cm (2⁷⁄₁₆ × 1³⁄₁₆ × ½ in.)

Pat McGrath

—BRITISH, B. 1966—

Understated and ethereal, glamorous and erotic, radical and mutant—makeup in the hands of Pat McGrath is utterly transformative. It not only complements the runway fashion, editorials, and ads it graces, but also elevates them. McGrath's makeup is definitive, setting a mood, illuminating a character, or driving a narrative. And in a career that has spanned over twenty years, her range and indefatigable innovation are astounding. She has created some of the catwalk's most iconic visages, using bold and neon colors, crystal embellishments, gold foil, exaggerated faux brows, ridiculously long lashes, and so much more. Particularly astonishing was the sequin, Swarovski crystal, and shell–studded mask McGrath created for the Givenchy Fall 2015 menswear collection. A follow-up to the jeweled masks McGrath created for Givenchy's Spring 2014 Ready-to-Wear collection, this latest mask is tribal and futuristic, a cross between a sinister, bearded figure and an exoticized Persian king. Since 2004, McGrath has also been global creative design director for Procter & Gamble, where she distills runway looks into some of makeup's biggest trends, including a selfie-proof matte liquid foundation. McGrath's encyclopedic range of aesthetic innovation leads her to constantly redefine notions of beauty as a visionary in her field. — ANDREA LIPPS

———What early experiences and/or inspirations led you to become a makeup artist?

My mother was obsessed with fashion, classic Hollywood films, and cosmetics, and her passion directly influenced my career as a makeup artist.

———The breadth of your work and creativity seems endless. What is the source of your ideas and inspiration?

As a visual artist, my inspirations come from so many different aspects of my life: books, films, photography, exhibitions, cosmetics, and, most notably, trends within the counterculture. As a teenager, I was surrounded by so many incredible makeup looks and amazing characters. I was obsessed with the outrageous looks of the Punks, the New Romantics, and the Blitz Kids. The way these artists embraced makeup so fearlessly expanded my perceptions of beauty and gave me an understanding of makeup as an artistic medium, as a means of self-expression and becoming a character. The makeup looks of Siouxsie Sioux, Jordan, and Leigh Bowery were so iconic and legendary. I was heavily influenced by all of these artists and how they uniquely challenged the conventional notions of beauty and makeup.

Today, my days are filled with artistic collaboration and inspiration, and I'm so blessed to be working with photographer Steven Meisel, who is an absolute genius, as well as some of the best creative teams in the world.

———What do you most enjoy about working with makeup?

Makeup is such an incredible medium to work with. It allows you to be whomever or whatever you want at any given moment, to create and to push the boundaries and conceptions of beauty. I believe it can be as limiting or limitless as you want—to each their own!

———What comes to mind when you hear the word "beauty"?

To me, beauty not only pleases the eyes but impacts the senses. I try to discern beauty in its purest form and to see beyond the surface. In pursuit of beauty in my work, I seek to further realize and question the duality of what beauty is and also what beauty can be.

———What is the most beautiful time of day?

The most beautiful time of day is watching the sunset overlooking the Hudson or against the trees in Hyde Park in the summertime. I become so mesmerized by of all of the brilliant purples, oranges, and pinks that light up the skies in New York and London, two of my favorite cities.

———What is the most beautiful place you've visited?

Without question, the Mediterranean islands are some of the most memorable places I have been. I'm drawn to the water, and I love swimming in the vivid turquoise sea. I'm completely enthralled by the exotic and strange landscape: the steep cliffs, consisting of congealed volcanic ash rising upward to the sky, and the pearlescent sand, which speaks to the unspoiled nature of a region rich in culture. One of my first impressions upon arriving to the islands was what a truly remarkable respite it is from the "modern" world.

— INTERVIEW WITH ANDREA LIPPS

Makeup by Pat McGrath for *W Magazine*,
March 2014; Photographed by Steven Meisel;
Styled by Marie-Amelie Sauve

Makeup by Pat McGrath for *Vogue Italia*, April
2013; Photographed by Steven Meisel; Styled
by Karl Templer

Hair styled by Guido Palau; Photographed
by David Sims; 2010

Guido Palau

—BRITISH, B. 1962—

Guido Palau is one of fashion's most influential hairstylists. His work spans over two decades, elevating hair as a definitive beauty statement. Palau was a major force in developing the dirty grunge look in the 1990s, and his vision can be credited to pivotal hair trends and styles since, seen on runways and in magazine editorials and ad campaigns. His work achieves a narrative expression imbued with gesture and mood, whether subtle and classic or dark and confrontational. Palau is deeply imaginative, drawing inspiration from history, art, music, and street style. He interprets and distorts these ideas, yielding iconic images that often challenge accepted notions of contemporary beauty. In this way, he consistently pushes the field, and our eye, forward. His recent book, *Hair* (2014), is evidence of this. Shot by renowned photographer David Sims (a long-standing collaborator), the images in the book present hair's artifice—tightly wrought, sculpted, and formed—as an abstracted point of view about the medium's possibilities. Here, hair provides social commentary. With it, Palau contrasts historicism and futurism, mixes androgyny and ambiguity, and evokes melancholy and beauty to examine hair's unnatural construction. — ANDREA LIPPS

———You have a wide range of references in your work—Dutch paintings, Japanese anime, neoclassical art, to name a few. What is the source of your ideas and inspiration?

When I'm thinking about hair, I first think of the character, of the feeling I want to create. As you say, that can come from various references—classical paintings, Dutch portraiture, manga, anime, musical references that I grew up with like Punk, New Romantic, New Wave, Goth. One of my biggest assets is that I do have this visual sensibility. When I see something once, if it makes a style impact on me, it goes into my visual library. When I want to create something or I have a feeling for something, all those references that I've stored come into play, and I take from various places.

———And then you use these references in unexpected ways.

I want the person looking at my work to be interested in the character portrayed. Most of the time there's some believability, some classicism to it. And there's also whatever element I might be playing with, like punk or futurism or skepticism or something. It's a moving scale. One viewer might look at some of my work and think it's almost classical, and then someone else can look at it and feel like it's futuristic. People have their own impression of it.

———There's something very familiar in your work, but then you twist it so it becomes unfamiliar, almost ungraspable. It's very intriguing.

I always love ambiguity in things, in people, in everything. When I was in my late teens, early twenties, I was going out to nightclubs in London and seeing this emerging street culture, when it first really became fashionable. I would see these people, and I wouldn't really know what they were. Did they really live this life, or was it something they put on in the evening? I was always intrigued, but I was never brave enough to become one of these people. I was a great observer, and I would make up my own story about these people that I would see around me. It's the same thing today, passing a picture or photograph or person on the street. You don't really know if it's a true representation. There's a mystery to it all. I love that. That's why I love creating these characters.

———Your latest book—*Hair*, made in collaboration with David Sims—presents an abstracted point of view about hair. Tell me more about this project.

In the book, I wanted to look back at different periods and play with the ideas of artifice, form, abstraction, strange shapes. These ideas were from other decades, when it was socially acceptable to be much more peacock-like. It showed wealth. It demonstrated that you had people doing your hair. Back in Louis XIV's days, the higher your hair, the more money you had. It was probably the same in the eighties. But now we've gotten to a decade where we're much less inclined to do that. To show your wealth, you probably show more your understated idea of beauty, which is a reversal. Women and men today are less adventurous to try things or to play out a fantasy with their look.

In the early nineties, I first got known in the fashion industry for grunge, this very undone kind of beauty. It was an anti-glamour. We'd just come out of the supermodel era, and there was this reaction to that. Twenty-five years on, my work has, of course, developed. I've learned and loved different kinds of hair.

Right now, we are at this very simple point in hair, which is great in one way. Beauty barriers have broken down the last couple of decades, and women quite rightly can walk around without having done anything to their hair. There's, of course, nuance of a good undone or a bad undone, but it's an acceptable idea of modern beauty.

———Hair is such an ephemeral medium. You wash it; it's gone. What are the advantages and the limitations of working in this way?

I once said that I'm one water bottle squirt from my work being destroyed. I like that. The lucky thing for me is now my work is photographed. In that way, it has some kind of posterity to it. But I suppose people don't take it as seriously because it is so disposable as a form. Maybe if it were something that could be kept, that you could hold, it would become more precious. I think that's why I wanted to do the book as well, to wave the flag for hairdressing so it can be more than just a pretty picture of pretty hair. You can say something with it. Hair is so important to people. It's so important to fashion. It indicates so much about a person or a style or a decade. It's such an indicator of where we are socially, politically, culturally.

———What comes to mind when you hear the word "beauty"?

I find the grotesque can be beautiful. I find things that are disturbing beautiful. I like beauty to sometimes shock me. I don't always like just the idea of classical beauty; I find it can be saccharine. There is beauty in everything, of course; it's just how you look at it. What would be considered ugly twenty years ago in hair is now considered the ultimate in luxury, meaning you don't bother with your hair and it's undone. It's amazing how our eye changes in beauty or how our aesthetic changes. But it's important to disturb or challenge the idea of what is beautiful. It's the way things progress. Otherwise, if there were only one idea of beauty, things would stay stagnant.

———What is the most beautiful time of day?

In the morning, when I get up and there's a time before I have to get going. It's six thirty, seven. I really like the stillness before the day's begun.

———What is the most beautiful place you've visited?

Greenland. It was like I landed on icebergs. There were incredible big night skies and the aurora borealis, all those things you think you will never see. It was otherworldly.

— INTERVIEW WITH ANDREA LIPPS

 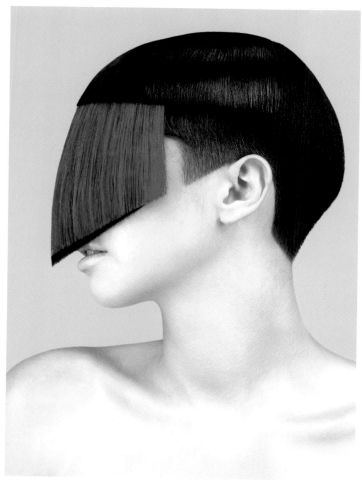

LEFT: Hair styled by Guido Palau;
Photographed by David Sims; 2014

RIGHT: Hair styled by Guido Palau;
Photographed by Fabien Baron; 2011

OPPOSITE: Hair styled by Guido Palau;
Photographed by Fabien Baron; 2013

Giambattista Valli

—ITALIAN, ACTIVE IN FRANCE, B. 1966—

Giambattista Valli is the embodiment of contemporary couture. Although his couture collection began in only 2011, he is already recognized as one of the key figures of Paris's Chambre Syndicale de la Haute Couture. Valli's collections are celebrated for their intense romanticism, blending fantasy with simple, clean lines in garments that are inherently wearable. Each piece is meticulously crafted, with decadent fabrics and impeccable tailoring. His is an elegant femininity. Highlights of Valli's Fall 2014 Haute Couture collection, for instance, included voluminous ball-gown skirts made of feathery tulle *dégradé* in candy-colored ombré. The look is dreamily indulgent, and when paired with tiny piped pajama tops in silk taffeta, it becomes sublimely balanced. The silhouette is extravagant and modern. Born in Rome and based in Paris, France, Valli studied fashion and illustration in Rome and London. He is a seasoned designer who has worked at Capucci, Krizia, Fendi, and Emanuel Ungaro. Valli launched his first collection, and eponymous house, in 2005. — ANDREA LIPPS

How does your day begin?

I like to have two days in one: one private, one professional. I live on the opposite side of Paris to my office, because I really love to separate my two personal and professional lives. So I live in Canal Saint-Martin. It's very bohemian; it looks like a village. I have a long breakfast, that is my silent moment; I'm getting energy and cleaning up my mind to come and start a new day. Normally I have a trainer come into the house. I do meditation, sometimes I do yoga. It's almost like a treat to go from that side of Paris to this side, the most historical and institutional one. It's a place very inspiring for the luxury profession. And then I come to the office, and the first thing is I have my tea. I drink tea all day.

What happens in the office? Do you draw?

When I sketch a collection, mostly I do it in my house, because it's the moment you are really naked with a white sheet of paper; it's the moment that you are the most fragile, with your mind, your soul, your emotions open. So I do it in private.

When you start a collection, where do the ideas begin?

Sometimes people ask, "Who's your muse?" and I always say the only muse I have is curiosity. I'm very curious about everything. I don't really think that you can bring out new clothes. A skirt is a skirt. A trouser is a trouser. A jacket is a jacket. But you can find new proportions of the clothes, and you can find a new way to put them together. This I think is my job: to refresh every season a wardrobe of a woman in a way unexpected.

How important is it to you to work on the human body?

It's extremely important. Sometimes I say I really don't want to do fashion; I just want to make clothes that real women are going to wear. I want to be with them in their happy moments. I want that they collect my clothes and they keep my clothes in their wardrobe as long as possible. I hate when somebody buys something in a season because it is the hottest thing, and then you drop the dress because you cannot wear it anymore; you are sick of the dress after a couple of times because millions of others have it, because there are millions of advertising pages all over. You know, I love that kind of having these relationships almost like old friends with your clothes, and sometimes you rediscover, like, a little black dress or something that really protects you, and when you're tired and you have to go to something, you rediscover it in your wardrobe and you say, "Oh, thank God," and you zip it on and you feel better.

Excerpt from Introduction, *A Magazine Curated by Giambattista Valli*, no. 10, 2010, p. 32

What is beauty?

[It is an] open [question], a muse for future expressions of beauty.

Real beauty is the one that touches the five senses, yes—you can almost say it strikes you—it can caress you, hit you right in the face, or worse, get you right in the stomach. Beauty is a stolen moment, gesture or encounter—often unexpected and unplanned. It surprises you; it can make you dizzy or erode you like an obsession. It can open new roads, it can frighten or irritate when unfamiliar. . . .

[M]y encounters with beauty . . . time and time again have brought me to new doors, to unknown rooms and landscapes. Sometimes I have stumbled upon beauty my mind was not ready to accept, but as Patti Smith wrote: "If you have a wall in front of you, kick it until it collapses." Next time something seems ugly or frightens you, stop and reflect—look at it because it's talking to you, it may be hiding something beautiful.

— INTERVIEW WITH VANESSA FRIEDMAN, excerpt from "Where Giambattista Valli Hangs His Hat," *The New York Times*, March 12, 2015.

Skirt and top, from Fall/Winter 2014–15 Haute Couture
collection, 2014; Tulle degradé, silk taffeta

Ensembles, from Fall / Winter 2014–15 Haute Couture
collection, 2014; Tulle degrade, silk taffeta

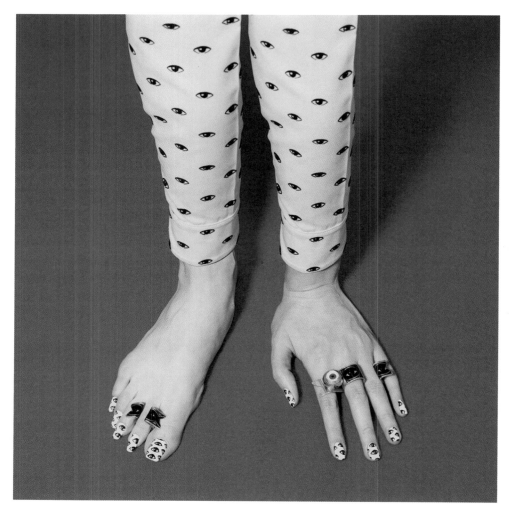

Naomi Yasuda

—JAPANESE, B. 1984—

For Naomi Yasuda, manicured nails are like jewelry. With her mesmerizing and intricate nail designs, the Nagoya-born manicurist has turned a cosmetic service into an art form. Yasuda typically uses color as a starting point for her designs, which run from the geometric to the illustrative. She often tops these tiny paintings with beads and ornaments, transforming the nails from flat canvases into sculptural works of art. Working in a wide range of styles, Yasuda believes that nail artists should be flexible enough to delight the imagination of any client. A love for doing nails led Yasuda to Chunichi Beauty College in her hometown after finishing high school. In 2007, she moved to New York City, where she has built a dedicated list of clients, including Alicia Keys and Madonna, as well as collaborations with Barneys New York, CoverGirl, Revlon, and Kenzo. — JUSTIN ZHUANG

How does your work start, and where do your ideas come from?

I look at fashion magazines to see what's new, what's hot, what are the cool patterns. I'm always looking at new magazines and art books and exhibitions. I carry a small notebook with me so that I can write down ideas. I've been seeing my clients for a long time, so they trust me. Sometimes they have an idea, but most of the time they're like, "Oh, just do whatever you want." If I'm doing a fashion shoot or working with celebrity clients, I usually see what they're going to wear or how they're going to take photos. Then I figure out what should I do.

As a designer, of course I want to try something new every time. I usually don't look at other nail artists' work because I don't want to get distracted and I don't want to copy anyone's designs. A lot of my friends are in the fashion business. They teach me what's cool, what's new, and what they are into now. That inspires me a lot.

When you have an idea in your head for a nail art design, do you make sketches?

Sometimes I have a clear vision in my head of what the nail is going to be, so I don't have to do a sketch. About half of the time, I do sketches first.

What do you think about the fact that nail art is so temporary?

That's the worst part of it. Sometimes it takes so long to create one nail that will only last for three weeks to a month, but at the same time, we can try something new every month. So it's fun, too.

A lot of your work is three-dimensional. Where do you get ideas for those pieces? Is it almost like making sculptures?

I love to go to the craft supply store and the bead store to find cool pieces—anything small that I can stick on the nails. The bead store is like a candy shop. So many good things.

What comes to your mind when you hear the word "beauty"?

Beautiful hair and makeup and nails and skin give women confidence, and confidence is a very important thing. A confident woman is beautiful. Personally, I don't have time to do my own nails, but I think it's important to take care of your nails. With hair and makeup, you need a mirror to see yourself. But nails you can always see for yourself, all the time.

What is the most beautiful time of day?

When I'm working during the day, finishing my clients' nails is the happiest moment. So is falling asleep. Before I go to bed, I get the most ideas. When I close my eyes, I think about what happened that day, and all of a sudden I get crazy nail ideas.

What is the most beautiful place you've visited?

I will say Japan. That's where I'm from. Recently I was in Japan to attend my sister's wedding. She had a traditional Japanese wedding. She wore a kimono, and we held the wedding at a beautiful temple with beautiful Japanese gardens. And it was kind of overwhelming, but at the same time, it was so peaceful.

— INTERVIEW WITH SUVI SALONIEMI

Nail designs, Eye See You, from Kenzo Fall / Winter collection, 2013; Gel

CLOCKWISE: Rainbow nails, 2014; Gel and rainbow film; Black and White Graph, 2015; Gel; Mystical Symbol, 2014; Gel; Nail design, 2014; Acrylic paint; Nail design, from Kenzo Fall / Winter collection, 2014; Blue flocking powder; Geometric marble nails, 2014; Gel

"Beauty always has a fracture, an error,
or a crack—and that makes it interesting.
Perfection is not beautiful anymore."

——— Kustaa Saksi